Critical Studies of the Asia-Pacific

Series Editor
Mark Beeson
University of Western Australia
Crawley, WA, Australia

Critical Studies of the Asia Pacific showcases new research and scholarship on what is arguably the most important region in the world in the twenty-first century. The rise of China and the continuing strategic importance of this dynamic economic area to the United States mean that the Asia-Pacific will remain crucially important to policymakers and scholars alike. The unifying theme of the series is a desire to publish the best theoretically-informed, original research on the region. Titles in the series cover the politics, economics and security of the region, as well as focusing on its institutional processes, individual countries, issues and leaders.

More information about this series at
http://www.palgrave.com/gp/series/14940

Ian Bowers

The Modernisation of the Republic of Korea Navy

Seapower, Strategy and Politics

palgrave
macmillan

Ian Bowers
Norwegian Institute for Defence
  Studies
Oslo, Norway

Critical Studies of the Asia-Pacific
ISBN 978-3-319-92290-4   ISBN 978-3-319-92291-1   (eBook)
https://doi.org/10.1007/978-3-319-92291-1

Library of Congress Control Number: 2018943264

Cover image: © US Navy Photo/Alamy Stock Photo
Cover design by Tjaša Krivec

Printed on acid-free paper

This Palgrave Macmillan imprint is published by the registered company Springer
International Publishing AG part of Springer Nature
The registered company address is: Gewerbestrasse 11, 6330 Cham, Switzerland

ACKNOWLEDGEMENTS

Any author will acknowledge that writing a book is a collaborative process. I started research on seapower and South Korean security in 2009 and over the years I have had the pleasure of discussing and arguing over the topics in this manuscript with countless academics, military officers, policymakers and friends. This book started life as a doctoral thesis at the Department of War Studies, King's College London. During my time there, I was fortunate to receive the help and guidance of my supervisors, Professor Andrew Lambert and Dr. Alessio Patalano. Both provided excellent feedback and their insights into seapower, naval history and Asian security continue to shape my work in the present day.

In South Korea, I have many people to thank. Mingi Hyun provided me with invaluable assistance, arranging interviews and bringing me on my first visit to a ROKN naval base. Without his help, I would not have been able to complete this project. Special mention must also go to Admiral An Byeong-tae, a former CNO of the ROKN who spent a number of hours with me explaining the origins of the ROKN's blue-water modernisation program. Admiral Song Keun-ho, Admiral Kim, Duk-ki, Captain Yoon Suk-joon, Captain Chung Sam-man and Dr. Lee Seo-hang all provided me with important insights and comments about the ROKN and South Korea's relationship with the sea. Academics and staff at the Korean Institute for Maritime Strategy, the Korean Institute for Defense Analyses, the Ministry of National Defense and the Institute of Foreign Affairs and National Security have all taken the time to enhance my knowledge of South Korean security and foreign policy decision making.

Since joining the Norwegian Institute for Defence Studies, I have had the pleasure to work with a very talented group of academics who have greatly advanced my understanding of international relations, military affairs and Asian security. Particularly, I would like to thank Jo Inge Bekkevold, Øystein Tunsjø, Paal Hilde, Lars Tore Flåten, Saira Basit, Bjørn Grønning and Christopher Weidacher Hsuing all of whom took the time to comment on draft chapters and have a created a stimulating and supportive environment in which to conduct research. At Palgrave, I would like to thank Sarah Roughley, Oliver Foster and Mary Fata for their enthusiasm about this project and their help in guiding me through the publication process.

I would be remiss if I did not thank my family in Dublin and in Seoul, who have supported me and without whose assistance I would not be where I am today. Finally, and most importantly, this book is for my wife Soon-kyun whose faith in my ability gave me the confidence to pursue a career in academia and whose love and support has it made it possible.

CONTENTS

ABOUT THE AUTHOR

Ian Bowers is Associate Professor at the Norwegian Institute for Defence Studies in Oslo, Norway. His research interests include East Asian security, seapower and naval modernisation, South Korean defence policy and the theoretical and policy aspects of conventional deterrence. He is co-editor of *Security, Strategy and Military Change in the 21st Century: Cross-Regional Perspectives* (Routledge, 2015). He has written journal articles and book chapters on South Korean seapower, conventional deterrence in the South China Sea, escalation at sea, the balance of naval operations and peacekeeping in maritime contexts. His work has been published in the *Journal of Strategic Studies*, the *Korean Journal of Defense Analysis* and *Global Asia*. Dr. Bowers teaches at the Norwegian Defence University College where he has lectured on international relations theory, maritime security and East Asian security. He holds a BA in History from University College Dublin (2001), an MA in War Studies from King's College London (2002) and a Ph.D. in War Studies in King's College London (2013).

ABBREVIATIONS

AAW	Anti-Air Warfare
AAV	Amphibious Assault Vehicle
ACV	Armoured Combat Vehicle
ADIZ	Air Defence Identification Zone
ANDVT	Advanced Narrowband Digital Voice Terminal
AIP	Air Independent Propulsion
AOE	Ammunition Oil Equipment (Replenishment Ship)
AORH	Ammunition Oil Resupply Helicopter (Replenishment Ship)
ARM	Anti-radiation Missile
AShM	Anti-ship Missile
ASROC	Anti-Submarine Rocket
ASUW	Anti-Surface Warfare
ASW	Anti-Submarine Warfare
ATS	Salvage and Rescue Ship
AWACS	Airborne Warning and Control System
C	Cruiser
C2	Command and Control
C4I	Command Control Communications Computers and Intelligence
C4ISR	Command Control Communications Computers Intelligence Surveillance and Reconnaissance
CINC USF	Commander in Chief US Forces Korea
CIWS	Close in Weapon System
CFC	Combined Forces Command
CMS	Combat Management System
CNO	Chief of Naval Operations
COMROKFLT	Commander, Republic of Korea Fleet

CPIC	Coastal Patrol Interdiction Craft
CTF-151	Combined Task Force 151
CV	Aircraft Carrier (Conventional)
DAPA	Defense Acquisition Program Administration
DD	Destroyer
DDG	Guided Missile Destroyer
DDH	Destroyer Helicopter
DE	Destroyer Escort
DMZ	Demilitarized Zone
DOD	Department of Defense
EBO	Effects Based Operations
EEZ	Exclusive Economic Zone
EW	Electronic Warfare
FIP	Force Improvement Program
FF	Frigate
FFX	Future Frigate Experimental
FMS	Foreign Military Sale
FMP	Force Modernization Plan
FRAM	Fleet Rehabilitation and Modernization
FS	Corvette
FTA	Free Trade Agreement
GCCS-M	Global Command and Control System-Maritime
IAMD	Integrated Air and Missile Defense
IMET	International Military Education & Training
JCS	Joint Chiefs of Staff
JMSDF	Japanese Maritime Self Defense Force
JSA	Joint Security Area
JVS	Joint Vision Study
KAMD	Korean Air and Missile Defense System
KCG	South Korean Coast Guard (Maritime Police)
KDX	Korea Destroyer Experimental
KIMS	Korea Institute for Maritime Strategy
KMA	Korean Military Academy
KMPR	Korean Massive Punishment and Retaliation
KNCCS	Korean Naval Command and Control System
KNOC	Korea National Oil Corporation
KNTDS	Korea Naval Tactical Datalink System
KPN	Korean People's Navy
KSS	Korea Submarine System
KVLS	Korea Vertical Launch System
LACM	Land Attack Cruise Missile
LCAC	Landing Craft Air Cushion

LCU	Landing Craft Utility
LCVP	Landing Craft Vehicle Personnel
LHD	Landing Helicopter Dock
LNG	Liquid Natural Gas
LPD	Landing Platform Dock
LPH	Landing Platform Helicopter
LPX	Landing Platform Experimental
LSF	Landing Ship Fast
LSM	Landing Ship Mechanised
LST	Landing Ship Tank
MANPAD	Man Portable Air-Defence System
MAP	Military Assistance Program
MASOC	Maritime Air Support Operations Centre
MBT	Main Battle Tank
MCBM	Maritime Confidence Building Measures
MDL	Military Demarcation Line
MHC	Minehunter Coastal
MINDEF	Minister of Defence (South Korea)
MND	Ministry of National Defense (South Korea)
MLEA	Maritime Law Enforcement Agency
MLRS	Multiple Launch Rocket System
MLS	Mine Laying Ship
MNF	Multi-National Force
MPA	Maritime Patrol Aircraft
MPC	Maritime Patrol Craft
MTF	Maritime Task Flotilla
MSH	Minesweeper Hunter
MTS	Maritime Task Squadron
NCW	Network Centric Warfare
NDPO	National Defense Program Outline
NDRC	National Defense Reform Committee
NLL	Northern Limit Line
NLOS	Non-Line-Of-Sight
NSC	National Security Council (US)
NWI	Northwest Islands
OECD	Organisation for Economic Cooperation and Development
OPCON	Operational Control
PACOM	Pacific Command
PCC	Patrol Craft Corvette
PK	Patrol Killer (Fast Patrol Boat)
PKG	Patrol Killer Guided-Missile (Fast Patrol Boat)

PKM	Patrol Killer Medium Fast (Patrol Boat)
PKMR	Patrol Killer Medium Rocket (Fast Patrol Boat)
PKO	Peacekeeping Operations
PKX	Patrol Killer Experimental
PLAAF	People's Liberation Army Air Force
PLAN	People's Liberation Army Navy
PRC	People's Republic of China
PRT	Provincial Reconstruction Team
PSI	Proliferation Security Initiative
RAM	Rolling Airframe Missile
RIMPAC	Rim of the Pacific Exercise
RMA	Revolution in Military Affairs
ROC	Requirement of Operational Capabilities
ROE	Rules of Engagement
ROK	Republic of Korea
ROKAF	Republic of Korea Air Force
ROKA	Republic of Korea Army
ROKMC	Republic of Korea Marine Corps
ROKN	Republic of Korea Navy
ROKS	Republic of Korea Ship
SAM	Surface to Air Missile
SAREX	Search and Rescue Exercise
SATCOM	Satellite Communications
SLOC	Sea Lines of Communication
SOF	Special Operations Forces
SSK	Attack Submarine (Conventional)
SSCS	Surface Ship Command System
TDL	Tactical Data Link
UN	United Nations
UNC	United Nations Command
UNCLOS	United Nations Convention on the Law of the Sea
UNMAC	United Nations Military Armistice Commission
UNPKO	United Nations Peacekeeping Operation
USFK	United States Forces Korea
USN	United States Navy
VLS	Vertical Launch System

LIST OF FIGURES

LIST OF TABLES

Note on Transliteration

For the transliteration of Korean terms this volume generally uses the Revised Romanization of Korean system with the exception of names, places and other well-known cases. Korean names are written with the family name first, then the given name, however, there are some exceptions (Syngman Rhee).

CHAPTER 1

Introduction

On a March day in 1995, the President of South Korea, Kim Young-sam stood before the graduating cadets of the Korean Naval Academy.[1] In his address, he called for these new Republic of Korea Navy (ROKN) officers to be part of a blue-water maritime era when, for the first time, South Korean warships would operate across the world.[2] The speech marked a moment when nascent ROKN ambitions to become a modern naval force received public political support. This was a major change and a long-term challenge for a navy that was both operationally and ideationally defined by the post-Korean War mission of deterring North Korea in the littoral waters of the Korean Peninsula.[3] To be successful, not only would it require a substantial leap in technological capability, it would need a shift in mindset within the ROKN, South Korean security stakeholders and the wider public about what a navy is for and the ultimate purpose of South Korean seapower. Is it solely to provide deterrence within the limited context of the North Korean threat or is the ROKN to become representative of a more advanced, independent and globally engaged South Korea?

This is the first English-language book to explore the ROKN and its ongoing process of blue-water modernisation. It examines how South Korea's understanding of seapower, its strategic environment and political situation has and continues to inform ROKN modernisation. It is a study of how the navy of a previously inward-looking nation, dealing with an existential threat on its only land border, began to look outwards

© The Author(s) 2019
I. Bowers, *The Modernisation of the Republic of
Korea Navy*, Critical Studies of the Asia-Pacific,
https://doi.org/10.1007/978-3-319-92291-1_1

towards the seas that surround it. Although the book delves into the origins of the ROKN, it primarily covers the period after 1988 when South Korea democratised and the foundations for blue-water modernisation were laid. In its current state, the ROKN is one of the world's most powerful and combat-experienced conventional navies yet it is often ignored within the wider literature on seapower and naval modernisation in Asia.

This book argues that a new perception of South Korea's maritime security requirements and the ever-evolving threat from North Korea combined with greater South Korean access to modern naval technology facilitated a new and still developing approach to naval operations and seapower, where mobility, multi-functionality, connectivity and lethality have primacy. These strategic and technological factors have coincided with a changing political and alliance landscape that has become more amenable to the concept of an expanded operational role for the ROKN. The book contends that the United States, South Korea's only ally, first constrained but now facilitates and encourages the ROKN's goal of an expanded operational role. The ROKN has also attempted to leverage the reduced impact of the army (ROKA) in South Korean society after democratisation to engage in a campaign to persuade the public and political elites of the importance of seapower and naval power to South Korea's security and prosperity. It is shown that this effort has been partially successful and the ROKN's ambitions and arguments for blue-water modernisation have matched the political and strategic vision of successive South Korean presidents. However, this volume emphasises that naval modernisation is a long-term project and resource-intensive endeavour and ROKN ambition remains vulnerable to changes in the strategic environment and the political orientation of the country.

What Is Blue-Water Modernisation?

South Korea has traditionally maintained a singular mindset regarding the development and application of the naval component of its seapower. The existential threat posed by North Korea on land since the end of the Korean War coupled with an asymmetric alliance relationship where the US once controlled the purse strings and still maintains wartime operational control (OPCON) of the South Korean military framed and constrained the development of the ROKN. Since the navy's inception in 1945, it has been overshadowed by the much larger ROKA.

The ROKN's operational approach betrayed its own limitations and the continental mindset of the South Korean government and Ministry of National Defense (MND). The understandable operational priority has been to maintain deterrence at sea in the context of North Korea. In war, the ROKN has been tasked with holding the line until the US Navy (USN) arrives and would, much like in the Korean War, perform missions that would complement their ally's operations.[4]

Even as South Korea grew economically and gained the ability to control the direction of its own procurement programs, the ROKN's mission set did not expand. Despite the modernisation of its platforms and the deployment of vessels such as *Gearing*-class destroyers that were capable of blue-water operations, the ROKN remained focused on the littoral waters around the peninsula. Its modernisation goals were framed by and reactive to the capabilities of the North Korean Navy (KPN) and the ROKN was rarely allowed to take the initiative in terms of the deterrent competition between the two sides. This book shows that the series of army-dominated governments prior to the democratisation of South Korea in 1980s did not consider South Korean seapower as something that could be separated from the strategic situation around the Korean Peninsula and while maintaining parity with the KPN was viewed as important, the investment needed to create a superior ROKN with a wider operational purview was not judged to be of substantial strategic benefit. The constant presence of the US 7th Fleet ensured that the South Korean leadership did not need to consider a more expansive use of South Korean naval power.

It is against this strategic and political background that in the early 1990s the ROKN sought to build its independence, expand its operational roles and make itself more central to South Korea's current and future security planning. The predominantly northward continental view of South Korean security still dominates in many areas of the MND and the South Korean Joint Chiefs of Staff (JCS), yet the introduction of democracy and the gradual expansion of South Korean security and foreign policy interests and goals provided the ROKN with the space to develop and then propose a new operational concept.

The ROKN has framed this modernisation process as the development of a blue-water or ocean-going navy. The term blue-water navy usually implies the ability to operate on the world's oceans and away from coastal waters, yet its generic nature provides little specificity.[5] The USN describes it as a non-doctrinal term referring generally to operations in the open ocean. This term is problematic as many navies with vastly different capabilities can perform effective operations outside of their home waters. For example, both the USN and the German navy can operate in waters far from their homeports, but their warfighting capability, sustainability, operational goals and strategic effect are vastly different. Some have tried to further deconstruct this term, dividing blue-water navies into groups delineated by their geographic reach. Todd and Lindberg, for example, argue that the term blue-water can refer to navies that can project power in four geographic categories outside of their home waters: Global-reach, limited global reach, multi/extra-regional and regional.[6] However, while the ROKN is ultimately seeking to possess the capability to project power in regional and even extra-regional settings, the term blue-water as commonly understood has little utility to describe what the ROKN is trying to achieve.

This book demonstrates that ROKN blue-water modernisation is fundamentally about creating a new navy that reflects the ambitions and geopolitical circumstances of South Korea. The ROKN is seeking sufficient capabilities to independently and cooperatively carry out the requisite range of operations to support South Korea's foreign and security policy requirements at home and abroad.[7] To achieve this, the ROKN is developing a balanced, technologically advanced naval force capable of network-centric warfare (NCW) and precision operations. As Table 1.1 shows, since 1990 the ROKN has introduced 20 new classes of warship, resulting in a modernised and expanded set of warfighting capabilities.

The book also disabuses the notion that ROKN blue-water modernisation ignored North Korea in favour of developing large platforms aimed solely at regional operations. In the context of North Korea, ROKN modernisation has two core goals. The first is maintaining deterrent superiority over the KPN. A long-term conventional deterrent relationship is dynamic and the ROKN has introduced capabilities to offset specific North Korean asymmetric operational approaches such as high-speed infiltration and amphibious craft and its numerous coastal and mini-submarines. Second, the ROKN is seeking to expand its strategic effect in relation to North Korea. Larger platforms that are blue-water capable have utility in a peninsular context. The introduction of sea-launched cruise missiles and other offensive capabilities, for the first time, gives the ROKN the capacity to perform both tactical and strategic strike

Table 1.1 ROKN vessels introduced since 1980. Displacement is calculated at full load

Name	Type	Displacement (tons)	Number in class	Notes
1980–1989				
Ulsan class	FF	2,180/2,300	9	To be replaced by Incheon/Daegu-class
Pohang class	PCC	1,220	24	To be replaced by Incheon/Daegu-class
Donghae class	PCC	1,076	4	Final vessel decommissioned in 2011
Ganggyeong class	MHC	520	6	
1990–1999				
Cheonji class	AOE	9,000	3	
Go Jun Bong class	LST	4,278	5	
Chung Haejin class	ASR	4,330	1	
KDX-I	DDH	3,855	3	Also known as *Gwanggaeto Daewang*-class
Wonsan class	MLS	3,300	1	
Chang Bogo class	SSK	1,285	9	1st in class constructed in Germany
Yangyang class	MSH	730	3	
2000–2009				
Dokdo class	LPH	18,800	1 (+1)	2nd in class under construction with modifications
KDX-III	DDG	10,290	3	Also known as *Sejong Daewang*-class
KDX-II	DDH	5,500	6	Also known as *Chungmugong Yi Sun-shin*-class
Son Won-il class	SS	1,860	7 (+2)	Nine planned in class
PKG	PKG	570	18	Also known as *Gumdoksuri*-class
2010–				
Soyang class	AOE	10,000	1 (+2)	Three planned in class
Cheon Wang Bong class	LST-II	7,140	4	
Tongyeong class	ATS	4,700	2	
Nampo class	MLS	4,240	1 (+3)	Four planned in class
Daegu class	FFG	3,592	1 (+7)	Eight planned in class
Incheon class	FFG	3,250	6	
New Mulgae class	LCU	940	6	
PKMR	PKMR	200	1 (+15)	16 planned in class

operations against North Korea. Further, given North Korea's development of nuclear weapons and ballistic missiles, the ROKN's installation of the Aegis system on its KDX-III destroyers means the platforms that in many ways symbolise the blue-water modernisation program are now a key component of peninsular defence. The commissioning of the 18,800-ton, amphibious assault ship ROKS *Dokdo* and its future sister ship ROKS *Marado* in combination with the introduction of a new class of four 7,100-ton landing ships will provide the ROKN with a much greater amphibious capability.[8] If resourced properly, these capabilities will strengthen the ROKN's ability to perform independent defensive and offensive operations on the peninsula in a time of war.

Of course, blue-water modernisation is not just about the Korean Peninsula. East Asia is a predominantly maritime theatre that now suffers from increased strategic tension, a heightened potential for arms racing and is the crucible where the rising power of China is pushing against the established power of the US and its allies. The US and Japan are reinforcing their navies and further south, the littoral nations of the South China Sea are undertaking the targeted procurement of key anti-access capabilities such as submarines and strike aircraft.[9] Seoul cannot afford to ignore these developments and therefore, ROKN modernisation is partially aimed at providing a hedge against instability in the maritime sphere. Although South Korea is a US ally, it is reluctant to choose sides in the East Asian maritime domain and views both Japan and China with a level of suspicion. The ROKN cannot compete in terms of manpower and resources with its Northeast Asian neighbours and therefore has set the target of maintaining sufficient independent capabilities to deter threats to its regional maritime interests and sea lines of communication (SLOC). The ROKN is looking to create a force that would represent South Korean interests and is commensurate with an independent, responsible middle power.

Even with the addition of new platforms, questions remain regarding the ability of the ROKN to carry out independent operations far from Northeast Asia. Operational requirements to manage the ever-evolving threat from North Korea and the pressure of increasing maritime strategic tension between China, Japan and the US will mean that ROKN platforms will need to remain in Northeast Asian waters. The goal of sustained independent operations in the wider East Asian region is currently a remote possibility and is more aspirational than realistic given South Korea's geostrategic environment.

Further, ROKN modernisation is not without its problems. It is an ongoing process and one that is fraught with difficulty given the level of suspicion that it generates among some South Korean security stakeholders who are unconvinced by its necessity. Due to the expense of naval modernisation the ROKN is vulnerable to trends in the nation's finances and political priorities. The sinking of the ROKS *Cheonan* by a North Korean submarine in 2010 and the subsequent shelling of Yeonpyeongdo a few months later led many in the South Korean media, political circles and even the public to call for an end to the blue-water program and for the ROKN to refocus on the threat from North Korea.

This was a misunderstanding of the goals of ROKN modernisation, but it exposed the vulnerability of the ROKN to accusations of ignoring peninsular operations. Publicly the ROKN dropped the language of blue-water modernisation but the plans themselves after some delay have continued. The future of the ROKN lies with the initial blue-water concept, but an outstanding question remains regarding the ability of the ROKN to cement its strategic importance within the minds of the public and policymakers.

SOUTH KOREA AND THE SEA

The sea has many attributes, it can be a medium for trade, commerce and cultural exchange, a resource to be exploited, a means of dominion, a barrier from attack and a potential strategic vulnerability.[10] For South Korea, the sea is all of these things. The free use of the maritime domain has facilitated South Korea's phoenix-like emergence from the ruin of the Korean War and its subsequent transformation into one of the world's most advanced trading economies. However, geopolitics and the division of the Korean Peninsula means that South Korea is essentially an island. The safety of its SLOC is therefore of enormous strategic importance as their disruption would imperil their economy and their population's well-being.

The constant threat from North Korea on land and at sea means that South Korea must constantly guard its 2413 km coastline and over 3300 islands, of which 482 are populated.[11] The Northern Limit Line (NLL), the de facto maritime border between the two states, is an area of great strategic tension and its security has meant that the ROKN has been deployed and ready for combat every day since the end of the Korean War in 1953.

South Korea is also sandwiched between two larger and rival powers. To the east and across the East Sea/Sea of Japan lies Japan, the ships of the US 7th Fleet and the route to the Pacific Ocean. To the west across the West Sea/Yellow Sea is the rising power of China.[12] To the south is the East China and the South China Seas, waters that provide a gateway to the Middle East and Europe but are rife with contentious geostrategic issues including disputed maritime territory, conflicting economic exclusive zones (EEZ) and Taiwan. Geostrategic tension in maritime East Asia has been a reality since the end of the Cold War but it is being exacerbated by China's drive to become the preeminent seapower in the region. This is an uncomfortable geostrategic position for South Korea as its vital maritime interests run through waters that are increasingly conflictual (Map 1.1).

South Korea has declared a territorial sea of 12 nm and a contiguous zone of 24 nm.[13] With the ratification and enactment of UNCLOS in 1996, Seoul also declared an EEZ of 200 nm.[14] However due to South

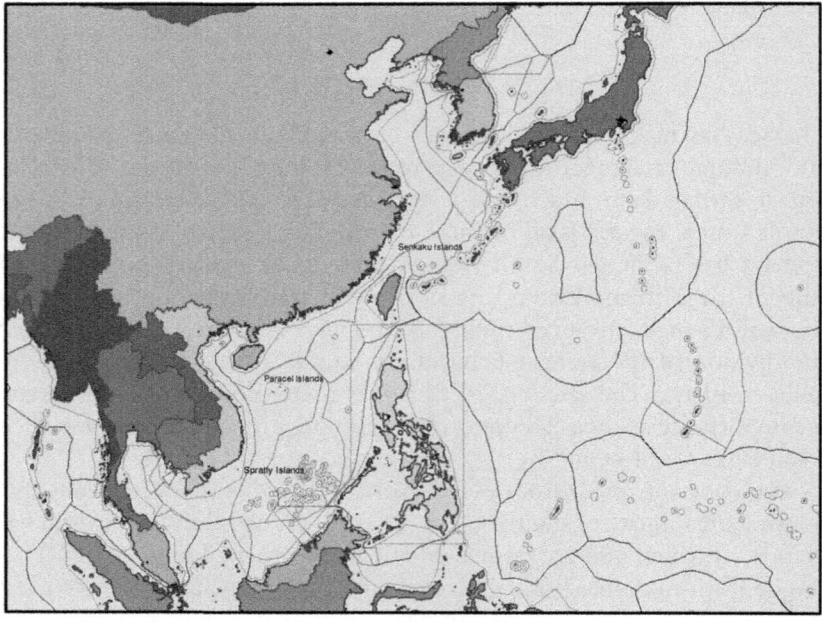

Map 1.1   East Asian Maritime Environment

Korea's proximity with Japan and China and outstanding differences over the ownership of islands, the measuring methods of EEZ and the limits of the continental shelf, neither South Korea's EEZ or continental shelf have been formally delimited.[15] The UNCLOS regime has heightened the strategic and economic importance of maintaining maritime rights and consequently protecting South Korean EEZ has become an important element in South Korea's maritime security thinking.

The economic importance of South Korea's EEZ lies in its maritime resource exploitation activities. The seas around South Korea are rich fishing grounds and although fisheries only account for approximately 0.2% of the country's GDP they are important as a source of food and employment.[16] The South Korean fishing fleet has over 67,000 powered vessels but it has been in slow decline over the past 15 years in part due to government schemes aimed at reducing the size of the fleet.[17] Nevertheless, fishing provided employment for over 200,000 people in 2015.[18] The majority of South Korea's fishing activity takes place within its EEZ. Declining stocks caused by over-fishing and other environmental factors have put increased emphasis on conservation measures and has ensured that the protection of maritime economic rights is a political priority.

So far minimal oil and gas deposits have been found in the waters surrounding the peninsula. In 1998 the Korea National Oil Corporation discovered a viable gas field in the East Sea. Called Donghae-1, it has modest reserves of around 186 billion cubic feet of natural gas.[19] Production started in 2004 and was scheduled to finish in 2016/2017, however the discovery of a second field 5.2 km away (Donghae-2) has extended production until 2019.[20] There is also hope that oil and mineral deposits will be discovered around the Jeju Basin in the East China Sea.[21]

The economic and strategic value of the sea for South Korea extends far beyond its EEZ. With a focus on manufacturing and exports, the economy of South Korea has shown some spectacular growth since the mid-1970s and in 2006 it joined the exclusive group of nations with a GDP of over one trillion dollars.[22] This growth is inextricably linked with the sea. Shipbuilding was identified in the 1960s as a key developmental area in South Korea's industrialisation efforts and received substantial government aid.[23] As Fig. 1.1 demonstrates, access to the sea is vital for South Korean economic growth and seaborne trade has shown

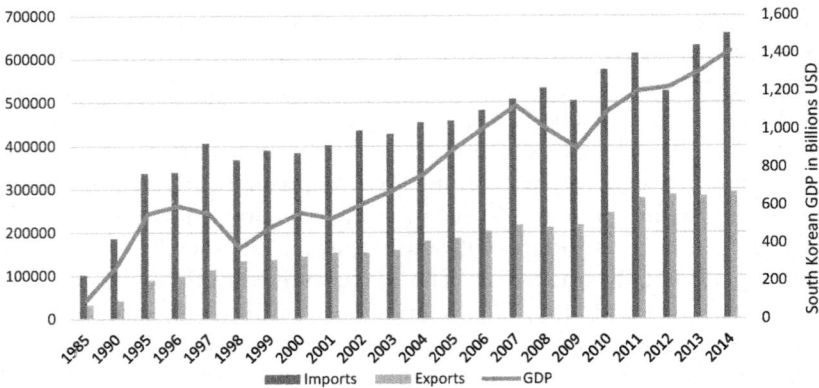

Fig. 1.1 South Korean seaborne trade volume (Thousand Tons) & South Korea GDP in constant US Dollars (*Source* The World Bank, *World Development Indicators*, Republic of Korea 3 January 2018, https://data.worldbank.org/country/korea-rep, accessed 19 March 2018; Korea Shipowners Association, *Korean Seaborne Trade Volume*, http://www.shipowners.or.kr/eng/ks_industry/ks_industry2.php, accessed 19 March 2018)

a steady increase since the 1980s with a clear connection between it and South Korean GDP.

Such growth has only been possible because of the ability to take advantage of the world's SLOC. By 2016, South Korea had become the world's 6th largest importer and 11th largest export of merchandise in the world.[24] In value terms, 85% of South Korea's GDP is carried over the ocean and over 99% of its traded goods.[25] Although South Korea has a population of approximately 51 million people, its largest port at Busan in the southeast of the country is world's 5th busiest container terminal handling over 19 million TEU in 2016.[26]

The size and modernity of the South Korean economy requires a substantial supply of energy. However, South Korea is resource dependent and has no energy pipelines and therefore maritime imports account for over 94% of its energy needs.[27] Figure 1.2 indicates that South Korea is heavily dependent on imports for coal, petroleum products and liquid natural gas (LNG).

It is the world's 5th largest importer of crude oil, 2nd LNG and fourth largest importer of coal for both energy and manufacturing.[28] Without the sea, South Korea would not be able to create the energy

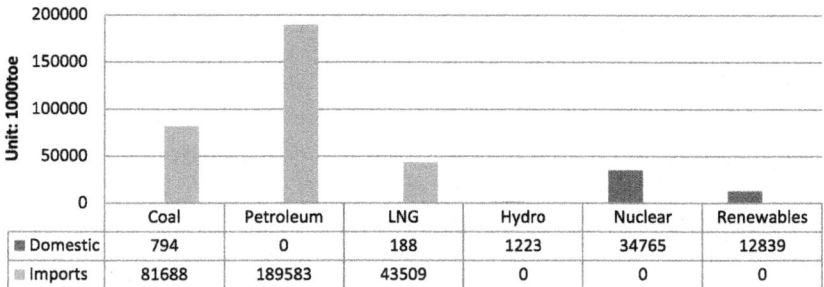

Unit: 1000toe	Coal	Petroleum	LNG	Hydro	Nuclear	Renewables
■ Domestic	794	0	188	1223	34765	12839
▨ Imports	81688	189583	43509	0	0	0

Fig. 1.2 South Korea's energy balance in 2015 (*Source* Korea Energy Economics Institute, *2016 Energy Info. Korea* (Ulsan: Korea Energy Economics Institute, 2017), 50–53)

required to sustain its economy. For both oil and LNG, South Korea is heavily reliant on imports from the Middle East, although there are indications that efforts to diversify its suppliers are bearing fruit as indicated by a substantial increase in energy imports from the US.[29]

SEAPOWER AND EAST ASIA

At the heart of this book is the relationship between seapower, naval power and the state. Noted US strategist, historian and naval officer Alfred T. Mahan coined the term seapower in the nineteenth century, yet he left its definition shrouded in ambiguity.[30] This has complicated the discourse surrounding the pursuit and exercise of power at the sea. Seapower, naval power and maritime power have been used by academic and practitioners interchangeably and often with different understandings of their meaning. The lack of clarity raises several questions. Is seapower analogous to naval power? Is it solely the size of a state's naval forces and their ability to project power overseas? Alternatively, is seapower a broader concept that includes a wider array of ocean-related attributes?

For this volume, seapower is not just about the application of military power at sea. It encompasses 'the entirety of the use of the sea by a nation'.[31] This, of course, comprises all military forces that can produce a strategic effect at sea, including navies, air forces and shore-based capabilities. It also includes civilian components such as merchant marine, maritime law enforcement agencies (MLEA), port facilities and maritime industrial capacity. Naval power as a component of seapower is the basis for the use of military force at sea.[32] It is determined by more than the total tonnage of a fleet or a calculation of ship numbers but rather how naval capabilities are utilised to carry out national strategy be it in the littorals or in vast expanses of the ocean.[33]

Seapower is about how these means are used to influence and 'determine events both at sea and on land'.[34] Seapower, therefore, can produce a number of diverse effects including the control or influence over international trade, the exploitation of maritime resources, the wartime application of power at and from the sea, and the peacetime use of both military and civil power for deterrence, compellence, diplomacy and influence.[35] In the modern world, naval power is the most important element of seapower. After all, the United States, through its navy, exercises substantial seapower and can achieve incredible strategic effect, yet it now does not possess a substantial merchant marine or fishing fleet.[36]

Importantly, seapower is not solely the preserve of major powers in possession of global power projection capabilities. Yet frustratingly the study of seapower and its use has mainly focused on large states.[37] All states that have a coast possess a minimum capability to achieve affect at sea and therefore exercise some form seapower.[38] As Till crucially notes, seapower is relative; 'some countries, and this is the point, have more or less than others, and it is that relationship that is strategically significant in peace and war'.[39]

A broad number of factors determine the level of seapower a state chooses to pursue. These include geostrategy, technological capability, threat perception, economic capacity, state policy and national identity.[40] History suggests that some states such as Venice, Britain or the Netherlands naturally develop seapower to offset economic or geostrategic weakness.[41] For such states, seapower is inculcated into their strategic culture. Other states choose to artificially pursue seapower as a means for power projection or other specific national interests. As Eric Grove argues, if a state wishes to impact international events and 'shape the contemporary security environment to reflect one's own and allies' geopolitical interests one has to be a major seapower or a significant contributor to a maritime coalition'.[42] Given this reality, it is no surprise that naval capability has been an often-used method to judge the relative power of states.[43]

It should also be accepted that for many states, the pursuit of substantial levels of seapower could be considered a luxury. This is particularly true if the level pursued exceeds what is minimally required for immediate national defence. The naval component of seapower is capital intensive and requires dedicated and long-term planning for its effective development. Further, states that face threats on their borders must make hard choices regarding the level of seapower and particularly naval power to be pursued as they risk diverting precious resources away from their key security concerns.[44] However, as Norman Friedman writes, for states that can afford it, naval power can provide substantial advantages.

> Given the combination of capital intensity and mobility, sea-based forces offer (or at least have offered) far more leverage per man than armies. For a high-industrialised country able to choose between land power and sea-power, seapower is a natural expression of national power.[45]

These considerations of seapower have substantial relevance in East Asia, a region dominated by its maritime system. In the twenty-first century, strategic competition will play out in the waters of the Indo-Pacific. This is a substantial difference from the twentieth century where the geo-strategic interests of the great powers collided on the plains of Western Europe. The exercise of seapower and its relative balance will play a central role in determining strategic stability in the coming decades.

In Northeast Asia, China, Japan and South Korea all possess the coastlines, technological capability, economic capacity and strategic need to pursue and operationalise seapower. These three states are among the strongest civil-maritime states in the world as they all rely on the sea for the import and export of goods, raw materials and energy. It should be no surprise that eight of the world's top ten busiest container ports are in Northeast Asia.[46] Chinese, South Korean and Japanese shipyards are the busiest in the world accounting for 92% of global deliveries in 2016.[47] All three countries are in the top ten in terms of ship-owning countries, with Japan in 2nd, China 3rd and South Korea 7th.[48]

This domination of many of the civil aspects of seapower is now replicated in the development of naval power in the region. By far the biggest change is China's pursuit of naval power and its integration of the numerous components of seapower into a coherent maritime strategy.

China is seeking to become something almost unique in world geopolitics, a preeminent continental power and simultaneously a preeminent seapower.

This is a long-term project, which has evolved in strategic and political importance for the leadership in Beijing. The origins of the China's naval power development can be found in the 1980s when Beijing determined that the Soviet Union was no longer a major threat and that smaller wars on China's periphery would become the major strategic challenge.[49] China's economic interests, capacity to create naval power and significant internal dynamics such as the ascendancy of Liu Huaqing to the head of the People's Liberation Army Navy (PLAN) combined to create a situation where naval power development could thrive. In an indication of its growing importance, in a 1992 speech, President Jiang Zemin spoke about the need to protect the country's 'maritime interests'.[50] Ten years later, in his work report at the 18th Party Congress, President Hu Jintao declared that China was to become a great maritime power.[51] Five years after that, China's 2015 Military Strategy declared:

> The traditional mentality that land outweighs sea must be abandoned, and great importance has to be attached to managing the seas and oceans and protecting maritime rights and interests. It is necessary for China to develop a modern maritime military force structure commensurate with its national security and development interests, safeguard its national sovereignty and maritime rights and interests, protect the security of strategic SLOCs and overseas interests, and participate in international maritime cooperation, so as to provide strategic support for building itself into a maritime power.[52]

It should be no surprise that this push to the sea comes at a time when China has secured the majority of its land borders and has become the world's second-largest economy. For the leadership in Beijing, the possession of seapower is about more than defence. It is an expression of China's growth and national power and signals a desire to influence events far from its littorals. China's development and utilisation of not just its navy, the (PLAN), but also its MLEA, maritime militia, fishing and merchant fleets to all produce strategic effect and exercise China's national policies is a true expression of seapower and one that is challenging the region and beyond. As Andrew Erickson highlights China is pursuing 'a naval strategy that has evolved from "near-coast defense" to a combination of "near-seas defense" and "far seas protection"'.[53] The combination of these seapower elements is allowing China to operationalize a maritime strategy of future military and civil peacetime dominance in the seas of North and Southeast Asia and beyond through the maritime component of the one-belt one road (OBOR) economic strategy and a coercive approach to controlling the economic resources of the South China Sea.[54]

For Japan, seapower is not a strategic luxury or tool to project power far from its own shores. As Japan is an island nation, both the military and civil components of seapower are viewed as central to the state's survival. Japan's first national security strategy written in 2013, placed the maritime domain as a core determinant of its security stating:

> Surrounded by the sea on all sides and blessed with an immense exclusive economic zone and an extensive coastline, Japan as maritime state has achieved economic growth through maritime trade and development of marine resources, has pursued "Open and Stable Seas".[55]

This text expounded a truth that has been present in Japanese defence planning since the end of World War II. Built upon the country's imperial history following the Meiji restoration, the Japanese Maritime Self Defense Force's (JMSDF) doctrine has, since the 1960s, focused on protecting its SLOC and during the Cold War complementing its major ally, the US, with mine warfare and anti-submarine warfare (ASW) forces aimed at containing the threat posed by the Soviet Pacific Fleet.[56] Since the end of the Cold War, Japan's naval development has continued to focus on SLOC protection while adding capabilities aimed at defending nation from the threat posed by North Korea, protecting Japanese territory (both the homeland and its outlying Island including Senkaku/Diaoyudao) and future asymmetric threats.

In this sense, Japan's maritime commitments and policies have not undergone substantial changes but rather a natural evolution reflecting altering security concerns.[57] Force modernisation and operational structures to deal with new threats such as the rise of China and the requirement to protect islands are designed to leverage modern multifunctional naval capabilities so that the capability to protect SLOC is always available. For Japan, the understanding of seapower is determined by the vulnerability that maritime geography imposes on it.

This leaves South Korea. Unlike China and Japan, South Korea faces an intractable and existential foe on its immediate border. Its approach to seapower was one of emphasis on the civil component to further its economic development, but its pursuit of naval power was framed and limited by the threat from North Korea. How naval power integrates with seapower and nature of South Korea as a state is a core theme in this volume. South Korea's linkage of economic security, naval power and its utility not just for national security but also for national prestige and influence must be weighed against the need to maintain naval forces in the littoral. Every country views seapower in a different manner and for South Korea, the bifurcated and multiple challenges it faces mean that its understanding of the relationship between seapower and the state is still evolving.

THE STRUCTURE OF THE BOOK

This volume uses a mix of primary and secondary sources including government and military publications, a small number of Korean and foreign works on the ROKN and South Korean seapower, newspaper reports and several available unpublished Master and PhD thesis written by serving ROKN officers. The author has also used formal and informal interviews with active and retired military officers, government officials, and academics. As this book concerns naval modernisation, I only explore the South Korean Coastguard and the Republic of Korea Marine Corps within the context of ROKN operations. Both play a vital role in South Korean maritime securityand I hope this book will be a platform for greater research into these organisations. Researching South Korean security is often problematic as the country's Military Secret Protection Act understandably ensures that military affairs and information are closely held. Consequently, sources are often in disagreement about the technical details of the South Korean military. In these cases, I have used my best judgement to decide the correct information, any errors in this volume are entirely mine.

The remainder of this book builds upon the themes introduced in this chapter. Chapter 2 examines how the threat from North Korea at sea influences ROKN modernisation. The chapter first discusses the operational geography in the littoral waters of the Korean Peninsula with a focus on the critical waters around the NLL. The chapter then turns to the nature of deterrence at sea and how ROKN modernisation is influenced by the need to respond to changes in North Korea's threat posture. The chapter concludes by highlighting the operational advantages that the multifunctional platforms introduced under the blue-water modernisation program provide the ROKN in the littoral waters of the Korean Peninsula.

Chapter 3 turns to South Korea's maritime strategic interests in non-peninsular contexts. It demonstrates that South Korea faces several direct and indirect security threats at sea. These include the challenge of maintaining their strategic maritime interests in an area of increased strategic competition, protecting their maritime resources and ensuring the security of their SLOC. The chapter argues that these threats have partially driven and shaped blue-water modernisation. However, the need to maintain deterrence around the Korean Peninsula pulls ROKN operations in different directions. The chapter concludes by describing how the ROKN is attempting to leverage the multifunctionality and mobility of modern naval platforms and integrate these capabilities into a force structure that can respond to threats in both peninsular and non-peninsular contexts. Chapter 4 discusses the nature of the ROKN's force modernisation effort since 1990. It explores the surface, subsurface and aviation capabilities that have been added to the ROKN fleet. It then assesses how these capabilities are being integrated into the ROKN force structure and training regimen.

Chapter 5 examines how the US alliance has influenced ROKN blue-water modernisation. This chapter starts at the end of the Korean War and traces how alterations in the US-South Korea alliance resulted in changes in the procurement and operational priorities of the ROKN. It concludes by arguing that although the US has historically acted as a constraint to ROKN blue-water modernisation it now encourages it, as a modern and capable ROKN is more able to support US naval operations. Chapter 6 turns to domestic matters and explores how the ROKN is attempting to engage the South Korean public and political elite in the blue-water modernisation effort. They are trying to achieve this through the creation of a naval identity which will ultimately result in naval power being a natural part of South Korean defence planning. The ROKN is leveraging history, utilising public relations strategies and collaborating with seapower advocates to inform both the public and elites about the necessity of blue-water operations, however, this is a long-term effort which is constantly challenged by the threat of North Korea. Chapter 7 continues with this theme by examining the relationship between naval modernisation and domestic politics. It explores four South Korean administrations between 1993 and 2013. The chapter argues that ROKN blue-water modernisation initially succeeded because the ambition for greater South Korean naval power matched the policies of three successive administrations.

The book concludes by tying these strands of naval modernisation together. It shows that naval modernisation is a multifaceted process which to be properly analysed requires the examination of internal and external strategic and political factors. It argues that ROKN blue-water modernisation is most likely going to continue but it is vulnerable to changes in the political and strategic circumstances of South Korea. It highlights some of the future challenges that South Korea may face in continuing along a path of blue-water modernisation including the cost of technology and alliance requirements. Even with successful and sustained blue-water modernisation the persistent problem of limited platform numbers and multiple missions sets will continue to dog the ROKN and determine their operational effectiveness around the Korean Peninsula and beyond.

NOTES

1. South Korea is also referred to as the Republic of Korea (ROK). In this volume, South Korea will be used except in the case of citations and when government publications are referenced.
2. Young-sam Kim, *Speech at the 49th Commencement Ceremony of the Korean Naval Academy*, 24 March 1995, http://pa.go.kr/research/contents/speech/index.jsp?spMode=view&artid=1308100&catid=c_pa02062, accessed 10 March 2017.
3. North Korea is also referred to as the Democratic People's Republic of Korea (DPRK). In this volume, North Korea will be used except in the case of citations and when government publications are referenced.
4. During the Korean War, the ROKN was tasked with mine clearance, coastal operations including raids and fire support, logistical operations and refugee relief operations. See: Paul M. Edwards, *Small United States and United Nations Warships in the Korean War* (Jefferson: McFarland & Co, 2008), 219.
5. United States Navy, *Naval Operations Concept 2010: Implementing the Maritime Strategy* (Washington, DC: United States Department of the Navy, 2010), 9.
6. See: Daniel Todd and Michael Lindberg, *Navies and Shipbuilding Industries: The Strained Symbiosis* (Westport: Praeger, 1996), 55–56.
7. The South Korean Military Glossary uses the term *Daeyanghaegun* which literally means ocean navy, to describe both an ocean-going

and blue-water navy. See: Republic of Korea Joint Chiefs of Staff, *Gunsayongeohaesol* [Military Glossary], http://www.jcs.mil.kr/user/indexSub.action?codyMenuSeq=71157&siteId=jcs&menuUIType=sub, accessed 19 January 2018.

8. Displacement figures on based on full-load measurements.

9. Ian Bowers, "Power Asymmetry and the Role of Deterrence in the South China Sea," *Korean Journal of Defense Analysis* 29, no. 4 (2017): 551–73.

10. Geoffrey Till, *Seapower: A Guide for the Twenty-First Century*, 2nd ed. (Oxon: Routledge, 2009), 23–32.

11. Republic of Korea Navy, *Gandanhago pyeonhage ilgeul su inneun haegungaideubuk* [An Easy and Simple to Read Navy Guide Book] (Gyeryong: Navy Headquarters, 2016), 175.

12. South Korea uses the name East Sea to describe the Sea of Japan and the West Sea to describe the Yellow Sea. For consistency this volume will use the South Korean names. This is not a judgement on their propriety.

13. U.S. Navy Judge Advocate General's Corps, "Korea, Republic of: Summary of Claims, DoD 2005.1-M," *Maritime Claims Reference Manual*, October 2014, http://www.jag.navy.mil/organization/documents/mcrm/Korea,South2014.pdf, accessed 10 February 2018.

14. Ibid.

15. Different ROKN publications provide different assessments of the total size of South Korean maritime territory (including EEZ), potentially due to the undermined nature of the EEZ. One 2008 publication states its maritime territory is 308,408 km^2, while a 2011 publication puts it at 443,000 km^2. See: Republic of Korea Navy *(Nuguna al su Issneun!) Haegunjakjeon Deuryeodabogi* [As Anyone Can See! Look into Naval Operations] (Seoul: Republic of Korea Navy, 2011), 10; Republic of Korea Navy Headquarters, *2008nyeondo haegunjeongchaek bogoseo* [2008 Naval Policy Report] (Gyeryong: ROKN Headquarters), 10.

16. Food and Agriculture Organisation of the United Nations, *Fishery and Aquaculture Profiles Republic of Korea*, June 2017, http://www.fao.org/fishery/facp/KOR/en, accessed 4 January 2018.

17. Food and Agricultural Organisation of the United Nations, *FAO Yearbook: Fishery and Aquaculture Statistics* (Rome: Food and Agricultural Organisation of the United Nations, 2017), 15.

18. Ibid., 17.

19. Korea National Oil Company, *Operations: E&P Worldwide*, https://www.knoc.co.kr/ENG/sub03/sub03_1_1_4.jsp, accessed 3 February 2018.

20. Jin-hai Park, "Donghae-1 Natural Gas Field," *The Korea Times*, 3 November 2015, http://www.koreatimes.co.kr/www/news/biz/2015/11/123_190136.html, accessed 3 February 2018.

21. Korea National Oil Company, *Operations: E&P Worldwide*.
22. Currently only 15 countries have GDP of over one trillion dollars. South Korea fell out of group following the 2008 financial crisis but quickly re-joined in 2010. All figures taken from: The World Bank, *GDP (Current US$) Korea, Rep. 1960–2016*, https://data.worldbank.org/indicator/NY.GDP.MKTP.CD?locations=KR, accessed 10 February 2018.
23. Kyoung-ho Shin and Paul S. Cicanntell, "The Steel and Shipbuilding Industries of South Korea: Rising East Asia and Globalisation," *American Sociological Association* 15, no. 2 (2009): 181.
24. Central Intelligence Agency, "Country Comparison: Imports," *The World Factbook*, Continuously Updated, https://www.cia.gov/library/publications/resources/the-world-factbook/rankorder/2078rank.html, accessed 3 February 2018.
25. Republic of Korea Navy (*Nuguna al su Issneun!*), 10.
26. Hong Liang Lee, "Busan Port Aims for 20m TEU Container Volume in 2017," *Seatrade Maritime News*, 24 January 2017, http://www.seatrade-maritime.com/news/asia/busan-port-aims-for-20m-teu-container-volumes-in-2017.html, accessed 10 February 2018.
27. Korea Energy Economics Institute, *2016 Energy Info. Korea* (Ulsan: Korea Energy Economics Institute, 2017), 6. The remainder consists of some LNG and renewable energy sources.
28. United States Energy Information Administration, *Country Analysis Brief: South Korea*, 19 January 2017, https://www.eia.gov/beta/international/analysis_includes/countries_long/Korea_South/south_korea.pdf, accessed 10 February 2018.
29. "S. Korea's U.S. Energy Imports Soar This Year," *Yonhap News Agency*, 20 December 2017, http://english.yonhapnews.co.kr/business/201 7/12/20/0501000000AEN20171220009300320.html, accessed 10 February 2018.
30. John Gooch, "Maritime Command: Mahan and Corbett," in *Seapower and Strategy*, ed. Colin S. Gray and Roger W. Barnett (London: Tri-Service Press, 1989), 31.
31. Milan N. Vego, "On Naval Power," *Joint Forces Quarterly* 50, no. 3 (2008): 9.
32. Ibid; Ian Speller, *Understanding Naval Warfare* (Oxon: Routledge, 2014), 41.
33. For this author littoral operations fall within the British Maritime Doctrine's open definition of '*coastal sea areas and that portion of the land which is susceptible to influence or support from the sea*'. See: United Kingdom Ministry of Defence, *British Maritime Doctrine, BR 1806*, 3rd ed. (London: The Stationary Office, 2004), 27.

34. Geoffrey Till, Seapower, 22.
35. Sam J. Tangredi, "Globalization and Sea Power: Overview and Context," in *Globalization and Maritime Power*, ed. Sam J. Tangredi (Washington, DC: National Defense University, 2002), 3.
36. Robert C. Rubel, *Navies and Economic Prosperity—The New Logic of Sea Power*, Corbett Paper No. 11 (London: Kings College London, 2012).
37. There is a small but growing body of work looking at how small and middle powers understand and exploit the sea. See: Ian Speller, Deborah Sanders, and Michael Mulqueen, "Introduction," in *Small Navies: Strategy and Policy for Small Navies in War and Peace*, ed. Michael Mulqueen, Deborah Saunders, and Ian Speller (Surrey: Ashgate, 2014), 1–14.
38. Geoffrey Till, Seapower, 22.
39. Ibid.
40. Sam J. Tangredi, "Globalization and Sea Power: Overview and Context," 3.
41. Colin S. Gray and Roger W. Barnett, "Introduction," in *Seapower and Strategy*, ed. Colin S. Gray and Roger W. Barnett (London: Tri-Service Press, 1989), xiii.
42. Eric Grove, "The Ever-Increasing Importance of Sea Power," *ISN, ETH Zurich*, 7 April 2014, https://www.files.ethz.ch/isn/188136/ISN_177612_en.pdf, accessed 5 March 2018.
43. Alessio Patalano and James Manicom, "Rising Tides: Seapower and Regional Security in Northeast Asia," *The Journal of Strategic Studies* 37, no. 3 (2014): 336.
44. Jakub Grygiel, "Geography and Seapower," in *Twenty-First Century Seapower: Cooperation and Conflict at Sea*, ed. Peter Dutton, Robert S. Ross, and Oystein Tunsjø (Oxon: Routledge, 2012), 19.
45. Norman Friedman, *Seapower as Strategy: Navies and National Interests* (Annapolis: Naval Institute Press, 2001), 43.
46. Seven are in China and one in South Korea. See "Top 50 World Container Ports," *World Shipping Council*, http://www.worldshipping.org/about-the-industry/global-trade/top-50-world-container-ports, accessed 3 March 2018.
47. United Nations Conference on Trade and Development, *Review of Maritime Transport 2017* (Geneva: United Nations Conference on Trade and Development, 2017), 22.
48. Ibid., 28.
49. Bernard D. Cole, *The Great Wall at Sea 2nd Edition: China's Navy in the Twenty-First Century* (Annapolis: Naval Institute Press, 2010), 16.
50. Office of the Secretary of Defense, *Annual Report to Congress: Military and Security Developments Involving the People's Republic of China* (Washington, DC: Department of Defense, 2011), 58

51. Michael McDevitt, "Beijing's Dream: Becoming a Maritime Superpower," *The National Interest*, 1 July 2016, http://nationalinterest.org/blog/the-buzz/beijings-dream-becoming-maritime-superpower-16812, accessed 3 March 2018.

52. Ministry of National Defense, The People's Republic of China, *Full Text: China's Military Strategy*, 16 May 2015, http://eng.mod.gov.cn/Press/2015-05/26/content_4586805_4.htm.

53. Andrew Erickson, "Numbers Matter: China's Three Navies Each Have the World's Most Ships," *The National Interest*, 26 February 2018, http://nationalinterest.org/feature/numbers-matter-chinas-three-navies-each-have-the-worlds-most-24653?page=show, accessed 3 March 2018.

54. M. Taylor Fravel, "China's Strategy in the South China Sea," *Contemporary Southeast Asia* 33, no. 3 (2011): 296; Tim Huxley and Benjamin Schreer, "Standing Up to China," *Survival* 57, no. 6 (2015): 130.

55. Prime Minister of Japan, *National Security Strategy*, 17 December 2013, http://japan.kantei.go.jp/96_abe/documents/2013/__icsFiles/afieldfile/2013/12/17/NSS.pdf, accessed 3 March 2017.

56. Alessio Patalano, "Japan as a Seapower: Strategy, Doctrine, and Capabilities Under Three Defence Reviews, 1995–2010," *The Journal of Strategic Studies* 37, no. 3 (2014): 410–11.

57. Peter J. Wooley, *Japan's Navy: Politics and Paradox* (London: Lynne Rienner, 1999), 17; Alessio Patalano, *Post-war Japan as a Sea Power: Imperial Legacy, Wartime Experience and the Making of a Navy* (London: Bloomsbury, 2015), 157–61.

CHAPTER 2

North Korea and Deterrence at Sea

The tragic sinking of the ROKS *Cheonan* in 2010 was a strategic shock for the ROKN. North Korea's use of a submarine exposed weaknesses in the ROKN's littoral ASW capabilities and forced a reassessment of the potential for severe escalatory acts in the waters around the Korean peninsula. The attack brought into focus the difficulties faced by the ROKN in maintaining deterrent superiority over North Korea while also managing South Korea's multiple other maritime strategic interests.

Since the end of the Korean War, ROKN planners have had to contend with an opponent that is continuously seeking to design around their deterrent measures. Deterrence in the littoral waters of the Korean Peninsula is about maintaining sufficient forces to prevent the outbreak of war and discourage North Korea from violating South Korean maritime territory. The same South Korean naval forces used to maintain deterrence 24 hours a day, 365 days a year must also be prepared for the sudden outbreak of fighting or full-scale war and therefore have to be able to seamlessly transition from deterrence, to combat, to defensive operations to offensive operations in short order. Even in an era of blue-water modernisation, when the ROKN has looked to expand the scope of its operations, managing the threat posed by North Korea at sea remains its primary task.

The geography of the Korean Peninsula and the evolving nature of the threat posed by the KPN determines how the ROKN carries out this mission. Given the secretive nature of the North Korean regime, it is

© The Author(s) 2019   23
I. Bowers, *The Modernisation of the Republic of
Korea Navy*, Critical Studies of the Asia-Pacific,
https://doi.org/10.1007/978-3-319-92291-1_2

impossible to completely understand the KPN's objectives under existing armistice conditions, but from what is known publicly about their operations and capabilities, traditional naval roles such as surveillance, fishery protection and littoral defence form part of the KPN's mission set.[1] Yet, it is the more offensive aspects of their operations that influence the ROKN's day-to-day strategy, tactics and deployments.

The KPN presents a consistent amphibious and subsurface threat to South Korean waters, islands and mainland areas close to the maritime border. This, along with the KPN's sustained and often aggressive contesting of the Northern Limit Line (NLL) requires the ROKN to maintain deployed and deployable forces on high alert on and near the NLL. Although, the KPN is qualitatively inferior to the ROKN, its development of asymmetric capabilities such as mini-submarines and high-speed amphibious craft ensures that the ROKN must continuously adjust its own capabilities to maintain deterrence.[2]

This chapter demonstrates that the long deterrent standoff on the Korean Peninsula ultimately affords the ROKN time to adjust to changes in North Korea's threat profile. South Korea's current superiority in terms of resources makes such adjustments easier, enabling them to react quicker and modernise faster than their North Korean opponents. However, this dynamic is not without cost, the sinking of the *Cheonan* highlights the dangerous nature of operations in the Korean littoral and the complexities of maintaining deterrence against an unpredictable opponent.

What follows in this chapter is a discussion of the threat North Korea's maritime forces pose and how the ROKN is forced to continuously adjust and modernise its operational posture and procurement priorities to it. This chapter first discusses the operational geography in the littoral waters of the Korean Peninsula with a focus on the critical waters around the NLL. The chapter then turns to the nature of deterrence at sea and the lessons provided by three surface clashes that occurred between 1999 and 2009. Next, the chapter addresses how the ROKN has attempted to adjust to the various threats that the KPN poses including the challenge of submarine warfare. The chapter concludes by highlighting the operational advantages that the multi-functional platforms introduced under the blue-water modernisation programme provide the ROKN in the littoral waters of the peninsula.

Operational Geography

Both the threat posed by the KPN and the ROKN's response to it are largely determined by the interaction of geography and capabilities. The KPN does not currently possess platforms that can operate efficiently outside of littoral waters and therefore North and South Korean naval forces do not interact on the high seas. Instead, the ROKN must manage the threat posed by North Korea within the littorals of the Korean Peninsula.

The division of the peninsula on land is what defines the area of operations at sea. The Military Demarcation Line (MDL) which forms the basis of the Demilitarized Zone (DMZ) separates the two sides on land. Established in 1953 as part of the Armistice Agreement, the MDL is protected by fencing, guard posts, minefields and all the other military capabilities one would associate with a fortified border. At sea, the NLL is the de facto maritime border between North and South Korea (Map 2.1). It extends out into the sea on both sides of the peninsula and functionally demarcates the maritime territory of both sides, yet unlike the DMZ, there are no markings to delimit the border and no barriers

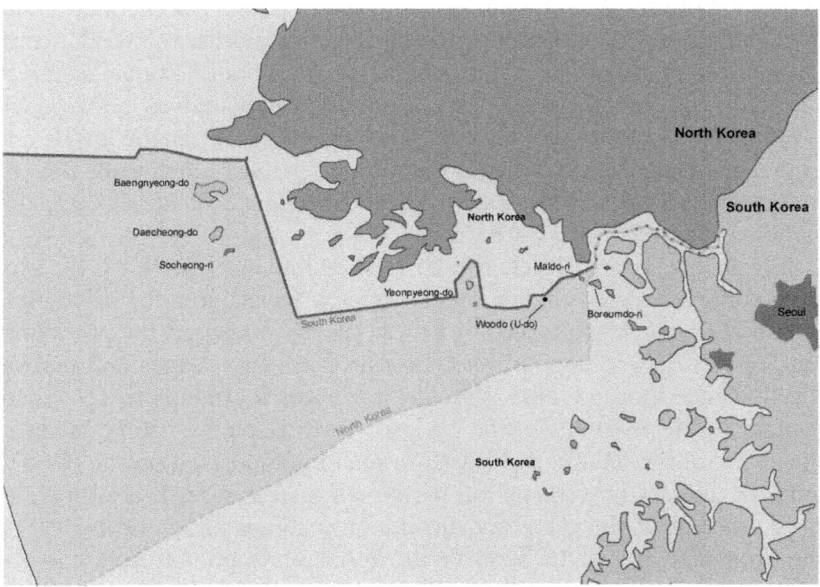

Map 2.1 The Northern Limit Line and Northwest Islands

to breach.[3] Consequently, as total control of the sea is impossible, both military and civilian actors of either side can enter and exit the territory of the other before being challenged. This poses an operational problem for the ROKN as naval vessels can move quickly and cover distances at a greater rate than ground forces thereby increasing the risk of surprise.[4] This heightens the potential for interaction between the opposing forces, thereby opening the door for clashes, escalation and the potential outbreak of hostilities.

The ROKN is tasked with deterring KPN ships and North Korean civilian vessels from crossing the NLL on both the surface and subsurface, monitoring the entire littoral of South Korea for signs of covert intrusion and deterring the outbreak of full-scale war. This requires the maintenance of sufficient surveillance capabilities and forces in situ both on the NLL and around the peninsula to demonstrate presence, immediately respond to North Korean actions and to provide reinforcements when conflict escalation occurs.

On the east coast of the Korean Peninsula, the NLL is a direct extension of the MDL and its legitimacy has never been challenged by North Korea.[5] On the west coast, the location of five South Korean-controlled islands, Woodo, Yeonpyeongdo, Baengnyeongdo, Daecheongdo and Socheongdo, collectively known as the Northwest Islands (NWI), complicated the demarcation of the NLL. To ensure South Korean access to the NWI, the NLL follows a position approximately midway between the NWI and the North Korean coast.[6] This deviates from the MDL and in practice extends South Korean maritime territory northward, thereby making North Korean access to the West Sea more difficult and arguably violating their territorial waters.[7]

On an operational level, the current delimitation of the NLL provides some strategic benefits for the ROKN. By including the five NWI in South Korean waters, access to these islands is secured thereby allowing South Korea to support the populations on the islands and making their defence more credible should North Korea attempt to take them by force.[8] The proximity of the NLL to North Korean territory enhances the ability of the ROKN and South Korean forces located on the NWI to monitor military movements on the North Korean side. It also provides early warning in the case of a surprise amphibious attack on the NWI, the proximate city of Incheon or the Seoul Metropolitan Area.[9] In the same manner, the NLL serves as a quasi-line of defence where infiltrating submarines and other craft can be blocked or intercepted, thereby increasing the protection of South Korea's territorial integrity, ports and littoral SLOC.

While these are operational advantages, the ROKN must contend with two fundamental challenges. The first is the proximity of the NLL to the North Korean coast which puts it in range of North Korean coastal weaponry such as heavy artillery, shore-based anti-ship missiles and multiple launch rocket systems (MLRS). It also places South Korean territory and forces in range of the North Korean air force (KPAAF). Although the KPAAF possesses a fleet of ageing aircraft and is inferior to the ROKAF and USAF, its potential presence in the airspace around the NLL complicates the operational environment and could endanger the operation of ROKN ASW aircraft.[10] This compressed area of operations also assists North Korea in carrying out operations against South Korean interests as it shortens the warning and consequent response time for the ROKN in the event of attack from the air, surface or subsurface.

The second challenge is the fact that North Korea contests the legitimacy of the NLL. The NLL was not initially introduced as legal maritime border, but as an operational line of control. The Armistice Agreement which established the MDL and DMZ did not include a maritime component and consequently the NLL was demarcated later in 1953 when the then Commander of United Nations Command saw the need to divide the respective territorial seas to minimise the prospect of violence erupting due to South Korean fishing vessels entering North Korean waters.[11]

For twenty years after the signing of the armistice, North Korea did not formally protest the maritime delimitation imposed by the NLL. And in fact, there is evidence that both sides used the NLL to divide the lucrative fishing grounds off the west coast.[12] However, at a December 1973 meeting of the UN Military Armistice Commission (UNMAC), Pyongyang raised an objection. They argued that while South Korea legitimately controlled the NWI, the islands were in North Korean territorial waters and South Korea would require permission to access them. They proposed moving the NLL further south and drawing it as a direct extension of the MDL. Both the UNC and South Korea rejected this proposal and the location of the NLL has remained unchanged.[13]

North Korea has undertaken periodic campaigns, notably in the 1970s—after their original complaints were rejected—and again in the

1990s, to contest the NLL. These have taken the form of deploying military and civilian vessels across the line, thereby forcing a South Korean response. This is a standard approach when contesting maritime borders and has been used across the world in contested maritime spaces such as the Gulf of Fonesca or the South China Sea. It is typically a low-cost strategy as withdrawal at sea is usually easy and no territory is permanently gained or conceded. But in the strategic context of the Korean Peninsula, such contestation operations both increase the risk of unintentional escalation and facilitate a strategy of escalation by choice.

The legal ambiguity and political status of the NLL further complicate ROKN operations as contesting the NLL by crossing it does not have the same potential political and strategic consequences for North Korea as violating the DMZ on land. As the NLL was not part of the original Armistice Agreement, the US and by extension UNC does not view North Korean vessels crossing the NLL as an armistice violation[14] However, acts of violence that have occurred as a direct result of North Korean vessels crossing the NLL have been classified as such.[15]

At the same time, the integrity of the NLL has become increasingly important in South Korean political and nationalist discourse. This raises the pressure on the ROKN to respond robustly to any North Korea violation of the NLL. As incidents along the NLL have become more serious, particularly the sinking of the *Cheonan* and the shelling of Yeonpyeongdo, maintaining the integrity of the maritime border has become a matter national pride. Both, politically and ideologically the NLL is now fundamentally linked to the idea of South Korean sovereignty and resistance against North Korean aggression.

South Korea's 2012 Defense White Paper became the first major MND document to assert that the NLL was the de facto maritime border, declaring that the waters 'south of the NLL are under ROK jurisdiction'.[16] In the same year a vicious political conflict erupted in Seoul, as allegations surfaced in South Korea's National Assembly that former President Roh Moo-hyun had secretly agreed to alter the status of the NLL during the 2007 inter-Korean summit with Kim Jong-il. While the allegations proved to have little merit, the tenor of the argument between the liberal and conservative sides of South Korean political divide demonstrated the political importance now placed on securing the NLL and the pressure on the ROKN to do so effectively.[17]

Further, the NLL sits across lucrative fishing grounds which heightens the potential for fishing vessels on either side to cross it in pursuit of catch. While South Korean fishing vessels have been culpable in this regard, their violations were brought under control in the 1970s as a result of new restrictions, heavier policing on the part of the ROKN and South Korean Coast Guard (KCG) and aggressive KPN actions which resulted in the capture and in some cases deaths of numerous South Korean fishermen.[18] In recent years North Korean fishing vessels have crossed the NLL, sometimes escorted by KPN patrol vessels but have always turned or been forced back. The situation is complicated by the fact that Chinese fishing vessels also operate legally and illegally on both sides of the NLL and often cross it to avoid arrest or seizure.[19]

Surface Clashes & Superiority

Collectively the above factors of geography, strategy and politics result in a complicated operational environment for the ROKN to manage. Deterrence at sea has periodically failed as the KPN's efforts to contest the NLL and defend its own maritime claims have resulted in the use of force and substantial casualties. In 1967, a ROKN patrol craft, the ROKS *Dangpo* (formerly the USS *Marfa*) was ensuring that South Korea fishing vessels did not cross the NLL when it was sunk by North Korean shore artillery four miles off the North Korean coast with the loss of 39 ROKN sailors killed and 15 wounded.[20] In 1974, a South Korean Maritime Police Patrol boat was also sunk following a two-hour firefight with KPN patrol boats in the East Sea resulting in 26 casualties.[21]

It should be noted that during this period, following heavy investment in missile-armed vessels, submarines and amphibious lift capability, North Korea held both quantitative and qualitative superiority over the ROKN.[22] As there were no US naval forces permanently stationed in the area to reinforce them, ROKN and South Korean maritime law enforcement vessels were vulnerable to periodic incidents of North Korean escalation. This balance began to shift in the late 1980s as South Korea's economy grew stronger and North Korea weakened. The ROKN has undergone near continuous fleet renewal since then, leveraging its industrial capacity to indigenously construct new vessels and using its economic strength to procure and design new weapons systems. Conversely, the KPN has struggled to keep pace with ROKN modernisation and its surface fleet has become increasingly obsolete. The blue-water modernisation period that began in the early 1990s built upon this trend and has served to increase the ROKN's relative superiority over the KPN.

The growing disparity between the two navies was revealed in three major surface confrontations on the NLL. The First and Second Battles of Yeonpyeong in 1999 and 2002 and the Battle of Daechong in 2009. Combined, they demonstrate how the ROKN's superior capabilities allowed them dominate surface engagements and provided them with a greater operational scope to adjust to changes in KPN tactics.

The origins of the First Battle of Yeonpyeong, which began on June 15, 1999, can be found nine days earlier when North Korea accused ROKN vessels of entering their territorial waters. What followed was several days of KPN and North Korean fishing vessels performing contestation operations by crossing the NLL. The ROKN maintained a force level in the area of operations that would allow them to secure military superiority should fighting break out.[23] This included up to 12 fast patrol boats (PKM) and four corvettes (PCC). On June 9th a KPN patrol boat that had crossed the NLL intentionally collided with a ROKN vessel. The ROKN responded by initiating bumping operations to push the North Korean boats in an effort to end the crossing, and by June 11th both sides were actively seeking to ram each other. Between June 7th and 14th, North Korean patrol boats and fishing vessels crossed the 114 times.[24]

The clash itself began when two ROKN vessels simultaneously bumped a KPN patrol boat. The KPN vessel responded with machine gun and cannon fire. At that time, there were approximately 20 North Korean fishing vessels in the area, escorted by seven KPN vessels; one submarine chaser, two large patrol boats, two small/medium patrol boats and three torpedo boats. The ROKN had deployed ten PKM and two PCC. The result of the battle was decidedly one-sided. Two ROKN vessels were slightly damaged and South Korean forces suffered nine-wounded, while one KPN torpedo boat was sunk and another five North Korean vessels were damaged. The KPN lost somewhere between 17 to 30 killed and over 70 wounded. The reason for this outcome was superior ROKN capabilities. The KPN vessels proved to be outgunned, firing manually-loaded and aimed cannon which left their crews vulnerable to the rapid-fire 20 mm miniguns, and electronically aimed 40 and 76 mm cannons aboard the ROKN vessels.[25] The KPN could not match the accuracy and weight of fire that the more advanced ROKN vessels could bring to bear.

The Second Battle of Yeonpyeong occurred on June 29, 2002. At approximately 10 am that morning, two KPN vessels, one medium and one large patrol craft, crossed the NLL seven miles apart from each other. According to the MND, two patrolling ROKN PKM moved to intercept the closer of the two KPN vessels and sent verbal warnings and used sirens in attempt to warn them against crossing the NLL. The KPN vessels continued on their course and when the distance between the two opposing sides closed the KPN vessel opened fire using its deck cannons and hand-held RPG.

Two nearby ROKN PKM and two PCC moved to reinforce the two engaged PKM. Under consequent constant ROKN fire the KPN vessels retreated back across the NLL. PKM-357, the ROKN vessel initially hit by KPN fire, suffered heavy damage and later sank while under tow. Six members of its crew were killed and a further 18 were wounded. One KPN vessel was reported as being heavily damaged, with 30 North Korean personnel being killed or wounded.

Despite losing a ship, the engagement demonstrated that the ROKN maintained overall superiority in terms of surface combat capability. The manner of ROKN deployments with PKM operating in pairs and heavier PCC acting in support allowed them to quickly reinforce the engaged vessels and achieve fire superiority. As with the First Battle of Yeonpyeong, the better capabilities of ROKN vessels were apparent. The PKM that was initially engaged and later sank still managed to expend its entire reserve of ammunition firing 1500 rounds at the KPN vessel with a reported hit rate of about 40%.[26] This despite the wheelhouse taking significant damage and the commander of the vessel being fatally wounded in the engagement.

To offset their inferiority the KPN had attempted to take advantage of a weakness in the ROKN's rules of engagement (ROE). At that time the ROE entailed a five-step process when dealing with intruding KPN vessels: (1) warning, (2) demonstration, (3) blocking, (4) warning shot, and (5) final engagement.[27] In naval warfare, there is a higher incentive to strike first as this raises the possibility of gaining a fatal or debilitating hit.[28] The ROKN's ROE exposed their vessels and crews to a KPN first strike as they were required to manoeuvre close to opposing vessels in an attempt to block their progress.

Following the battle, the ROKN and the MND sought to close this vulnerability by shortening the engagement sequence in the ROE and giving the commander of each vessel greater operational autonomy over when to use force. The current ROE have a three-phase process, (1) warning & demonstration, (2) warning shot, and (3) final engagement, which means that ROKN vessels are not required to manoeuvre close to KPN patrol craft.[29]

The utility of these new rules became evident during the 2009 Battle of Daechong when a single KPN patrol boat crossed the NLL. Seemingly operating to support a fishing vessel which was caught approaching the NLL, the KPN vessel crossed the NLL despite being verbally warned by the responding ROKN vessels. The ROKN had two PKM (336 and 325), two PCC and one frigate deployed in the area.[30] After broadcasting that warning shots would be fired, the ROKN's PKM-336, under instructions from Second Fleet headquarters fired three warning shots close to the KPN vessel.[31] The KPN boat responded by firing approximately 50 rounds at PKM-325. All ROKN craft returned fire and approximately three minutes after the first warning shot was fired, the heavily damaged KPN vessel began to retreat north of the NLL.[32]

The use of warning shots is now common when dealing with intruding KPN or civilian North Korean vessels.[33] In 2014, reports emerged of KPN vessel responding to ROKN warning shots with 37 mm cannon fire which ultimately fell short. The KPN vessel retreated after three ROKN patrol boats engaged them.[34] While, the current ROE do not always deter North Korean boats crossing the NLL, they so far have been broadly successful in deterring further escalation on the surface and cutting off opportunities for the KPN to attack ROKN assets.

THE MAINTENANCE OF DETERRENCE

The three surface engagements demonstrated the ROKN's surface warfare superiority and ability to adjust to the KPN's tactics. They also showed that the general strategic stability the long-term conventional deterrent standoff provides for the Korean Peninsula is in an underlying state of flux. Within conventional deterrence relationships, the success of one side demonstrating its operational superiority or capabilities will ultimately lead to some form of response from the opponent to undermine these capabilities. As Edward Rhodes writes, 'if used against an intelligent and motivated opponent, every conventional deterrent threat contains the seeds of its own demise'.[35] North Korea, despite severe economic and industrial limitations, has not and does not stand still in terms of its force development. As the KPN learned that it was unable to compete in surface warfare, its procurement and operational focus has increasingly shifted to asymmetric capabilities designed to offset its weaknesses. The ROKN's operational challenge is to both understand the changes in the KPN's capabilities and to design appropriate countermeasures. What the sinking of the *Cheonan* revealed was that such a process is difficult and imperfect, but South Korea's superiority in resources and technology allows them to them close off their weaknesses through force modernisation in a way that North Korea cannot.

KPN Surface Capabilities

The KPN has proved to be incapable of rapidly modernising its surface fleet in the same manner of the ROKN. Despite impressive numbers on paper, most of their surface vessels are either of, or are based on Soviet and Chinese designs and many are reaching the end of their useful service life. Most of these platforms are designed for inshore operations and are incapable of operating far from the coast, in bad weather or at night. Questions also remain regarding the serviceability of their platforms given reports that two boats sank in 2013 while on operations in the West Sea.[36] Of those that are in an operational condition, there are few suited to a modern combat environment. The KPN suffers from a lack of advanced weaponry, surveillance and command and control systems (C2). They are particularly weak in terms of surface to air missile (SAM) and anti-ship missile (AShM) capabilities. Open-source intelligence sources disagree on the exact number of currently operational vessels with missile capabilities, with estimates ranging between 15 and 35 depending on the number of vessels that have been laid-up of discarded. Those that are operational are largely North Korean versions of the Soviet-designed *Osa* and *Komar* class fast attack craft. Each vessel has four KN01 AShM, which are North Korean missiles based on the now obsolete Russian P-15 Termit and Chinese Silkworm missiles. Range estimates vary on this system with some reports suggesting that North Korean modifications have increased the range to over 160 km. Given the age of this system and ROKN countermeasures, it is likely vulnerable to both the hard and soft-kill capabilities currently deployed on ROKN ships.[37]

The KPN has pursued some modernisation of its surface fleet and its weapons systems. However, assessments of this modernisation are largely speculative given the closed nature of the North Korean regime. What is evident is that this modernisation has occurred slowly but some improvements in the KPN's operational lethality are to be expected. Open questions remain regarding the long-term success of new ship and missile designs, the ability of the KPN to integrate new capabilities into their existing fleet and how the KPN intends to use such capabilities to achieve operational effects given their lack of C2 and networked sensor systems. The ROKN's current force modernisation program is most likely sufficient to manage these new threats given their technological superiority, the likelihood of supremacy in the air and the KPN's inability to introduce new platforms at a rate sufficient to overwhelm current ROKN defences. Evidence has surfaced that the KPN has built two to four new *Nampo*-class corvettes.[38] Their armament has not been confirmed, yet it likely to include improved ASW and AShM capabilities. Construction of these vessels began in 2006–2007 and they were launched between 2011–2012.[39] It is not yet clear if they are operational as design changes seem to have occurred after launch and the slow speed of their introduction demonstrates the difficulties the KPN has in sustaining the construction of new vessels.

The KPN has also developed a new class of surface effect ship (SES).[40] These *Nongo*-class vessels have some stealthy characteristics and the SES design, if successful, will allow them to operate at high speeds in good to moderate sea states.[41] The KPN has built six of these vessels with some different configurations, but possibly only two are operational. One variant, revealed in North Korean government photos, carries launchers for four AShM attached aft of the superstructure, forward and aft mounted close in weapons systems (CIWS), four 14.5 mm crew-serviced Gatling guns and potentially two short-range SAM launchers.[42]

A third new KPN capability is the introduction of a class of very slender vessel (VSV). They are approximately 30 metres long and 5 metres wide and can travel at over 50 knots depending on the weather conditions. They are primarily designed to perform infiltration operations, taking advantage of their high speed and low profile. [43] South Korean media reports from 2015 suggest that 10 of these vessels were constructed, with seven deployed close to the NLL.[44]

The operational impact of these new classes of vessels is ultimately a function of the weapons systems placed on-board. The KPN is developing a new AShM. Named the Kumsong-3, it is based on the Russian Kh-35. The Russian variant has a range of approximately 130 km and is designed to operate in modern high-intensity electronic warfare environments.[45] The KPN have also produced a coastal version of this weapon, the KN19, which has several upgrades including the ability to perform multiple waypoint manoeuvres and more advanced terminal guidance sensors.[46] The KPN is deploying the Kumsong-3 on its new vessels, and if they successfully integrate them they would represent a substantial step-up in capability. However, the KPN's weaknesses in sensors and networked capabilities will undermine the potential of these new systems. Without over the horizon radar, satellite systems or effective radar on networked aviation assets the KPN will struggle to find targets at the higher-end of the Kumsong-3's range. The KPN will need to find some method to identify the initial approximate location of targets before firing the missile after which, when the missile comes close enough, on-board terminal targeting systems would take over. These missiles could of course be launched closer to the target, but this leaves the launching vessels vulnerable to longer-ranged ROKN and US capabilities.

Even with the introduction of these new system, existing classes of vessels including the KDX-I and KDX-II destroyers have or are planned to undergo upgrades which will improve their capacity to defend against missile attack. The KDX-III destroyers, the new Incheon and *Daegu*-class frigates, *Cheong Wang Bong*-class LST and *Dokdo*-class LPH all possess either advanced point or air area air-defence systems, decoys and electronic countermeasures. Although, smaller ROKN patrol craft lack some of these hard-kill capabilities, their superior AShM weapons, electronic countermeasures and ability to operate in a networked environment mitigates against this vulnerability. Further, the ROKN's construction policy of building new classes of vessels in batches provides the opportunity to modernise systems and respond to developments on the North Korean side. While this capacity to respond through the introduction of new capabilities does not guarantee that North Korea will not attempt to engage an ROKN vessel it does mean that the ROKN can maintain warfighting superiority.

KPN Submarine Capabilities

The KPN's large submarine fleet poses a different and more difficult challenge to the ROKN. Even though the ROKN and its allies have clear advantages in technology and training, ASW is a complex exercise. This is particularly true in the cluttered shallow waters of the Korean littoral, which makes detecting small diesel-electric vessels especially difficult. The largest submarines the KPN operates are 20 *Romeo* class boats. The KPN deploys them on the east coast and most likely tasks them with sea denial and mine-laying operations. However, these vessels are an obsolete design, and some have been in service for nearly forty years. As an indication of their limited operational use, US defence officials highlighted the fact that two *Romeo* class vessels undertook a week-long patrol in the East Sea.[47] Their noisy propulsion systems make them easy to track and they would be vulnerable to the combined ASW capabilities of the ROKN, USN and JMSDF.

More threatening is North Korea's fleet of 35+ *Sang-o* and 10+ *Yono* coastal and mini-submarines. The Sang-o class is armed with four bow 533 mm torpedo launchers. At about 325 tons submerged and 34 metres long, these small coastal submarines can carry special warfare troops, conduct anti-shipping operations and if configured, perform mine warfare.[48] A second, stretched variant was introduced in 2011; this vessel most likely has a higher speed and greater operational range. In 1996, South Korean forces captured a *Sang-o* class after it ran aground while attempting to infiltrate troops onto South Korean territory. The *Yono*-class is a smaller 130 tons (submerged) mini-submarine. Armed with two torpedo tubes, these vessels have the same mission set as the *Sang-o* class.[49]

The KPN's emphasis on both developing and building these vessels is an indication that they recognise the operational benefits that submarines, even if they are technologically limited, provide. As former NATO Supreme Allied Commander Admiral James Stavridis notes, 'destroying a submarine is the hardest task in naval warfare'.[50] The sinking of the *Cheonan* on March 26, 2010 was a shift in tactics for the KPN. Operating at night and in rough seas, a *Yono*-class vessel successful struck the *Pohang*-class vessel with a single 533 mm torpedo. The vessel broke in half and sank approximately eight minutes later killing 46 South Korean sailors. The sinking exposed the ROKN to substantial criticism. A government report into the sinking of the *Cheonan* legitimately argued that the ROKN had largely focused on gaining superiority over North Korean surface and shore capabilities which resulted in a lack of readiness to deal with the threat of submarines.[51] This criticism reveals the difficulty of maintaining conventional deterrence over a sustained period where the opposition is always seeking to design new methods to gain operational advantage.

Since the sinking, the KPN has continued to build and operate these small submarines. In 2015, North Korea in an unprecedented show of force deployed 70% of their subsurface fleet at one time.[52] This stresses the operational importance the leadership in Pyongyang places on the platforms and it highlighted the core difficulty the ROKN and US may have in dealing with such a challenge. Despite their limited range, endurance and capabilities the sheer number of vessels made it impossible for US and South Korean forces to maintain a complete operational picture of their whereabouts.

As is the case on the surface, the ROKN has the potential to offset North Korean subsurface developments. In sinking the *Cheonan*, North Korea may have increased their short-term deterrent potential by demonstrating their warfighting capabilities but consequently there has been a strong reaction on the part of the ROKN. After achieving surface superiority, the ROKN has turned towards developing effective countermeasures to the ASW threat.

There has been an increased ROKN and US emphasis on ASW training and operations. South Korea has invested large sums in the R&D and procurement of added ASW capacity. For example, South Korea has introduced networked undersea monitoring capabilities, particularly designed to protect ports and other strategic areas.[53] They also constructed a geomagnetic map of the sea floor around the NLL, which was reported to be finished in 2013.[54] The ROKN has upgraded and increased its fleet of P3C Orion fixed-wing ASW aircraft and in 2013 launched a competition to procure modern maritime surveillance aircraft.[55] Similarly, in 2013, the ROKN acquired eight new AW159 Wildcat ASW helicopters to operate from their *Incheon*-class frigate and has launched a competition to buy more.[56] The newer vessels that the ROKN are introducing will also have increased ASW capability, for example, a core design requirement for the new KDX-III Batch-II destroyers is to have an ASW capability three times more effective than the design that preceded it.[57]

KPN Amphibious Capabilities

A second substantial deterrent challenge for the ROKN is to develop and maintain capabilities that can prevent the KPN from using its formidable array of amphibious platforms. North Korea's development of this capability and South Korea's reaction encapsulates the action-reaction dynamic that long-term conventional deterrence creates.

North Korea has two Special Forces Navy Sniper Brigades, one stationed on either side of the peninsula. Their missions include amphibious assault and covert infiltration. To deliver them onto South Korean territory, the KPN operates ten ageing medium landing ships (LSM), but its greatest threat comes from its multiple high-speed infiltrations and landing ships. These include over 130 *Kongbang* II & III hovercraft that can carry between 40 and 50 troops at 50 knots in ideal sea and weather conditions. These can be supplemented by large numbers of small conventional landing ships and a small number of *Chaho* fire-support ships.

These vessels are vulnerable to South Korean fire, but their strength lies in their ability to overwhelm South Korean defence through stealth, speed and platform numbers. As with submarines, it is evident that the North Korean leadership has identified this capability as one to be invested in. The hovercraft craft operate out of two main bases on the west coast, Kibong-dong and Tasa-ri and two on the east coast, Tapch'on-ni and Anjin-dong.[58] By deploying hovercraft from Kibong-dong the KPN could theoretically land a force of 2700 troops on Baegnyongdo with a journey time of between two and four hours.[59] In 2018, Joseph S. Bermudez revealed that the KPN had built two new hovercraft bases closer to the NLL in 2012 and another base at Yonbong-ni was under construction as of 2017.[60] These allow KPN hovercraft to reach Baegnyongdo in 30 minutes, thereby substantially the available reaction time of defending South Korean forces. By maintaining and developing this capability, North Korea can potentially open a small number of fronts in the South's rear areas during wartime, while in peacetime the ability to threaten the NWI provides important political leverage.

The South Korean government has not stood still in their response to this threat. The shelling of Yeonpyeongdo in 2010 concentrated minds in Seoul regarding the defence of the NWI. A new Northwest Island command was established under the South Korean Marine Corps (ROKMC). While some teething problems were found regarding delineating operational responsibilities, these were resolved and there is now an increased emphasis on joint ROKMC, ROKN and ROKAF operations.[61]

Further, new surveillance and weapons capabilities are being introduced and designed. In 2013, the ROKN introduced a new mobile maritime surveillance radar designed to replace the ageing fixed sensors that were on the NWI.[62] The new system has a range of 25 km and is linked to the ROKN's C2 system, the Korean Naval Tactical Data System (KNTDS). South Korea also purchased the Israeli-made Spike NLOS missile system and has deployed it on the NWI and on its Wildcat helicopters. This has a range of 25 km and can target both hardened ground targets and moving vessels.[63]

The ROKN has considered how their larger platforms can be used in this scenario. The KDX-III Aegis destroyers' superior surveillance capabilities, can provide early warning and command and control to assist air assets such as helicopters, to stem any massed amphibious strike.[64] As the Battle of Bubiyan demonstrated during the 1991 Iraq war, small surface vessels operating without the protective cloak of air superiority or possessing anti-air capabilities are extremely vulnerable to attack from the air.[65]

Future systems are also being developed to cope with the numerical that the KPN's amphibious forces pose, among them is a land-based mobile guided rocket system, known as the Bigung which can fire 36 70 mm rockets at moving targets.[66] Similarly, the PKMR patrol boat, the first of which was delivered in late 2017, is armed with a 130 mm guided rocket system which was specifically designed to engage high-speed moving targets such as the KPN's hovercraft.[67]

Linked to the KPN's continued development of its amphibious capabilities is its maintenance of infiltration capabilities. This has been a long-standing operational priority for the ROKN since the end of the Korean War. South Korean government figures do show a significant drop in the number of infiltrations since the 1990s, but these do not include successful covert attempts.

While the west coast has been the primary route, the east coast is also used, thereby forcing the ROKN to maintain constant patrol coverage, not just around the west coast NLL but also on the east and south coasts also. Significant infiltration incidents include the 1968 landing of between 120–130 commandos off the east coast of the peninsula and the previously mentioned 1996 discovery of a grounded KPN *Sang-o* class submarine, which had dropped off a North Korea surveillance team.[68] The crew of the submarine fled into the South Korea in an effort to get to the DMZ, but most were either killed or captured.

1998 seemed to be a turning point in such operations when three North Korean infiltration operations were exposed. In June of that year a North Korean *Yugo*-class mini submarine was caught in a South Korean trawler's drift net. The submarine itself sunk or was scuttled when the ROKN was towing back to port, but evidence found on the crews' body indicated that they previously infiltrated South Korean territory. Later in the same year a KPN semi-submersible, presumed to be attempting to covertly crossing the NLL was spotted and chased off by two ROKN patrol boats. In December, another semi-submersible was spotted near the South Korean coast off Yeosu in the south of the country. After a chase involving numerous ROKN vessels and a P-3 Orion, the semi-submersible was sunk by ROKN cannon fire. Among the wreckage was the body of a North Korean spy, who had been in South Korea contacting South Koreans sympathetic to the North.[69] This was the last discovery of a North Korean infiltration operation by sea and revealed the range of capabilities that the ROKN could bring to bear to prevent such activities. The drop in North Korean infiltrations can be partially attributed to the ROKN's increasing ability to maintain maritime domain awareness although it is possible that North Korea has since successfully carried out such operations undetected. The KPN's continued pursuit of infiltration capabilities such as VSV indicates that as is the case in surface and subsurface warfare the deterrent dynamic continues to shift.

New Deterrent Roles

So far, this chapter has shown that ROKN modernisation is aimed at countering specific North Korean threats at sea. However, ROKN blue-water modernisation now plays an important role in South Korea's response to Pyongyang's pursuit of ballistic missile and nuclear capabilities. The South Korean government is developing a triad of operational concepts aimed at deterring and defending against North Korean nuclear and missile attack; the Kill Chain, the Korean Air and Missile Defense System (KAMD) and the Korean Massive Punishment and Retaliation (KMPR) strategy.[70]

The Kill Chain and KMPR are both concepts which require precision deep-strike capabilities. The former (the Kill Chain) is designed to attack North Korean offensive capabilities such as missiles, launchers and command and control facilities. The latter (KMPR) is designed to 'punish and retaliate' following a North Korean conventional or nuclear strike.[71] This would target leadership facilities including bunkers and military headquarters. In essence, this is a strategy aimed at decapitating the senior North Korean leadership. Newer ROKN platforms including the KDX-III class destroyers and *Sohn Won-il*-class submarines all carry indigenously designed land attack cruise missiles (LACM). These include, the Hyunmoo-3C cruise missile with a 500 kg warhead and 1500 km range, the Haesong-II with a shorter, 500 km range and

Haesong-III which is designed to be launched by submarine. These ships are now an integral part of the efforts to operationalise both deterrence concepts. Future ROKN vessels including the next batch of the Aegis destroyers, the *Daegu*-class frigates and the KSS-III will all have land attack capability which will vastly increase the ROKN's ability to contribute to these approaches.

Similarly, the Aegis destroyers form an integral part of the intended KAMD system. The SPY-1D radar will connect with other surveillance systems to provide warning and tracking information for ground-based interceptors. While the three destroyers can perform surveillance and tracking their version of the Aegis system does not provide for full BMD capability. The three new Aegis destroyers will have the improved Aegis Baseline 9 version of the combat system combined with the BMD 5.1 system.[72] Consequently, these vessels will have Integrated Air and Missile Defense (IAMD) capabilities, although it is unclear if ROKN vessels will carry the SM-3IIA interceptor designed for use with the BMD 5.1 system.

Further, North Korea's reported development of the *Sinpo*-class conventional ballistic missile submarine (SSB) has increased pressure on the ROKN to further develop its ASW capabilities. It has also led some senior politicians including President Moon Jae-into call for the development of an indigenously designed nuclear-power attack submarine (SSN). This would theoretically provide the ROKN with the ability to sit submerged outside KPN submarine bases, lying in wait for these SSB to be deployed. Many open questions remain regarding this development including, US opposition to such a plan and whether the ROKN and MND could sustain the R&D and operational costs of such a platform. Further, as retired ROKN Captain and naval analyst Yoon Sukjoon points out, publicly available documents suggest that the ROKN does not operate beyond the NLL and cannot conduct ASW patrols against North Korean targets on or above North Korean waters.[73] While either a conventional or nuclear submarine would allow the ROKN to loiter undetected outside of North Korean submarine bases, the public acknowledgement of such operations would be a major shift in South Korean security policy.

WARTIME MISSIONS

Despite the deterrent standoff that has existed since the end of the Korean War, preparing for the outbreak of war is a constant feature in ROKN planning. Unlike the deterrent operations which the ROKN carries out independently every day, in wartime operations, the ROKN will become subordinate to the US Navy. In the event of an extended conflict, the majority of ROKN assets would be tasked with supporting US naval operations, most likely by ensuring security in the littoral and providing added protection to US carrier and amphibious groups.[74]

Yet in the initial phases, assuming North Korea started the conflict, the ROKN would act as a first responder, transitioning from deterrent to defensive operations to secure the waters and littoral areas around the Korean Peninsula from initial North Korean attacks. The ROKN has an advantage in maintaining its readiness to go to war as the forces currently deployed to deter by denial would have equal utility in wartime and would be readily available.[75]

ROKN documents state that the navy is tasked with three broad interrelated wartime missions: sea control, the protection of maritime transportation and power projection.[76] The ROKN understands sea control as a condition which allows for the free use of littoral waters at specific times and places.[77] This is an acknowledgement that complete sea control is a difficult to achieve. It does not imply that enemy ships do not operate, instead it means that the enemy does not have a significant ability to interfere with operations at sea.[78] This fact is particularly important in littoral operations, where the enemy can attempt to deny the secure use of the sea using a multitude of systems including mines, aircraft, submarines and coastal artillery.

Therefore, the pursuit of sea control is an ongoing series of operations. As the superior force, allied with the most powerful navy in the world, ROKN sea control operations will have both offensive and defensive elements. The former involves searching for and destroying the enemy fleet, taking out shore installations and conducting amphibious operations.[79] The latter would be the continuous protection of the South Korean coast, ASW operations and the full spectrum protection of maritime trade in the littoral.[80] This role will form an important part of the ROKN's mission set as ensuring free access to South Korea would be vital for the protection of US augmentation forces and logistical support.

The delineation between defensive and offensive would most likely be blurred in the opening phases of any Korean conflict. The ROKN's role would be to destroy the KPN's forces close to the NLL to remove their offensive capabilities. As these capabilities are degraded, the ROKN and US forces could concentrate on moving up the peninsula with the aim of destroying the KPN's littoral operating capacity to secure the ability to project power unimpeded.

Power projection in the ROKN's thinking is the application of force from the sea onto land.[81] For much of its history, the ROKN has possessed a limited power projection capability. Lacking aviation capabilities or long-range weapons, it had no ability to attack inland enemy targets and maintained a minimal fire-support capacity. Further, its capacity to independently carry out amphibious operations was constrained by a lack of amphibious capabilities and a limited ability to perform or support contested landings. Consequently, the ROKN has previously viewed power projection in defensive terms, with an emphasis on small-scale disruptive amphibious operations aimed at blunting a North Korean attack.

Mine warfare will be a consideration in any wartime scenario. During the Korean War, North Korea leaned heavily on defensive mining to protect strategically important areas such as vulnerable parts of their coast and port facilities. A number of North Korean vessels are capable of laying naval mines and certainly the ROKN and USN will be required to carry out minesweeping operations along the North Korean coast in order to conduct amphibious operations and on the vital Korea Strait SLOC which links southern Korea with Kyushu.[82] The ROKN currently operates eight mine-hunting vessels, a force which retired Japanese Admiral Yoji Koda described as 'not yet sufficient for the current security and military situation around the peninsula'.[83] The ROKN is also investing in its own offensive and defensive mine-laying capability with introduction of the *Wonsan*-class and *Nampo*-class mine laying vessels (MLS) in 1998 and 2017 respectively.

With the introduction of new capabilities including land attack cruise missiles, the ROKN can now undertake strike operations, engaging enemy targets from the sea. Given this capability, the ROKN has now greatly enhanced its wartime role, gaining the ability to engage tactical targets such as KPN shore facilities and strategic targets such as leadership and command and control facilities. In addition, the construction of the *Dokdo*-class LPH, a new class of four LST and the procurement of aviation assets is aimed at developing a multi-dimensional (land and air) amphibious capability which could in the future land and support a division-sized force of South Korean marines under contested conditions.[84] Although when compared to the US, the ROKN's ability to project power onto land remains small, it is increasingly formidable and South Korea is now capable of limited independent operations from the sea.

CONCLUSION

In this chapter, I have argued that maritime geography exposes the ROKN to greater risk than South Korean forces on land as the tracklessness of water provides North Korean forces with the opportunity to enter and exit South Korean territory without interception. Further, long-term conventional deterrence is a constantly shifting relationship, for example, North Korea's inability to operate effectively on the surface probably resulted in a shift to subsurface operations.

The sinking of the *Cheonan* demonstrated the KPN's capabilities in this area but also exposes it to the inevitable ROKN response. South Korea's superior resources in many ways allows them to respond faster than North Korea can change tactics. However, the difficulty of ASW operations means that for the ROKN, achieving total dominance in subsurface warfare may be impossible. Nevertheless, the investment in ASW capabilities will likely increase the ROKN's deterrence credibility.

This flexibility in deterrence is also demonstrated in the ROKN's response to North Korea's amphibious capabilities and its role in South Korea's response to North Korea's nuclear program. The ROKN is a key element in Seoul's multi-faceted nuclear deterrence and defence posture, which will also have to adjust as North Korea advances its own capabilities. The ROKN's short and long-term operational requirement in relation to North Korea is the continuous adjustment of its defence posture and modernisation of its capabilities to maintain deterrence and operational superiority.

Often such adjustments are resource intensive and take time to implement. Of course, the ROKN can predict its future operational requirements in deterring North Korea, but such a strategy is risky as in a deterrent relationship the opponent can undertake operational, tactical and strategic shifts. As long as North Korea exists as a threat, the ROKN will be required to continuously evolve to meet both its deterrence and warfighting obligations. The blue-water modernisation initiative allows the ROKN to meet this requirement. The focus on modern, multi-functional and networked platforms produces capabilities that are equally as effective against North Korea as the future regional threats that the ROKN is trying to address.

NOTES

1. Andrew Scobell and John M. Sanford, *North Korea's Military Threat: Pyongyang's Conventional Forces, Weapons of Mass Destruction, and Ballistic Missiles* (Carlisle: Strategic Studies Institute, 2007), 52.
2. Marine Corps Intelligence Activity, *North Korea Country Handbook* (Quantico: Marine Corps Intelligence Activity, 1997), 39–40.
3. Norman Friedman, *Seapower as Strategy: Navies and National Interests* (Annapolis: Naval Institute Press, 2001), 40–41; James John Tritten, "Is Naval Warfare Unique?" *Journal of Strategic Studies* 12, no. 4 (1989): 497.
4. Tim Benbow, "The 'Operational Level' and Maritime Forces," *The RUSI Journal* 160, no. 5 (2015): 56.
5. Suk-kyoon Kim, *Maritime Disputes in Northeast Asia: Regional Challenges and Cooperation* (Boston: Brill Nijhoff, 2017), 19.
6. Terence Roehrig, *Korean Dispute Over the Northern Limit Line: Security, Economics or International Law?, Issue 3 of Maryland Series in Contemporary Asian Studies* (Baltimore, MD: University of Maryland at Baltimore, 2008), 7.
7. Ibid.
8. Republic of Korea Navy *(Nuguna al su Issneun!) Haegunjakjeon Deuryeodabogi* [As Anyone Can See! Look into Naval Operations] (Seoul: Republic of Korea Navy, 2011), 54.
9. Ibid.
10. Republic of Korea Government, *Cheonanham pigyeoksageon baekse* [The Warship Cheonan Attack White Paper] (Seoul: Republic of Korea Government, 2011), 34.
11. There is some dispute regarding the origins of the Northern Limit Line, as Terence Roehrig argues points out there are contradictory documents surrounding the exact date of its implementation. See: Terence Roehrig, "The Origins of the Northern Limit Line Dispute," *North Korea International Document Project, E-Dossier #6, The Origins of the Northern Limit Line Dispute* (May 2012), 2.
12. Central Intelligence Agency, *Korean Fishing Areas in the Yellow Sea—Spawning Ground for Maritime Conflict*, GCK-RP 75-20, May 1975, Central Intelligence Agency Library, 4, https://www.cia.gov/library/readingroom/docs/CIA-RDP86T00608R000600140005-7.pdf, accessed 10 December 2017.

13. In 1999, Pyongyang proposed a new maritime boundary which followed the MDL but included a 2 nm access corridor to the NWI. This was also rejected by UNC.

14. Narushige Michishita, *North Korea's Military Diplomatic Campaigns, 1996–2008* (Abingdon, Oxon: Routledge, 2010), 63–64.

15. Jon M. Van Dyke, Mark J. Valencia, and Jenny Miller Garmendia, "The North/South Korea Boundary Dispute in the Yellow (West) Sea," *Marine Policy* 27 (2003): 146.

16. Republic of Korea Ministry of National Defense, *2012 Defense White Paper* (Seoul: Republic of Korea Ministry of National Defense, 2012), 59.

17. "Endless, Wasteful Brawls," *The Korea Times*, 8 October 2013, http://www.koreatimes.co.kr/www/opinion/2017/08/202_143904.html, accessed 10 August 2017.

18. Andrew Forbes and Sukjoon Yoon, "Old and New Threats from North Korea Against the Republic of Korea," in *Korean Maritime Strategy: Issues and Challenges*, ed. Geoffrey Till and Sukjoon Yoon (Seoul: Korea Institute for Maritime Strategy, 2011), 26–27.

19. Lisa Collins, "Between a Rock and a Grey Zone: China-ROK Illegal Fishing Disputes," *AMTI*, 6 July 2016, https://amti.csis.org/rock-grey-zone-china-rok-illegal-fishing-disputes/, accessed 20 November 2017.

20. Robert E. Newton, *The Capture of the USS Pueblo and Its Effect on SIGINT Operations, United States Cryptological History, Special Series Crisis Collection Volume 7* (Fort Meade, MD: Centre for Cryptologic History National Security Agency, 1992), 4.

21. Mischishita, *North Korea's Military-Diplomatic*, 55–56.

22. CIA National Foreign Assessment Center, *Intelligence Memorandum: Military Balance on the Korean Peninsula* (10 May 1978), RPM-78-10196.

23. Mischishita, *North Korea's Military-Diplomatic*, 145.

24. Ibid., 146.

25. Min-Seok Kim and Myo-ja Ser, "South Korea Navy Dominating," *Korea JoongAng Daily*, 13 May 2008, http://koreajoongangdaily.joins.com/news/article/article.aspx?aid=2889732, accessed 2 February 2018.

26. Bruce E. Bechtol, *Red Rogue: The Persistent Challenge of North Korea* (Washington, DC: Potomac Books, 2007), 71.

27. Republic of Korea Navy, *Gandanhago pyeonhage ilgeul su inneun haegun-gaideubuk* [An Easy and Simple to Read Navy Guide Book] (Gyeryong: Navy Headquarters, 2016), 159.

28. Ian Speller, *Understanding Naval Warfare* (Abingdon, Oxon: Routledge, 2014), 109.

29. Ibid.

30. ROKN documents suggest that this is the standard deployment pattern along the NLL.
31. Republic of Korea Ministry of National Defense, *2010 Defense White Paper* (Seoul: Republic of Korea Ministry of National Defense, 2010), 320.
32. Ibid.
33. "South Korea Fires Warning Shots at North Patrol Boat Near Border," *Reuters*, 25 October 2015, https://www.reuters.com/article/us-north-korea-southkorea-shooting/south-korea-fires-warning-shots-at-north-patrol-boat-near-border-idUSKCN0SJ03L20151025, accessed 10 January 2018.
34. Byong-su Park, "S. Korean Navy Vessel Attempted to Damage N. Korean Patrol Boat," *Hankyoreh*, 14 October 2014, http://english.hani.co.kr/arti/english_edition/e_northkorea/659698.html, accessed 10 January 2018.
35. Edward Rhodes, "Conventional Deterrence," *Comparative Strategy* 19, no. 3 (2000): 226.
36. Joshua Cohen, "The Korea People's Army Naval Force," *Naval Forces*, no. 3 (2014): 14.
37. Republic of Korea Government, *2007nyeondo gukjeonggamsagyeolgwa sijeong min cheoriyogusahange daehan cheorigyeolgwagoseo (Gukbangbu Sogwan)* [Report on the Completion of the 2007 National Assembly Audit Results and the Completion of the Corrective and Handling Requirements (Ministry of National Defense)], January 2008, 56.
38. Chad O'Carroll, "Exclusive: New Low-Visibility Corvette Spotted in North Korea," *NK News*, 8 November 2016, https://www.nknews.org/2016/11/exclusive-new-low-visibility-corvette-spotted-in-north-korea/, accessed 3 February 2018.
39. Joseph S. Bermudez, "New North Korean Helicopter Frigates Spotted," *38 North*, 15 May 2014, https://www.38north.org/2014/05/jbermudez051514/, accessed 1 December 2017.
40. "Nongo Surface Effect Ship," *Global Security*, https://www.globalsecurity.org/military/world/dprk/p-nongo.html, accessed 26 January 2018.
41. The Norwegian Navy's *Skjold* class corvette has a similar SES design and can operate at speeds of up to 60 knots in calm waters.
42. Joseph S. Bermudez, "The Korean People's Navy Tests New Anti-Ship Cruise Missile," *38 North*, 8 February 2015, https://www.38north.org/2015/02/jbermudez020815/, accessed 1 December 2017.
43. Ankit Panda, "Meet North Korea's Speedy, Stealthy Boats," *The Diplomat*, 29 May 2015, https://thediplomat.com/2015/05/meet-north-koreas-speedy-stealthy-boats/, accessed 26 January 2018.

44. Yong-soo Jeong and Myo-ja Ser, "North Has New and Fast Submersible," *Korea JoongAng Daily*, 28 May 2015, http://koreajoon-gangdaily.joins.com/news/article/article.aspx?aid=3004696, accessed 3 February 2018.
45. Rosoboronexport Naval Systems, *Uran-E*, http://roe.ru/eng/catalog/naval-systems/shipborne-weapons/uran-e/, accessed 1 December 2018.
46. Ankit Panda, "North Korea's New KN19 Coastal Defense Cruise Missile: More Than Meets the Eye," *The Diplomat*, 26 July 2016, https://thediplomat.com/2017/07/north-koreas-new-kn19-coastal-defense-cruise-missile-more-than-meets-the-eye/, accessed 2 August 2017.
47. Zachary Cohen and Ryan Browne, "US Detects 'Highly Unusual' North Korean Submarine Activity," *CNN*, 2 August 2017, http://edition.cnn.com/2017/07/31/politics/north-korea-ejection-test-submarine-activity/index.html, accessed 8 February 2018.
48. Eric Wertheim, *The Naval Institute Guide to Combat Fleets of the World, 16th Edition* (Annapolis: Naval Institute Press, 2013), 401.
49. Ibid., 402.
50. As cited in William Perkins, *Alliance Airborne Anti-Submarine Warfare: A Forecast for Maritime Air ASW in the Future Operational Environment* (Kalkar: Joint Air Power Competence Centre, 2016), 7.
51. Republic of Korea Government, *Cheonanham pigyeoksageon baekse*, 34.
52. "50 N.Korean Submarines Vanish from Radar," *The Chosun Ilbo*, 24 August 2015, http://english.chosun.com/site/data/html_dir/2015/08/24/2015082401139.html, accessed 14 September 2015.
53. LIG Nex1, *SONAR Surveillance System*, https://www.lignex1.com/eng/product/product02_03.jsp, accessed 5 January 2018.
54. Republic of Korea Government, *2010nyeondo gukjeonggamsagyeolgwa sijeong min cheoriyogusahange daehan cheorigyeolgwagoseo* (Gukbangbu Sogwan) [Report on the Completion of the 2010 National Assembly Audit Results and the Completion of the Corrective and Handling Requirements (Ministry of National Defense)], April 2011, 72.
55. "Boeing, Saab Compete to Win S. Korea's Maritime Patrol Aircraft Deal," *Yonhap News Agency*, 22 October 2017, http://english.yonhapnews.co.kr/search1/2603000000.html?cid=AEN20171022000200320, accessed 10 January 2017.
56. Chi-dong Lee, "S. Korean Navy Deploys 4 More Wildcat Choppers," *Yonhap News Agency*, 5 July 2017, http://english.yonhapnews.co.kr/search1/2603000000.html?cid=AEN20170705004000315, accessed 2 February 2018.
57. Republic of Korea Defense Acquisition Program Administration, "Gwanggaeto-III Batch-II tamsaekgaebal saeop gyeyak chegyeol [Gwanggaeto-III Batch-II Conclusion of Exploratory Development

Contract Business]," *Defense Acquisition Program Administration Press Release*, 24 June 2016.

58. Joseph S. Bermudez, "North Korean Special Operations Forces: Hovercraft Bases (Part I)," *Beyond Parallel CSIS*, 25 January 2018, https://beyondparallel.csis.org/north-korean-special-operations-forces-hovercraft-bases-part-1/, accessed 28 January 2018; Joseph S. Bermudez, "North Korean Special Operations Forces: Hovercraft Bases (Part III)," *Beyond Parallel CSIS*, 15 February 2018, https://beyondparallel.csis.org/north-korean-special-operations-forces-hovercraft-bases-part-iii/, accessed 20 February 2018.

59. Joseph S. Bermudez, "North Korean Special Operations Forces: Hovercraft Bases (Part I)".

60. Joseph S. Bermudez, "North Korean Special Operations Forces: Hovercraft Bases (Part II)," *Beyond Parallel CSIS*, 5 February 2018, https://beyondparallel.csis.org/north-korean-special-operations-forces-hovercraft-bases-part-ii/, accessed 8 February 2018.

61. Republic of Korea Government, *2011nyeondo gukjeonggamsagyeolgwa sijeong min cheoriyogusahange daehan cheorigyeolgwagoseo (Gukbangbu Sogwan)* [Report on the Completion of the 2011 National Assembly Audit Results and the Completion of the Corrective and Handling Requirements (Ministry of National Defense)], February 2012, 57.

62. Republic of Korea Defense Acquisition Program Administration, "Seobukdoseo haesang jeollyeok 24sigan gamsichegye guchuk [Construction of a 24-Hour Surveillance System for the Maritime Military Power of the Northwest Islands]," *Republic of Korea Defense Acquisition Program Administration Press Release*, 2 September 2013.

63. Tamir Eshel, "Seoul to Equip Its New Maritime Helicopters with Israeli Spike Missiles," *Defense Update*, 6 January 2014, http://defense-update.com/20140106_seoul-equip-new-maritime-helicopters-israeli-spike-missiles.html#.U3y0WsJOUdV, accessed 10 March 2017.

64. Interview with Admiral Song Keun-ho, April 2011.

65. Robert J. Schneller, *Anchor Resolve: A History of the U.S. Naval Forces Central Command Fifth Fleet* (Washington, DC: Naval Historical Center, 2005), 28.

66. "ADEX 2017: ROK Marine Corps Showcasing Bigung for the 1st Time," *Army Recognition*, 18 October 2017, https://www.armyrecognition.com/adex_2017_online_show_daily_news/adex_2017_rok_marine_corps_showcasing_bigung_for_the_1st_time.html, accessed 19 November 2017.

67. LIG Nex1. *130mm Guided Rocket System*, https://www.lignex1.com/eng/product/product01_02.jsp, accessed 9 February 2018.

68. Andrew Forbes and Sukjoon Yoon, "Old and New Threats," 24–25.

69. Sebastian Roblin, "A Short History of North Korea's Long Mini-Submarine Spy Campaign," *War Is Boring*, 25 March 2017, https://medium.com/war-is-boring/a-short-history-of-north-koreas-long-mini-submarine-spy-campaign-958b4ac7024b, accessed 4 April 2017.

70. Republic of Korea Ministry of National Defense, *2016 Defence White Paper* (Seoul: Republic of Korea Ministry of National Defense, 2016), 69–72.

71. Ibid., 71.

72. "Lockheed Martin to Bring Aegis Ballistic Missile Defense to the Latest US Korea and Japan Destroyers," *Lockheed Martin*, https://www.lockheedmartin.com/us/news/press-releases/2016/august/160815-mst-aegis-ballistic-missile-defense-to-latest-us-korea-and-japan-destroyers.html, accessed 10 December 2017.

73. Suk-joon Yoon, "Expanding the ROKN's Capabilities to Deal with the SLBM Threat from North Korea," *The Naval War College Review* 70, no. 2 (Spring 2017): 63.

74. Under current US-South Korea agreements, in the event of war US augmentation forces on the Korean Peninsula could include up to 160 naval vessels. See: ROK Ministry of National Defence, *2016 Defence White Paper*, 53.

75. Michael Gearson and Daniel Whiteneck, *Deterrence and Influence: The Navy's Role in Preventing War* (Alexandria, VA: Centre for Naval Analyses, 2009), 44.

76. Republic of Korea Navy, *Haegun [Navy]* (Gyeryong: ROKN Troop Information and Public Relations Office, 2011), 22.

77. Ibid.

78. Milan Vego, *Maritime Strategy and Sea Control: Theory and Practice* (Abingdon, Oxon: Routledge, 2016), 24.

79. Ibid., 7–8.

80. Ibid.

81. Republic of Korea Navy, *Haegun [Navy]*, 22.

82. Yoji Koda, "The Emerging Republic of Korea Navy: A Japanese Perspective," *The Naval War College Review* 60, no. 2 (Spring 2010): 30.

83. Ibid., 25.

84. Republic of Korea Ministry of National Defense, *2016 Defense White Paper*, 111; Republic of Korea Ministry of National Defense, *2008 Defense White Paper* (Seoul: Republic of Korea Ministry of National Defense, 2008), 60.

CHAPTER 3

To the Blue-Water

The unique and constant operational challenge posed by North Korea in the littoral waters of the Korean Peninsula does not relieve the pressure that the wider East Asian strategic environment places on South Korea. Since the early 1990s, the Ministry of National Defense (MND) and South Korean security stakeholders have publicly acknowledged that the difficulties presented by the East Asian strategic environment but have been reluctant to develop strategies to deal with it as the threat from North Korea continues to dominate strategic thinking. Despite this reluctance, as Northeast Asia is a predominantly maritime strategic environment, the Republic of Korea Navy (ROKN) has been allowed to develop a long-term operational plan to create a force capable of meeting South Korea's immediate and future security requirements in the region and beyond.

The ROKN's modernisation goal has the moniker of developing a blue-water navy. But it is much more than creating a force capable of operating in waters away from the littorals of the Korean Peninsula. Blue-water modernisation is predicated on leveraging multifunctionality and modern technology to create a force with strategic utility in both peninsular and non-peninsular contexts. At no point has the ROKN's blue-water plan signalled a reneging on its commitment to deterrence around the Korean Peninsula rather it is about increasing its operational independence and broadening its the ability to create a strategic effect in any number of scenarios.

© The Author(s) 2019
I. Bowers, *The Modernisation of the Republic of Korea Navy*, Critical Studies of the Asia-Pacific,
https://doi.org/10.1007/978-3-319-92291-1_3

The drive to expand the navy's mission set required a substantial shift in South Korea's understanding of the utility of South Korean naval power. The civil elements of South Korean seapower have grown since the 1960s and as trading nation, South Korea has become reliant on the sea for economic prosperity. Such prosperity coincided with democratisation in 1988 and the desire for South Korea to become a responsible international stakeholder. Combined these two factors increased the salience of the sea as a strategic interest, something that has only become more acute since the end of the Cold War, the rise of China and the growth in regional strategic instability. Situated between China and Japan, the ROKN is now required to ensure that South Korea's regional maritime interests are protected in what are increasingly congested and contested waters. At the same time, South Korea must ensure that its Sea Lines of Communication (SLOC) in the littorals, the region and beyond are secure. Not only is South Korea's export-based economy reliant on the world's SLOC to carry its goods across the globe, the country's dearth of natural resources means that the sea is vital for the import of the energy, raw materials and food needed to sustain the population and industry.

The chapter proceeds by examining South Korea's maritime security interests in Northeast Asia, its perception of SLOC security including its role in the South China Sea and its desire to become a central tool in South Korea's implementation of its global foreign and security policy. The chapter then addresses how the ROKN plans to balance the requirements for peninsular deterrence and warfighting with its future more expansive mission set and the difficulties it currently faces in meeting all of South Korea's maritime security requirements.

New Threats

Following the end of the Korean War, South Korea's understanding of its strategic environment and what constituted a threat to its security was narrowly framed and focused on North Korea, anti-communism and the management of the US alliance. This perception began to change at the end of the Cold War. While North Korea remains the dominant factor in security planning, South Korea's growing economic and political power resulted in expanding regional and global interests. These interests collided with fundamental shifts in East Asia's post-Cold War security architecture. The collapse of the Soviet Union, the rise of China and uncertainty surrounding the United States and its role in Asia required defence planners to give greater appreciation to non-North Korean security threats. At the heart of Seoul's broader assessment is the paradox of Asian economic growth and interdependence contrasted with increasingly competitive security behaviour.

As Fig. 3.1 shows, successive MND White Papers have highlighted the emergence of arms build-ups, if not races, maritime territorial and resource disputes, and the risks surrounding the shifting balance of power in the region due to China's re-emergence and its challenge to US primacy.

Much of South Korea's concern is not that such developments will result in direct conflict, but rather this environment will have a harmful indirect effect on their security. Effectively, South Korea's security identity outside of the Korean Peninsula, is informed by its understanding of history, where the actions of the great powers surrounding it have often left Korea exposed to external manipulation and control.[1] This concept is popularly encapsulated by the cliché of South Korea being a shrimp among whales. As the relatively weakest power in Northeast Asia (with the exception of North Korea) South Korea has little room for geopolitical manoeuvre and is often faced with choosing from poor strategic options.[2]

However, acknowledgment of threat does not necessarily result in sustained strategic planning to meet it. Due to the threat from North Korea, developing military options to deal with the broader Asian security environment has never been an immediate priority in the MND or the Joint Chiefs of Staff (JCS). The Republic of Korea Army (ROKA), by far the largest of the three services and a dominant presence within the MND and JCS was and is understandably fixated on deterring North Korean actions on the peninsula.

Assessing the operational requirements for a more competitive East Asian strategic environment required a shift in thinking away from the continent and towards the sea as East Asian strategic geography means that future threats will by and large be maritime in their nature. As the MND and JCS were not able or willing to make this conceptual leap, since 1990 the ROKN has taken the lead in formulating what type of navy is required to manage South Korea's security interests in the competitive strategic environment of East Asia.[3]

Senior leadership within the ROKN believed that it should develop a force commensurate with South Korea's growing political and economic

---

2003

- Despite the rise in economic interpdependence within the Northeast Asian region, which has emerged as one of the strategically important pillars of the world, the security environment continues to remain in a state of flux as a result of diverse sources of potential disputes, conflict of interests and competition for influence among countries.

2008

- The existence of disputes over territorial sovereignty between China and Japan, or between Japan and Russia is the cause of yet more unrest in the region. There are also historic issues: China's so-called Northeastern Project; the distortion of the history textbook by Japan; and Japanese politicians' visits to the Yasukuni Shrine are all factors contributing to the regional instability. Besides these, the establishment of an EEZ to utilize oceanic resources has become a potential factor for disputes as nations in the region adhere to the position that is advantageous to their own country.

2014

- In Northeast Asia the so-called "Asia's Paradox" has been in place in which economic interdependency grows without a commensurate level of advancement in security cooperation. Individual nations intend to increase their influence and continue an arms race. With the United States presently maintaining military superiority, China, Japan and Russia have strengthened their military power, focusing on naval and air forces. The "Rebalance to the Asia-Pacific Region" strategy of the United States and the rise of China will make their bilateral relations of cooperation and competition a key variable in the security order of Northeast Asia.

2016

- Against the backdrop of the U.S.-China relationship resting upon a dual structure of strategic cooperation and competition, Japan and Russia are also bolstering their militaries to increase their clout in the region while the level of instability and uncertainty continues to grow as the alliances and the cooperation and conflict dynamic among the regional nations persist.

Fig. 3.1 Ministry of National Defence assessments of the East Asia security environment (*Source* Republic of Korea Ministry of National Defense, *Participatory Government Defense Policy* (Seoul: Republic of Korea Ministry of National Defense, 2003), 22–23; Republic of Korea Ministry of National Defense, *2008 Defense White Paper* (Seoul: Republic of Korea Ministry of National Defense, 2008), 17; Republic of Korea Ministry of National Defense, *2014 Defense White Paper* (Seoul: Republic of Korea Ministry of National Defense, 2014), 14; Republic of Korea Ministry of National Defense, *2016 Defense White Paper* (Seoul: Republic of Korea Ministry of National Defense, 2016), 13)

power, and therefore, one that would be independently capable of dealing with potential non-North Korean threats while maintaining deterrence in the littoral waters of the Korean Peninsula.[4] This has allowed

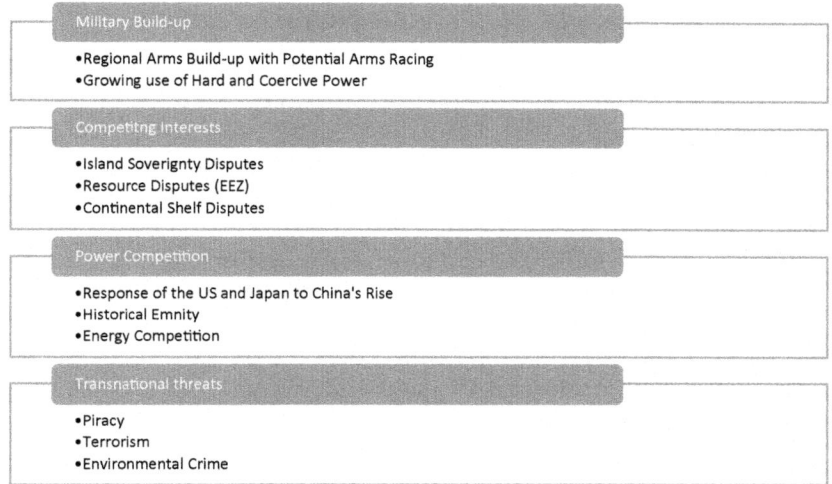

Military Build-up
- Regional Arms Build-up with Potential Arms Racing
- Growing use of Hard and Coercive Power

Competitng Interests
- Island Soverignty Disputes
- Resource Disputes (EEZ)
- Continental Shelf Disputes

Power Competition
- Response of the US and Japan to China's Rise
- Historical Emnity
- Energy Competition

Transnational threats
- Piracy
- Terrorism
- Environmental Crime

Fig. 3.2 ROKN assessments of threats to South Korean security (*Source* Republic of Korea Navy *(Nuguna al su Issneun!) Haegunjakjeon Deuryeodabogi* [As anyone can see! Look into naval operations] (Seoul: Republic of Korea Navy, 2011), 12; ROKN Headquarters, *2008nyeondo haegunjeongchaek bogoseo* [2008 naval policy report] (Gyeryong, ROKN Headquarters), 1))

the navy to translate South Korean perceptions of its regional security environment and its national interests into a set of future operational requirements. Figure 3.2 shows the ROKN's assessment of potential threats to South Korean security beyond those posed by the regime in Pyongyang.

The ROKN has determined that the East Asian strategic maritime environment creates a host of interlinked operational roles that must complement the ongoing deterrence operations in South Korean waters.[5] These include: maintaining forces suited for a conventional strategic deterrent posture within the context of the regional power structure and future potential instability; providing security for South Korean maritime resource exploitation in Korean waters; protecting South Korean SLOC, not only in littoral waters but also in the South China Sea and beyond; and supporting South Korean national foreign policy goals and global interests by participating in cooperative international multinational operations, such as UN PKO, disaster relief and counter-piracy operations.

Deterrence in a Tough Neighbourhood

For the ROKN, its power asymmetry in relation to China and Japan is of significant short and long-term operational concern (Map 3.1). Although Russia has been a factor in South Korean regional security assessments, its current lack of naval capabilities and the absence of contentious maritime issues means that it does not figure prominently in the ROKN's current strategic calculus.

The root of the ROKN's naval asymmetry can be found in the ratio of available resources. China and Japan are the world's second and third largest economies and in 2017, their GDP's were, respectively, ten and four times larger than that of South Korea.[6] This gives them greater actual and potential capacity to build and maintain superior military forces. Further, the requirements of maintaining deterrence on the peninsula divert resources away from the ROKN, thereby reducing their ability to match the People's Liberation Army Navy (PLAN) or Japanese Maritime Self Defense Force (JMSDF). In contrast, China currently faces no substantial threat on its land borders, while Japan, although in a contentious maritime strategic relationship with China, is not threatened

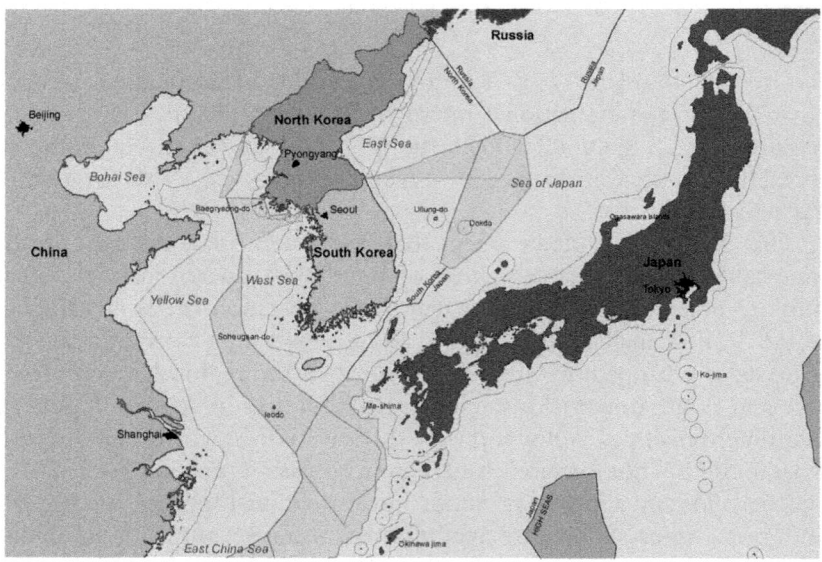

Map 3.1   Waters around the Korean Peninsula

Table 3.1 PLAN, JMSDF & ROKN shipbuilding between 2000 and August 2017

	SSBN	SSN	SSK	CV	C	DD	FF	FS	LHD	LPD	AOE/H	AORH
PLAN	4	6	28	1	1	23	31	43	–	5	1	8
JMSDF	–	–	16	4	2	12	–	–	1	–	2	–
ROKN	–	–	9	–	4	6	10	17	–	1	1	–

Source International Institute for Strategic Studies, "Chapter Two: Comparative Defence Statistics," *The Military Balance* 118, no. 1 (London: International Institute for Strategic Studies, 2018), 26

with invasion. This allows both countries to invest substantial sums in the pursuit of naval capabilities. Table 3.1 demonstrates the extent to which South Korea can't match the major platform development of its two neighbours.

The ROKN, no matter how strong, will most likely always be weaker in terms of capabilities than its two neighbours and how this is assessed as a threat is worthy of further elaboration. The ROKN fears both indirect and direct challenges to South Korea's maritime security. As an indirect threat, the fractious maritime relationship between China and Japan and the US role as a Japanese ally has raised concerns that a conflict at sea in Northeast Asia could erupt and either drag South Korea in or imperil their free use of the sea. This fear is not unreasonable as China has made the development of seapower one of its military priorities.[7] Beijing's coercive use of its maritime power and development of anti-access capabilities strike directly at the heart of Japanese security.[8] Tokyo has identified the sea as a national security priority and in reaction to China's actions is gradually increasing the deterrent strength of its armed forces.[9] The flashpoint that is the Senkaku/Diaoyudao Islands creates fluctuating levels of tension but the long-term trend is one of increased competition for capabilities to ensure maritime dominance and the spectre of conflict arising from either intentional or unintentional escalation is ever-present. In such a scenario, South Korea requires the requisite capabilities to ensure its own maritime security and economic interests are met, despite its comparatively weak position in terms of power.

Beyond the risk of regional conflict at sea, the ROKN does perceive direct challenges to its security from both Japan and China. Certainly, South Korea's understanding of Japan as potential competitor or even threat puzzles many external observers and is a constant hindrance in Washington's efforts to build closer trilateral cooperation.[10] Despite being democracies, US allies and countries with often-matching security priorities, political interactions between Seoul and Tokyo can be fractious and are punctuated with bouts of tension. From a South Korean perspective, this tension is due to Japan's colonial legacy and the perception in South Korea that Tokyo has not fully accepted Japanese culpability for atrocities committed during this time. Several outstanding issues exacerbate this tension including the status of Korean comfort women, divergent understandings of history and its teaching, and importantly for the ROKN, the status of Dokdo/Takeshima.[11]

To the west of the country, South Korea probably does not view China's rise as a direct threat in the same way that Japan or Washington does. However, as a relatively smaller country, it is very wary of China's increasing military strength. Chinese involvement in a Korean War scenario is also a matter of concern for ROKN planners.[12] It is unknown what role China would play if conflict broke out on the Korean Peninsula. Potentially, it could be on the side of North Korea, or Chinese forces could attempt to carve out a buffer zone between China's border and the approaching US-South Korean forces. Whatever the scenario, unlike during the Korean War, the capabilities of the PLAN cannot be ignored and will have a substantial impact on naval operations in the Yellow Sea. However, the advantage for the ROKN is in that any such scenario, US forces would most likely be engaged to balance the PLAN's superiority.

In general Seoul's freedom of action when dealing with Beijing is constrained by a growing economic dependence and the need to maintain good relations with China to manage North Korea.[13] South Korea is forced to walk a rather fine-line to keep both China and the US happy and the former's economic and political reaction over the 2017 US deployment of the THAAD missile defence system in South Korea highlighted the difficulties that Seoul has in managing the relationship between China and the United States.[14]

To mitigate its weaker regional presence, the ROKN has sought to adopt a strategy in line with the tenets of deterrence by denial. Such a strategy can be successfully enacted through convincing an opponent that the use of force to achieve a specific goal will be prohibitively costly or time-consuming, thereby reducing the benefits of aggression.[15] Under this strategy, the role of military forces is to increase the opposition's uncertainties and heighten their potential costs even if a full defence is impossible.[16] Therefore, it does not require forces that match or defeat the enemy, but rather it must have the capacity to inflict substantial damage. Publicly available ROKN documents highlight the potential for the ROKN to face a conflict under such asymmetric conditions and the need to develop capabilities and strategies that would enhance the lethality of the ROKN's combat power.[17]

In the words of Admiral An Byeong-tae, one of the founders of the blue-water operational concept, the ROKN has the long-term intention of building capabilities '*big enough to be counted by them*'.[18] This is in direct contrast with South Korea's strategic maritime deterrent dynamic with North Korea. In that case, South Korea is the stronger power and maintains sufficient to dominate the North Korean Navy (KPN) in times of conflict. The challenge for the ROKN is to maintain deterrence as the superior power in the littoral waters of the Korean Peninsula in relation to North Korea and maintain deterrence as the weaker power in the context of regional strategic competition.

The deterrence by denial strategy also fits within the ROKN's approach to managing some of the outstanding maritime issues that exist between South Korea and its two neighbours. The relationship at sea with Japan has been problematic since the founding of South Korea. Preventing illegal Japanese fishing activity was an operational requirement for the ROKN even during the Korean War. The two countries signed a fisheries agreement to manage this tension in 1965. After both countries ratified United Nations Convention on the Law of the Sea (UNCLOS) in 1996, Japan cancelled the 1965 agreement and in 1998, Tokyo and Seoul signed a new provisional fishing treaty. This established 35 nm Exclusive Economic Zone (EEZ) from the baselines of each country's territorial waters, delimited an EEZ along an equidistant line in the Korea Strait and created two joint fishing zones, one in the East Sea and one in the East China Sea.[19]

The inability to agree a permanently delimited EEZ in the East Sea can attributed to the contested nature of Dokdo. The island is composed of two large and 32 smaller rocky outcrops and is uninhabited except for approximately 50 South Korean police officers and two residents. It is located 47 nm from the South Korea's Ulleungdo and 86 nm from Japan's Oki Islands.[20] The final status of Dokdo is important as it will determine where the EEZ between the two countries can be set. South Korea argues that it should be on a median line between Dokdo and the Oki Islands, Japan argues that Dokdo can generate an EEZ and the median line should be drawn between Dokdo and Ulleungdo.[21]

For South Korea, Dokdo is one of the symbols of the South Korean state and its independence from Japan. In South Korean politics and in the public discourse, the status of Dokdo is not an issue for negotiation and Japan's efforts to contest its status feeds the mistrust that exists between South Korea and Japan. Declarations of Japanese ownership and the inclusion of Dokdo in Japanese Defense White Papers frequently draw swift rebukes from the South Korean Ministry of Foreign Affairs and politicians.

It is unlikely that the ROKN or South Korea regard Japan as an immediate direct threat and the odds of Tokyo attempting the takeover of Dokdo by force are extremely slim. However, the need to ensure the ability to maintain control coupled with underlying suspicion of Japan's motives indicates that a need to hedge against Japan's military power is a constant consideration in their defence planning.

In operational terms, the day to day responsibility for securing maritime territory and the waters around Dokdo lies with the South Korean Coast Guard (KCG). They undertake air and sea patrols of the area on a weekly basis and in response to Japanese patrols around the islands which according to KCG figures occurred on average 96 times per year between 2006 and 2015.[22] In 2006, a well-publicised incident occurred where the Japanese government intended to dispatch two Japanese Coast Guard vessels to carry out a maritime survey of the waters surrounding Dokdo. In response, the KCG deployed 18 vessels and threatened to seize any Japanese ships operating in the area around Dokdo.[23] This incident was resolved politically as are most maritime incidents between the two countries, but it did reveal the operational procedures regarding how the South Korean government manages such disputes.

The South Korean Government, the MND and the ROKN all include the protection of Dokdo as one of the military's missions. Following a round of particularly tense relations over Dokdo, the 2012 South Korean Defense White Paper significantly heightened the MND's commitment to defending Dokdo stating:

> In particular, the ROK military is maintaining a strong readiness posture based on the unwavering resolve to safeguard Dokdo, which is undoubtedly the territory of the ROK in terms of geographical and historical facts and international law.[24]

By having capabilities which may not match, but can compete with Japan, the ROKN fulfils part of this mandate. Additionally, the ROKN holds several joint exercises and highly publicised patrols in the waters around Dokdo. These exercises produce a number of benefits. Primarily, they increase interoperability between the ROKN, the KCG, the Republic of Korea Air Force (ROKAF) and the Republic of Korea Marine Corps (ROKMC). In 2017, two major one-day exercises were held in the waters around Dokdo.[25] The capabilities used included, five ROKN and KCG vessels, one P-3C MPA and F-15K strike fighters.[26] Part of the exercise includes the quick dispatch of marines to the island. Such exercises signal to the MND, South Korean politicians and members of the public that the ROKN has an operational value beyond that of North Korea. They also send a message to Japan regarding South Korean resolve over Dokdo; this is an important element when managing contested maritime territory.

Such signalling operations are in many ways replicated in South Korea's maritime interactions with China. Although the two countries have no contested islands, Seoul and Beijing have failed to agree to a permanent delimitation of an EEZ in the West Sea and the East China Sea due to differing methods of measuring territorial claims.

A flashpoint between the two countries is Ieodo, a submerged rock approximately 150 km away from the South Korea island of Marado. Although both sides agree that it is not a territorial dispute, it is situated within a zone where claimed EEZ overlap. In 2003, South Korea officially opened a marine research station that it had constructed over the rock. The area has the potential for oil and gas deposits and for China, there is strategic value as the rock is close to the route its naval vessels leaving Qingdao naval base take to get to the Pacific.[27] As with the East Sea, the KCG has primary responsibility for ensuring South Korea's maritime sovereignty in this region and performs 2–3 patrols per week in the area surrounding Ieodo.[28] The KCG report an average of 30 Chinese air or sea patrols per year around Ieodo between 2006 and 2015.

When China declared an Air Defence Identification Zone (ADIZ) without prior consultation in 2014, it covered the area over Ieodo. One element of the South Korean government's response was for the ROKN to undertake a series of exercises in the areas around the disputed rock, including one with JMSDF. This forms part of a pattern

Table 3.2 Number of Chinese vessels seized in Korean waters, 2001–2017

	2001–2005	2006–2010	2011	2012	2013	2014	2015	2016	2017
Total	1617	2199	534	467	487	341	568	405	247
Number of vessels seized in the EEZ	1314	1960	504	426	447	316	543	355	230
Number of vessels seized around the NLL	303	239	30	41	40	25	25	50	17

Source Korean Coast Guard, *Junggugeoseondansokyeonhwang* [Status of Chinese fishing boat control], December 26, 2017. http://www.index.go.kr/potal/main/EachDtlPageDetail.do?idx_cd=1622. Accessed 10 January 2018

where the ROKN has an increasing role in back-stopping the KCG and signalling to the Chinese the South Korean military presence in disputed waters.[29]

This sort of backstopping is being replicated over the issue of illegal Chinese fishing in South Korean waters. Due to the failure to settle an EEZ, a provisional fishing agreement between the two countries, similar in composition to the South Korea–Japan agreement, into effect in 2001.[30] However, this agreement failed to alleviate the consistent problem of illegal Chinese fishing activity in South Korean waters. As Table 3.2 shows, a substantial number of Chinese fishing vessels have been seized since the agreement came into effect, including vessels operating around the sensitive NLL.

The number of vessels seized does not reveal the level of violence that the Chinese fishermen have used against KCG officers. In recent years, Chinese fishermen have murdered two South Korean KCG officers and sank one small KCG vessel.[31] The tactics used by the Chinese vessels include chaining together to prevent seizure, the use of hand-held weapons and ramming. In response, the KCG has eased restrictions on the use of force and has stepped-up operations in illegal fishing hot spots.[32] Several Chinese fishermen have also been injured or killed in clashes with South Korean law enforcement.[33] As of yet, no Chinese government vessels have intervened to protect their fishermen as is the case in the South China Sea. This is most likely due to the 2001 agreement and the fact that China does not claim the entirety of the West Sea. However, the Chinese government has complained about the excessive use of force and seems unwilling to completely reign-in its fishermen by punishing them under Chinese law.

Due to the level of violence, the ROKN has come under political pressure to provide support to the KCG. This has resulted in heightened cooperation between the two services and the creation of a manual for joint-operations in 2017.[34] In an example of a joint-operation, one naval vessel supported nine coast guard ships and two aircraft for three days.[35] This operation led to seven seizures, and the retreat of 158 Chinese fishing vessels from South Korean waters.

Illegal Chinese fishing became a strategic issue when vessels were detected in the Han River Estuary, an area that is under United Nations Military Armistice Commission (UNMAC) control. This was first discovered in 2011, but the number of incidents sharply escalated in 2015 resulting in the UNMAC declaring that the Chinese vessels were in violation of the armistice.[36] The UN response, in accordance with the armistice agreement, was to deploy KCG and South Korean Military Police on four speedboats flying South Korean and UN flags.[37] The MND argues that this was a successful joint operation between the military, KCG and United Nations Command (UNC). They also engaged diplomatically with the Chinese government, which in contrast with the illegal activity in South Korean waters, responded by acting to stop its fishermen from operating in the estuary.[38]

As China is likely to continue to exercise its seapower in the region, the ROKN will be required to maintain its presence in the West Sea and East China Sea. Operationally, the management of potential future coercive activities similar to those observed in the South China Sea will logically form part of the ROKN's strategy to ensure the integrity of South Korea's maritime resources. The operational interactions at sea between the maritime forces of the littoral nations of the South China Sea and China show the need for a credible surface capability to demonstrate presence and to discourage coercive activity.[39] This requires the possession of vessels, of a size that can credibly contest the presence of their Chinese opponents, in sufficient numbers to be deployed on a sustained basis. This is not a capability that the ROKN or KCG has traditionally possessed. In 1991, when Admiral An was commander of the Second Fleet, a 4,000-ton PLAN vessel was detected approaching a South Korean-contracted oil exploration vessel operating in international waters in the West Sea. While this approach was legal and non-aggressive, the South Korean admiral felt that the ROKN must dispatch its own vessel, but the largest available was a 1,500-tons frigate. This was not deemed sufficient to show presence in case of an encounter turning hostile and so a maritime surveillance aircraft was dispatched instead.[40] Given reports that the ROKN has already come under Chinese pressure to curtail its operations in the Yellow Sea, and the seemingly inexorable increase in the number of Chinese naval and maritime law enforcement platforms, managing Chinese coercion will be a consistent issue in future ROKN operations.[41]

SLOC PROTECTION

Since the end of the Korean War, SLOC protection has been part of the ROKN's mission set. For South Korea, the maintenance of open sea lanes is vital to ensure US access to South Korean ports during times of war. Consequently, the ROKN has developed the operational capability to protect its SLOC in its littoral waters against any North Korea threat. However, it has been reliant on the United States and other major navies to ensure wider maritime stability and international order at sea to provide a safe maritime environment for South Korea's global commercial maritime interests. Since the ROKN began is a drive for blue-water modernisation it has used South Korea's reliance on the sea for its economic advancement as a justification for expanding its SLOC protection role from the confines of the littoral to the regional waters of East Asia and beyond.

The ROKN in its long-term planning has recognised a need for both a cooperative and independent capacity to protect their SLOCs. Optimal cooperation with the United States and other partners to ensure maritime security requires interoperable platforms that are capable of sustained operations alongside westernised navies. Cooperative operations at sea to protect SLOC leverage the fact that it is in every country's interest to maintain stable commercial maritime activity. Being able to contribute to maritime security operations both directly benefits South Korean commercial activities but also promotes the image of South Korea as a contributor to the international maritime order and therefore as a provider of global public goods. The ROKN has already demonstrated its commitment to this type of operation by maintaining a destroyer on counter-piracy operations in the Gulf of Aden since 2009.

The desire for an independent capability is driven by the ROKN's concern that a third-party conflict in Asia could impact their SLOC. This is particularly true in the context of the South China Sea, Taiwan and the China–Japan competition over the Senkaku/Diaoyudao islands. Currently, South Korea has no direct involvement in these disputes and yet there is a legitimate concern that these points of contention may leave South Korea exposed with no specific guarantee of security for its shipping in any conflict zone. However, there are outstanding questions regarding the ROKN's ability to carry out this kind of independent SLOC protection role in high threat environments contested by great powers. At times of heightened tension, ROKN vessels could escort vital shipping to South Korean ports but at a time of war, such shipping would be forced to either find alternate routes or avoid the conflict zone.

The ROKN has designated four major SLOC as being vital to the country's survival: Korea–China, Korea–Japan, a Southeast SLOC and a Southwest SLOC.[42]

- The Korea–China SLOC

The Korea–China sea lane links South Korea with its largest trading partner. Any interference with this SLOC would have substantial effects on the South Korean economy. Disruption to this SLOC would more likely arise from a political or strategic disagreement between China and South Korea and thus would not immediate operational concern for the ROKN. North Korea's ability to interfere with this SLOC outside of the littoral waters of the Peninsula is also limited. If war broke out on the Korean Peninsula the security of this route would be determined by China's position in any conflict and the consequent type of strategic and operational interaction between Chinese and US/South Korean forces.

- The Korea–Japan SLOC

The security of the Korea-Japan SLOC is determined by the geopolitical situation at the time. In peacetime, political issues or sovereignty disputes between Japan and South Korea are unlikely to result in any trade disruption between the two countries. However, in wartime this route would be of paramount importance as a large proportion of supplies and reinforcements will arrive via Japan. The ROKN, USN and JMSDF would provide protection to this SLOC in a time of war. A secondary threat to this route is posed by the potential for conflict between China and Japan. It is a plausible planning consideration that shipping on this route may be vulnerable in such a scenario.

- The Southeast SLOC

This route provides access to the United States, Latin America and Australia, while important for trade purposes and energy purposes, it is also essential for wartime augmentation of forces and equipment. As with the South Korea–Japan SLOC, protection for this route is provided by the ROKN, USN and the JMSDF and as such naval cooperation and friendly relations are vital to its security in any wartime scenario.

- The Southwest SLOC

This SLOC is critical for South Korea's energy supply from the Middle East and is the most efficient route to Europe. It is also one of South Korea's most vulnerable as it passes through several areas of dispute including Taiwan, the Senkaku/Diaoyudao Islands and the contested waters of the South China Sea. Additionally, this route passes through some areas with incidents of piracy and an ever-present threat of terrorism. The security of this route has historically been secured through international cooperation particularly in relation to counter-piracy efforts in the Straits of Malacca and the Gulf of Aden. However, the ROKN also views the potential destabilising effects of conflict in the region and particularly in North and Southeast Asia as direct threats to the security of the SLOC. It is this potential that has in part determined the ROKN's requirements for an independent SLOC protection capability not just in the littorals of the peninsula but also in the South China Sea.

Despite the difficulties of independently protecting their SLOC in a regional setting, the stated pursuit of such a capability is in many ways motivated by Seoul's reluctance to become entangled in regional disputes and its seeming policy of intentional opacity regarding its position on sensitive maritime territorial issues. This position is driven by a desire to avoid alienating either Washington or Beijing. In 2005, when discussing negotiations over strategic flexibility, President Roh Moo-hyun said that 'it should be clarified that we will not be embroiled in any conflict in Northeast Asia against our will'.[43] This was a direct message to the United States regarding South Korea's freedom of action over Taiwan and the role of US forces stationed on the Korean Peninsula in any none scenario.

A similar position is now evident in the South China Sea, where South Korea has not been as vocal as Japan, the United States or other powerful maritime states in criticising China's coercive activities in the region. The South Korean government has publicly posited that disputes in the region should manage peacefully and that 'freedom of navigation and commercial aviation in the South China Sea should be guaranteed'.[44] Notably, South Korea is not part of the burgeoning cooperation between the United States, Japan, India and Australia aimed at maintaining the rules based maritime system.[45] This does not mean South Korea is completely uninvolved. ROKN naval vessels pass through the South China Sea on a regular basis, usually when transiting to the Gulf of Aden. Further, South Korea has sold naval vessels including submarines to Indonesia, the Philippines, Malaysia and Thailand.[46] It has also donated one ageing *Pohang* class corvette to the Philippines and another to Vietnam.[47]

It should be acknowledged that if conflict breaks out or tensions heighten significantly this policy of ambiguity and no direct involvement will become increasingly difficult to execute as pressure from the United States may become hard to resist. The ROKN's calculation is that having a force capable of independently protecting South Korean maritime interests will provide some room for political manoeuvre. However, possessing such a naval force may be a double-edged sword. If South Korea has the spare capacity to provide independent protection of its SLOC with modern interoperable warships it may face greater expectations from the United States in terms of contributing forces to allied operations. In the past, South Korea has not been considered as a naval power outside of the Korean Peninsula. The build-up of naval forces may ultimately place greater pressure on the South Korean government to become involved in the region.

THE ROKN AND SOUTH KOREAN FOREIGN POLICY

South Korea's position as a major economy and country with global interests increases its responsibilities as a member of the international community. Slowly but surely, the MND and the South Korean armed services have made contributions to both UN PKO and multinational force operations such as those in Iraq and Afghanistan, with the first dispatch of troops on UN PKO duties occurring in 1993.[48]

Supporting these efforts and contributing to South Korean security is therefore an important method for the ROKN to show its added value to the MND and gives it the opportunity to gain operational experience in a context outside of the Korean Peninsula. Naval forces have some

Table 3.3 ROKN international operations

Operation	Date	Type	Units deployed
Vietnam War	1965–1973	Logistical and deployment support	LST & LSM
East Timor	2000–2002	Logistical and humanitarian support	LST
Afghanistan	2001	Logistical and humanitarian support	LST
Asian Tsunami	2005	Logistical and humanitarian relief	LST
Gulf of Aden	2009–	Counter-piracy	DDG
Typhoon Haiyan (Philippines)	2013	Humanitarian relief	LST

unique qualities in this regard. The fact that they are considered national territory, are capable of multiple missions at the same time and can traverse distances quickly means that their deployment provides governments with numerous options in times of emergency. The development of a blue-water capability provides Seoul with the capacity to contribute to both international and South Korean security on a global scale.

As Table 3.3 shows, the ROKN's previous contributions to international operations have largely been limited to the provision of logistical support for troops on the ground and for disaster relief efforts. The stand-out operation has been the deployment of a destroyer on counter-piracy duties to the Gulf of Aden since 2009. The South Korean government authorised the dispatch of a single KDX-II destroyer on rotating four to five-month deployments to operate as part of the international counter-piracy task force CTF 151.[49] Not only has this mission clearly demonstrated South Korea's ability to sustain an operation in waters far from the Korean Peninsula, it has also served to demonstrate to the South Korean government the utility of naval forces to serve the national interest and signalled to South Korea's allies and partners that it is fully capable of contributing to global maritime security.

From an operational perspective, the mission can so far be considered a success. Between 2009 and 2016, the deployed ROKN ships escorted over 2000 vessels of both South Korean and international origin. The ROKN has led the task force on several occasions, the first being in 2010. They have also participated in over 270 specific maritime security operations. One of the most famous being the rescue of 21 crewmembers of the Norwegian-owned by South Korean-operated *Samho Jewelry* chemical tanker. During the operation by ROKN SOF, eight pirates were killed and five captured. By maintaining a ship in the

Gulf of Aden and leading an international task force, the ROKN has gained substantial operational experience.[50] Further, the utility and flexibility of modern naval forces were demonstrated on two occasions when the ROKN used vessels assigned to CTF 151 to rescue South Koreans and other nationalities from the wars Libya in 2011 and Yemen in 2015. The navy's actions in these two cases aided the South Korean government in fulfilling their duty to protect South Korean citizens who are now based all over the world.

FINDING THE BALANCE

For the ROKN to broaden its operational role and meet the strategic requirements posed by the post-Cold War maritime environment it needed to articulate a strategic plan and procurement strategy that would allow it to maintain deterrence and prepare for war in the waters around the Korean Peninsula, while at the same working towards building the capacity to deal with current and future regional threats.[51] This concept is at the heart of the ROKN's blue-water modernisation program and represents more than the development of new platforms. It is the expression of the ROKN's new way of thinking about its role and future of South Korea seapower.

The initial proposal for dealing with this bifurcated operational requirement was made in 1995, when Admiral An Byeong-tae won approval for the construction of a blue-water navy from President Kim Young-sam. This was a seminal moment for the ROKN who had harboured such ambitions since 1990 but could not receive approval for them. Kim Young-sam was the first civilian president since the 1960s and he had an ambition for South Korea to become a globalised country and responsible international stakeholder. A blue-water navy matched such ambitions.

The blue-water navy concept was articulated in *Navy Vision 2020*, a document that set out the ROKN's potential future roles and capabilities for the year 2020. Published in 1999, the document argued that following unification on the Korean Peninsula, the maritime domain would become South Korea's primary strategy concern.[52] To prepare for this future, the document called for the ROKN to develop larger more technologically advanced platforms which could be used to maintain deterrence around the Korean Peninsula while also providing the navy with the capabilities necessary to cope with the contingencies outlined above.[53]

The ROKN was not seeking to abrogate its responsibilities in and around the Korean Peninsula in favour of force modernisation aimed at blue-water operations. Instead, it looked to leverage technology to enhance its lethality and surveillance capabilities and take advantage of the inherent multifunctionality that advanced, large naval platforms possess to perform North Korea-related operations while at the same time laying the groundwork for an expanded mission set. Nine-years later, the ROKN published Navy Vision 2030. This document built upon many of the concepts of Navy Vision 2020, but it did not predicate itself on a unified future, rather it highlighted how a modern blue-water ROKN which would be fully operationalised by 2030 would provide game-changing strategic benefits for South Korea in the waters around the Korean Peninsula and beyond.[54]

Submarines are good example of how the ROKN has sought to manage the problem of regional asymmetry while at the same time increasing capabilities in relation to North Korea. The ROKN has identified their submarine capability as the primary tool to carry out deterrence within the context of Northeast Asia. A 2008 ROKN publication stated that it is 'carrying out the principal of sea area defense and the protection of sea lanes by utilising submarines in spite of the intense military strength competition all over Northeast Asia'.[55] Both Navy Vision 2020 and 2030 describe the strategic deterrence and sea denial capability of their future submarine force suggesting that their utility not only lies in the context of the Korean Peninsula but also as a force capable of mitigating the ROKN's weaknesses when compared with the PLAN and JMSDF.

The challenge for the ROKN has been to transfer these concepts into workable operational structures. The solution the ROKN has developed is the Strategic Mobile Fleet concept. Future modernisation plans indicate an intention to keep ROKN's existing fleet structure of the three core fleets determined by the geography of the peninsula. These would be modernised to increase their effectiveness in relation to North Korea, while at the same time building capabilities of equal utility in a regional context.[56]

The Strategic Mobile Fleet concept is designed to take advantage of the mobility and flexibility of naval vessels. The proposal contained in both Navy Vision 2020 and Navy 2030 was for three mobile flotillas of between six to eight modern naval vessels capable of independently and cooperatively carrying out multidimensional warfare.[57] These flotillas would be self-contained, able to operate for long periods without returning to port and would have the capacity to operate as far south as the Malacca Straits.[58] The proposed mobility of these groups is the key to their potential strategic effect. The ROKN intends to use these mobile flotillas to respond emergencies in regional waters and to reinforce the sea fleets on either side of the peninsula in case of heightened tensions or war with North Korea.

The difficulty the ROKN faces is one of critical mass. The future force structure it calls for in Navy Vision 2020 and 2030 requires substantial investment and time. Further, as chapter two highlights the North Korean threat is constantly evolving thereby requiring continuous reassessments of ROKN force requirements. While technology and multifunctionality can partially alleviate this problem, it is not a catch-all solution. This reality could hinder the consistent build-up of the forces required to undertake the multitude of missions the ROKN envisages.

The ROKN's larger blue-water surface platforms, the three KDX-III and six KDX-II destroyers have now been organised into Maritime Task Flotilla 7. The intention is that this will be transformed into a mobile fleet when more platforms are added.[59] Even with the existing nine vessels, the ROKN has learned that increasing their commitments far from the Korean Peninsula and taking on new roles significantly reduces available platforms. Due to the requirements of training and maintenance, most navies expect to achieve about a 30% deployment rate and the ROKN is no different.[60] The commitment of one KDX-II destroyer to the counter-piracy mission in the Gulf of Aden takes away three vessels due to maintenance, transit and training requirements. This reduces the available force of 4,000-ton destroyers for operations around the Korean Peninsula by 50%.[61] At one stage, due to the South Korean contribution to the Rim of the Pacific Exercise (RIMPAC) and the dispatch of one vessel to an international fleet review, only one KDX-II destroyer was on deployment in the ROKN's immediate area of operations.[62] Similar limitations can be assumed for the KDX-III class, where having only three ships reduces training and maintenance time during periods of high-operational tempo and will have significant long-term effects on combat readiness and platform durability.[63]

The sinking of the *Cheonan* forced a temporary revaluation of the navy's priorities and the prior procurement of platforms capable of blue-water operations drew substantial political, media and public criticism. The ROKN temporarily pulled back from its blue-water ambitions and the *already existing* development programs for new classes of patrol boat and frigate were accelerated. However, the ROKN's view of the broader maritime environment, including future force requirements for advanced operations around the Korean Peninsula was not incorrect. The pressures of China's rise and regional strategic competition on South Korean security quickly ensured that long-term blue-water development was funded. That the ROKN continued to pursue such capabilities and was given the budget to procure them is an acknowledgement by security stakeholders in South Korea that the country requires an independent naval force to meet all of its contingencies. In 2013, three years after the sinking of the *Cheonan*, ROKN CNO Adm. Choi Yoonhee stated that:

> The navy will go beyond the current maritime operations concept under which it relied on the U.S. Navy...it is illogical to passively operate the current Korea-U.S. operational capabilities. (We) will seek to change the current paradigm by swiftly securing maritime superiority and projecting naval power.[64]

Questions during parliamentary audits and publicly available statements regarding future force development all highlight that South Korea cannot ignore the naval modernization that is occurring in Northeast Asia.[65] Consequently, current force improvement plans including three KDX-III Batch-II destroyers, six smaller KDDX destroyers and its ongoing submarine development program are aimed at bolstering the ROKN's core goal of building capabilities for any number of peninsular and non-peninsular scenarios.[66]

CONCLUSION

This chapter has demonstrated that the ROKN is trying to fundamentally alter how South Korea understands and utilises its naval power. This effort is encapsulated in the blue-water modernisation program. This program is much more than the simple introduction of new platforms or the extension of the ROKN's area of operations. It is about engaging with South Korea's changing security circumstances in the region and recognising that South Korea must have the ability to secure its own strategic interests while also contributing to global security.

As a middle power with a strong economic relationship with and reliance on the sea, South Korea is vulnerable to the shifting geopolitical undercurrents of instability that characterize the East Asian maritime environment. As China continues to challenge the United States and Japan for primacy in the waters of the region, the strategic trend is one of competition and potential conflict. The possession of sufficient naval power to protect South Korea's economic interests in its EEZ and SLOC is of paramount importance as the United States may not be a reliable provider of maritime security in the future. Further, the possession of modern platforms allows South Korea to contribute to international security operations and take its place as a reliable international stakeholder.

Of course, developing sufficient capabilities to perform such operations while also maintaining deterrence around the Korean Peninsula is extremely difficult. The navy's solution has been to leverage the multifunctionality of large platforms which could provide it with a greater independent capability within the context of the North Korean threat. The same platforms have the capacity to meet some but currently not all South Korea's requirement in regional waters away from the Korean Peninsula. In the setting of North Korea, the ROKN largely enjoys supremacy over the KPN. However, in a regional setting, the ROKN must cope with its asymmetric power relationship with China and Japan. Further, the challenges of maintenance, training and the distance substantially reduce available platforms and threaten to weaken ROKN capabilities despite its attempted exploitation of the mobility of naval platforms to offset this problem.

As long as the threat from North Korea exists the majority of the ROKN fleet will remain tied to the littoral waters of the Korean Peninsula, however, the navy must continue to seek further operational independence in non-North Korean contexts. The geostrategic reality, as acknowledged by the ROKN, is that the security environment in East Asia cannot be ignored no matter what North Korea does. With the introduction of new surface vessels and submarines, the ROKN's ability to sustain naval power at sea will continue to develop. However, it remains to be seen how South Korea and the ROKN will utilize its naval power in the future and if the navy will continue to enjoy such funding should strategic circumstance change.

Notes

1. Sang-hoon Park, "Korea's Security Policy," *Institute for Foreign Affairs and National Security Review* 4, no. 3 (1996): 7.
2. Gilbert Rozman, In-taek Hyun, and Shin-wha Lee, "Overview," in *South Korean Strategic Thought Toward Asia*, ed. Gilbert Rozman, In-taek Hyun, and Shin-wha Lee (New York: Palgrave Macmillan, 2008), 4.
3. Sang-yup Lee, "Ships, Security, and Symbols: A Constructivist Explanation of South Korea's Naval Build-Up" (PhD Dissertation, Rutgers University, 2013), 243–44.
4. Successive Defense White Papers highlight the fact that while the ROKN would continue to maintain deterrence on the Korean Peninsula, it would also prepare for future threats. This is in contrast with the ROKA and ROKAF. Both service branches' force development was focused on North Korea.
5. ROKN Headquarters, *Haegun bijeon 2020* [Navy Vision 2020] (Gyeryong: ROKN Headquarters, 1999), 96–103; ROKN Headquarters, *Haegun bijeon 2030* [Navy Vision 2030] (Gyeryong: ROKN Headquarters, 2008), 18–19.
6. The International Monetary Fund, *World Economic Database* (October 2017).
7. The State Council the People's Republic of China, *China's Military Strategy* (27 May 2015), http://english.gov.cn/archive/white_paper/2015/05/27/content_281475115610833.htm, accessed 20 June 2016.
8. Ian Bowers and Bjørn Gronning, "Protecting the Status Quo: Japan's Response to China's Rise," in *Strategic Adjustment and the Rise of China: Power and Politics in East Asia*, ed. Robert Ross and Øystein Tunsjø (New York: Cornell University Press, 2017), 140–42.
9. Ministry of Defense of Japan, *National Security Strategy*, 17 December 2013 (Tokyo: Ministry of Defense of Japan, 2013), 2.
10. The US often acts as the facilitator of South Korea–Japan security cooperation and views it's a central to future regional security. See: The White House Office of the Press Secretary, *Remarks by President Obama, President Park of the Republic of Korea, and Prime Minister Abe of Japan*, 25 March 2014, http://www.whitehouse.gov/the-press-office/2014/03/25/remarks-president-obama-president-park-republic-south-korea-and-prime-minister, accessed 12 January 2015; Samuel J. Locklear, *Statement of Admiral J. Locklear, U.S. Navy Commander, U.S. Pacific Command Before the Senate Armed Services Committee on U.S. Pacific Command Posture*, 16 April (Washington, DC: Senate Armed Services Committee, 2015), http://www.armed-services.senate.gov/imo/media/doc/Locklear_04-16-15.pdf, accessed 19 April

2015; "S. Korea, U.S., Japan Agree to Bolster 3-Way Cooperation," *The Korea Herald*, 17 April 2015, http://www.koreaherald.com/view.php?ud=20150417000168, accessed 20 April 2015.

11. For an overview of these issues and their impact on South Korea-Japan relations see: Brad Glosserman and Scott A. Snyder, *The Japan-South Korea Identity Clash: East Asian Security and the United States* (New York: Columbia University Press, 2015).

12. Michael A. McDevitt, *Report on the KIMS-CNA Conference "The PLA Navy's Build-Up and ROK-USN Cooperation"* (Alexandria: Centre for Naval Analysis, 2009), 5.

13. Ellen Kim and Victor Cha, "Between a Rock and a Hard Place: South Korea's Strategic Dilemmas with China and the United States," *Asia Policy*, no. 21 (January 2016): 101–21.

14. It is reported that South Korea, following negotiations with Beijing, agreed not join a trilateral networked MD system with the US and Japan. See: Ankit Panda, "China and South Korea: Examining the Resolution of the THAAD Impasse," *The Diplomat*, 13 November 2017, https://thediplomat.com/2017/11/china-and-south-korea-examining-the-resolution-of-the-thaad-impasse/, accessed 10 December 2018.

15. Michael S. Gearson, "Conventional Deterrence in the Second Nuclear Age," *Parameters* 39, no. 3 (Autumn 2009): 37; John J. Mearsheimer, *Conventional Deterrence* (New York: Cornell University Press, 1983), 24.

16. Samuel P. Huntington, "Conventional Deterrence and Conventional Retaliation in Europe," *International Security* 8, no. 3 (1993–1994): 36.

17. ROKN Headquarters, *Haegun bijeon 2020*, 94.

18. Author conducted interview with Adm. An Byeong-tae, April 2011.

19. Min-gyo Koo, *Island Disputes and Maritime Regime Building in East Asia: Between a Rock and a Hard Place* (New York: Springer, 2009), 179.

20. Seok Woo Lee, "South Korea's Maritime Challenges and Priorities," in *Maritime Challenges and Priorities in Asia*, ed. Joshua H. Ho and Sam Bateman (Oxon: Routledge, 2012), 219–30, 226.

21. Seok Woo Lee and Hee Eun Lee, *The Making of International Law in Korea: From Colony to Asian Power* (Leiden: Brill Nijhoff, 2016), 253.

22. Republic of Korea Government, *2012nyeondo gukjeonggamsagyeolgwa sijeong min cheoriyogusahange daehan cheorigyeolgwagoseo* (Gukbangbu Sogwan) [Report on the Completion of the 2012 National Assembly Audit Results and the Completion of the Corrective and Handling requirements (Ministry of National Defense)], March 2013, 66.

23. Suk-kyoon Kim, *Maritime Disputes in Northeast Asia: Regional Challenges and Cooperation* (Leiden: Brill Nijhoff, 2017), 72.

24. Republic of Korea Ministry of National Defense, *2012 Defense White Paper* (Seoul: Republic of Korea Ministry of National Defense, 2012), 60.

25. Seok-jong Lee, *Haegun*, "Jeongnyejeok Dokdobangeohullyeon [Navy, Regular Dokdo Defense Training]," *National Defense Daily*, 18 December 2017, www.kookbang.dema.mil.kr/kookbangWeb/view.do?bbs_id=BB-SMSTR_000000000005&ntt_writ_date=201712229&parent_no=5, accessed 16 February 2018.
26. Ibid.
27. Kim, *Maritime Disputes*, 60–61.
28. Republic of Korea Government, *2012nyeondo gukjeonggamsagyeolgwa*, 66.
29. Yong-soo Jeong and Sarah Kim, "Korean Navy Conducts Drill Close to Ieodo," *Korea Joongang Ilbo*, 4 December 2013, http://koreajoongang-daily.joins.com/news/article/article.aspx?aid=2981469, accessed 10 March 2016.
30. Republic of Korea Ministry of Foreign Affairs, "Korea-China Fisheries Agreement Comes into Effect," *Press Release*, 29 June 2001, http://www.mofa.go.kr/eng/brd/m_5676/view.do?seq=296187, accessed 10 January 2018.
31. One KCG officer was killed in 2008 when he drowned after been struck by an iron bar. Another was stabbed to death by a trawler captain in 2011. See: Johnathan Watts, "South Korean Coastguard Stabbed to Death While Seizing Chinese Boat," *The Guardian*, 12 December 2011, https://www.theguardian.com/environment/2011/dec/12/south-korean-coastguard-stabbed-boat, accessed 10 February 2018; "Chinese Fishing Vessels Ram Korean Coast Guard Boat," *Maritime Executive*, 10 October 2016, https://www.maritime-executive.com/article/chinese-fishing-vessel-rams-korean-coast-guard-boat#gs.0LOK=_Q, accessed 10 February 2018.
32. Ju-min Park, "South Korea Vows Greater Force Against China Fishing Boats," *Reuters*, 11 October 2016, https://www.reuters.com/article/us-southkorea-china-fishermen/south-korea-vows-greater-force-against-china-fishing-boats-idUSKCN12B09O, accessed 10 February 2018.
33. As an example, in one incident the KCG used flash bang grenades when boarding a Chinese vessel which started a fire causing three Chinese fishermen to die from asphyxiation. See: "Three Chinese Fishermen Killed in Confrontation with South Korea Coastguard," *Reuters*, 30 September 2016, https://www.reuters.com/article/us-southkorea-china-fishermen/three-chinese-fishermen-killed-in-confrontation-with-south-korea-coastguard-idUSKCN1200DQ, accessed 10 March 2017.
34. Republic of Korea Government, *2016nyeondo gukjeonggamsagyeolgwa sijeong min cheoriyogusahange daehan cheorigyeolgwagoseo* (Gukbangbu Sogwan) [Report on the Completion of the 2016 National Assembly Audit Results and the Completion of the Corrective and Handling Requirements (Ministry of National Defense)], (February 2017), 134.

35. Ibid.
36. Republic of Korea Ministry of National Defense, *2016 Defense White Paper*, 238–39.
37. Park Boram, "S. Korea, UNC Crack Down on Illegal Chinese Fishing in Neutral Waters Between Koreas," *Yonhap News Agency*, 10 June 2016, http://english.yonhapnews.co.kr/northkorea/2016/06/09/0401000000AEN20160609003852315.html, accessed 15 September 2017.
38. Republic of Korea Ministry of National Defense, *2016 Defense White Paper*, 240.
39. As an example, Indonesia has found that its own maritime law enforcement vessels are not large enough to manage their interactions with their Chinese counterparts and have subsequently taken to dispatching more powerful naval vessels. In this type of scenario at sea, the relative size and power of the vessels involved does matter. See: Lyle J. Morris, "Indonesia-China Tensions in the Natuna Sea: Evidence of Naval Efficiency over Coast Guards?" *The RAND Blog*, 5 July 2016, https://www.rand.org/blog/2016/07/indonesia-china-tensions-in-the-natuna-sea-evidence.html, accessed 12 February 2018.
40. Interview with Admiral An Byeong-tae, April 2011.
41. Yong-soo Jeong, "China Tried Muscling South Korea in the Yellow Sea," *Korea Joongang Ilbo*, 30 November 2013, http://koreajoongangdaily.joins.com/news/article/article.aspx?aid=2981288, accessed 2 April 2014.
42. Michael McDevitt, "Final Report," in *Workshop Report: The Future of ROK Navy-US Navy Cooperation*, ed. Michael McDevitt (Alexandria: Centre for Naval Analysis, 2007), 3; Republic of Korea Navy, *(Nuguna al su Issneun!)*, 8–9; William D. Sullivan, "Chapter 1: Old Issues and New Threats," in *Korean Maritime Strategy: Issues and Challenges*, ed. Geoffrey Till and Sukjoon Yoon (Seoul: The Korea Institute for Maritime Strategy, 2011), 3–16, 12.
43. Moo-hyun Roh, *Address at the 53rd Commencement and Commissioning Ceremony of the Korea Air Force Academy*, 8 March 2005.
44. ROK Ministry of National Defense, *2016 Defense White Paper* (Seoul: RON MND, 2016), 167; *Statement by the Spokesperson of the Ministry of Foreign Affairs of the Republic of Korea on the South China Sea Arbitration Award*, ROK Ministry of Foreign Affairs, 13 July 2016, http://www.mofa.go.kr/eng/brd/m_5676/view.do?seq=316765, accessed 10 August 2017.
45. Tanvi Madan, "The Rise, Fall and Rebirth of the 'Quad'," *War on the Rocks*, 16 November 2017, https://warontherocks.com/2017/11/rise-fall-rebirth-quad/, accessed 10 February 2018.
46. SIPRI, *SIPRI Arms Transfer Database: Trade Registers*, http://armstrade.sipri.org/armstrade/page/trade_register.php, accessed 21 February 2018.

47. It should be noted that South Korea also donated one Pohang Class corvette to Egypt and this seems to be a business development strategy rather than an explicit maritime capacity building effort. "Egypt Receives New Warship Donated by South Korea," *APA News*, 26 October 2017, http://apanews.net/en/pays/egypte/news/egypt-receives-new-warship-donated-by-south-korea, accessed 17 February 2017.

48. See: Ian Bowers, "South Korea," in *Asia-Pacific Nations in International Peace Support and Stability Missions*, ed. Chiyuki Aoi and Yee-Kuang Heng (New York: Palgrave Macmillan, 2014), 87–111.

49. Republic of Korea National Defense Committee, *Gukgunbudaeui somallia haeyeok pagyeon donguian geomto* [Review of the Motion to Dispatch Korean Military Forces to Somalia Waters] (Seoul: National Defense Committee, 2009).

50. Terence Roehrig, "South Korea's Counterpiracy Operations in the Gulf of Aden," in *Global Korea: South Korea's Contributions to International Security*, ed. Scott Bruce, John Hemmings, Balbina Y. Hwang, Terence Roehrig, and Scott A. Snyder (Washington, DC: Council on Foreign Relations, 2012), 41.

51. Author conducted interview with Admiral An Byeong-tae, April 2011.

52. Republic of Korea Navy Headquarters, *Haegun bijeon 2020*, 93–94. It should be noted that Kim Dae-jung was South Korean President in 1999 and engaged in the Sunshine Policy, which was a policy of engagement with North Korea. By emphasising a post-unification security environment, the ROKN was leveraging the political climate at that time.

53. Ibid., 91–92.

54. Republic of Korea Navy Headquarters, *Haegun bijeon 2030*, 37.

55. Republic of Korea Navy Headquarters, *Daehanminguk haegu=The Republic of Korea Navy* [The Republic of Korea Navy=The Republic of Korea Navy] (Chungnam: Republic of Korea Navy Headquarters, 2008), 56.

56. Ibid., 24.

57. Republic of Korea Navy Headquarters, *Haegun bijeon 2020*, 113; Republic of Korea Navy Headquarters, *Haegun bijeon 2030*, 33.

58. Interview with Admiral An Byeong-tae, April 2011.

59. See Chapter 4.

60. Jo Inge Bekkevold and Ian Bowers, "A Question of Balance: Warfighting and Naval Operations other the War," in *International Order at Sea: How It Is Challenged, How It Is Maintained*, ed. Jo Inge Bekkevold and Geoffrey Till (London: Palgrave Macmillan, 2016), 246.

61. The Government of Korea, *2011nyeondo gukjeonggamsagyeolgwa sijeong min cheoriyogusahange daehan cheorigyeolgwagoseo* (Gukbangbu Sogwan) [Report on the Completion of the 2011 National Assembly Audit Results

and the Completion of the Corrective and Handling Requirements (Ministry of National Defense)] (February 2012), 58.

62. Song-kyu Hong, "ROK Daily: ROK National Assembly Confronts Military over Response Deficiencies," *Seoul Sinmun Online*, 21 September 2011, http://wnc.eastview.com/wnc/article?id=32816050, accessed 5 March 2014.

63. Korean National Assembly Audits revealed that in 2013, ROKN DDGs were operating beyond their targeted operational rate due to the need to respond to North Korea's nuclear program. The Government of Korea, *2013nyeondo gukjeonggamsagyeolgwa*. 79.

64. "Navy Pushes Blue-Water Operations," *The Korea Herald*, 7 February 2013, http://m.koreaherald.com/view.php?ud=20130207000954&ntn=0, accessed 10 March 2013.

65. Republic of Korea Government, *2012nyeondo gukjeonggamsagyeolgwa*, 65; Republic of Korea Government, *2013nyeondo gukjeonggamsagyeolgwa sijeong min cheoriyogusahange daehan cheorigyeolgwagoseo* (Gukbangbu Sogwan) [Report on the Completion of the 2013 National Assembly Audit Results and the Completion of the Corrective and Handling Requirements], March 2014, 75.

66. Republic of Korea Defense Acquisition Program Administration, *Je95hoe bangwisaeopchujinwiwonhoe gyeolgwa* [Results of the 95th DAPA Committee], 15 May 2016.

CHAPTER 4

Force Modernisation and Integration

To create a force and structure which can correctly exploit South Korea's potential naval power is a challenge for the ROKN given the divergent challenges it faces at sea. In developing force modernisation plans, the ROKN is required to maintain forces that are capable of operating under conditions where in relation to North Korea, they are superior and in relation to the rest of the region, they are inferior. The result has been a qualitative force modernisation effort aimed at replacing old capabilities and introducing new ones. The start of this effort can be traced back to the ROKN's initial plans for force modernisation in the mid-1980s and since the first *Chang Bogo*-class submarine was commissioned into service in 1993 there has been a consistent emphasis on quality over quantity.

ROKN force modernisation encompasses more than the introduction of new vessels. It includes weapons, sensors, training and structural alterations aimed at improving the ROKN as a fighting force. This ongoing effort is having a transformative effect on the ROKN. It is transitioning from a platform-centric navy with limited multifunctionality to a network-centric force with the ability to perform a wide array of operations on the surface, subsurface and in the air.

What follows in this chapter is a description and assessment of the ROKN's force modernisation since 1993. Surface, subsurface and aviation capabilities are first examined with a combined analysis of new weapon and sensor systems. The ROKN's current and future structure is

© The Author(s) 2019   81
I. Bowers, *The Modernisation of the Republic of
Korea Navy*, Critical Studies of the Asia-Pacific,
https://doi.org/10.1007/978-3-319-92291-1_4

then explored to assess how new capabilities are being integrated into the fleet. This allows for an assessment of deployment and operational priorities. Finally, the ROKN's training regime will be explored to assess what this reveals about current and future missions and capabilities.

NATURE OF MODERNISATION

Most commentary on the ROKN's modernisation focuses on platforms with little analysis on the long-term thinking behind force modernisation choices. However, such examinations of what the ROKN is introducing does not allow for a sufficient understanding of the navy's modernisation goals.

The objectives of the ROKN's force modernisation are based on leveraging the Revolution in Military Affairs (RMA) and the long-term development of four interconnected core outputs; multifunctionality, mobility, lethality and connectivity. In combination, the four outputs are designed to transform the ROKN into a force that can perform effective operations in relation to its current and future threat environments. This means that the ROKN is developing forces that have utility in both peninsular and non-peninsular contexts.[1] Larger platforms and new weapons, sensors and command and control systems are the inputs from which to achieve this objective.

Multifunctionality and mobility are at the centre of the ROKN's modernisation plans. The ability to perform operations in a multidimensional threat environment is a notable feature in publicly available modernisation documents.[2] This includes maintaining a warfighting operational capacity on the surface, subsurface and in the air.[3] The majority of new ROKN vessels, as with modern warships around the world, now to varying degrees possess this attribute of multifunctionality. Mobility is an inherent trait in naval vessels that the ROKN is seeking to leverage to be able to respond to several concurrent threats in different parts of South Korea's area of operations. By ensuring that modern ROKN platforms have good seakeeping capabilities in combination with the life support and crew comfort systems to sustain operations, the ROKN is seeking to mitigate the operational difficulties imposed by geostrategy and the possession of a limited number of platforms.

The goal of multifunctionality in individual vessels is being augmented with a complementary emphasis on leveraging network centric warfare (NCW) operations to allow ROKN vessels and capabilities from other services to work cooperatively to fight and win in all dimensions of the maritime environment.[4] NCW involves the creation, display and distribution of 'large amounts of tactical data between disparate units, resulting in shared situational awareness between vessels, aircraft and ground stations'.[5]

The ability to convert this type of warfare into effective operational outcomes is dependent on advanced surveillance capabilities, data processing, highly trained personnel and precision weaponry.[6] The emphasis on NCW heightens the ROKN's ability to engage in lethal, precision warfighting. The ROKN is developing into a force that can engage in modern warfare both at sea and from the sea with introduction of advanced, indigenously developed weapon systems. It is now in an exclusive club of world navies with both tactical and strategic land attack capabilities.

This approach to modernisation closely matches a broader trend within South Korea's military that has sought to integrate RMA technologies and new capabilities both to remain interoperable with the United States and to develop a greater independent warfighting capability.[7] This effort has been described in various forms since it was first publicly articulated in the early 1990s, but there has been a consistent emphasis on joint operations, NCW and indigenously developed sensor to shooter capabilities. In its latest iteration, the 2016 Defense White Paper describes the culmination of this effort as 'offensive integrated operations' which would allow for networked joint, precision offensive operations in the land, air, sea and cyber domains.[8]

The first ROKN command and control (C2) system was the Korea Naval Tactical Data System (KNTDS). The ROKN signed a contract in 1989 with US firm Litton Industries to design the first version of the system.[9] The platform has since undergone several upgrades to improve connectivity and prevent system outages.[10] The KNTDS connects major ROKN units, aircraft, radars and headquarters through Link-11 Tactical Data Links (TDL) and landlines, creating a common operating picture and providing commanders with real-time information of the tactical situation.[11]

In 2007, the ROKN introduced a C4I system called the Korean Naval Command and Control System (KNCCS). This system forms part of the wider cross-service C4I Korean Joint Command and Control System (KJCCS) aimed at enhancing joint operations and facilitating sensor to shooter operations. The KNTDS feeds information command and control information into the KNCCS. These two systems were designed at different times and use different technologies. Current upgrade work on both systems will result in the full integration of the KNTDS into the KNCCS.[12] Publicly, available information indicates that all new ROKN vessels will be integrated into the KNCSS and will be equipped with the indigenous Korean TDL, Link-K, which is reported to be equivalent to and interoperable with Link-16.[13]

Of course, the need to respond to specific changes in the peninsular threat environment also determines South Korea's force modernisation pathways. Urgent operational requirements can force changes and reprioritisations in long-term development plans. This is evident in the heightened focus on ballistic missile defence technologies that has occurred since North Korea substantially accelerated its nuclear program in 2015. At sea, a platform such as the PKMR is specifically designed to counter the KPN's focus on high-speed, high-volume attack capabilities in the Korean littoral. However, the connecting red-line of ROKN modernisation even when it is in response to a specific rather than general strategic need is an RMA inspired focused on high-technology, connected, precision warfare.

Sources of Modernisation

The ROKN's modernisation reveals an increasing reliance on indigenous sources for both platforms and systems. Since the 1970s successive South Korean governments have sought to develop an indigenous defence industry. This resulted in the domestic construction of new platforms such as the *Pohang*-class corvette and *Ulsan*-class frigate in the 1980s, however, these vessels were equipped with foreign-designed weapons and sensor systems. An emphasis on R&D, developing close ties with the private sector and technology transfer agreements with foreign sources have resulted in an increasingly capable domestic defence industry with higher rates of indigenous output.[14]

Major naval shipbuilding contracts are often shared between the large South Korean shipbuilders including Hyundai Heavy Industries, DSME, Hanjin Heavy Industries and STX Offshore & shipbuilding.[15] Consequently, two or more shipyards will construct different batches of the same class of vessel. Naval weapons and sensor technology is concentrated in a small group of South Korean arms manufactures with LIG Nex 1 and Hanwha having a dominant presence in recent ROKN procurement. Newer classes of ROKN vessel are now largely equipped with domestic technology for weapons, sensors and combat control systems. However, some components remain sourced from foreign suppliers, these include data links that are interoperable with the United States, advanced radar and combat management systems such as Aegis, propulsion systems including engines and turbines and aviation assets.[16] In many of these cases, South Korea is developing its own technology through R&D and technology transfer agreements but this is a long-term process and although the trend is for increasing indigenisation, the ROKN will continue to rely on foreign sources for key components into the foreseeable future.

SURFACE FLEET MODERNISATION

The heart of the ROKN's blue-water surface modernisation program is the KDX series of destroyers. The ROKN conceived the first class of this series in the early 1980s and it was intended as a replacement for the ROKN's *Gearing*-class destroyers. As blue-water modernisation concepts took hold in ROKN operational planning and new technologies were introduced into the designs, three ship classes were developed.

The ROKN initially conceived of the first in the series of KDX vessels, the 3,900 tons KDX-I (*Gwanggaeto Daewang*-class) in 1981. The initial time frame was for construction to begin in 1990, but delays caused by the addition of further operational requirements mid-design, meant that the first in class was laid down in 1995 and launched one year later.[17] The initial plan called for between 17 and 20 vessels in this class but the ROKN only procured three.[18] The delay in construction and the consequent resource squeeze reduced the class buy as the following and more capable KDX-II and KDX-III vessels took priority.[19]

This ship represented a step-change in ROKN capabilities. Although it was not the first ROKN vessel constructed in South Korea, its sensors, computing power, weapons complement and seakeeping brought about a qualitative leap in capability for the ROKN. The KDX-I is equipped with a SSCS MK-7 combat management system (CMS). This British-built system is based on the CMS used in the Royal Navy's *Type-23* frigates.[20] It was the first modern CMS installed in an ROKN vessel and connects all weapons and sensor systems. The KDX-I is also fitted with the KNTDS which allows it to act as a command and control vessel.[21]

Armed with the RIM 7 M Sea Sparrow SAM system and two Signaal Goalkeeper CIWS, the KDX-I has superior point air defences to any previous ROKN ship. It also carries two quad launchers for Harpoon and six 324 mm torpedo tubes armed with the Mark 46 ASW torpedo. The ROKN enhanced the vessel's ASW capability with the installation of a German hull-mounted active sonar and a Korean-designed passive towed array.[22] The ship can also support one Super Lynx helicopter that strengthens its surface and subsurface combat capability. The installation of an advanced combat management system allows this vessel to operate in a multi-threat environment. They are currently tasked to provide support to the smaller patrol boats that operate in the littoral waters of the peninsula and each vessel in the class serves as a flagship to one of South Korea's three Fleet Commands. At the time of writing, this class of vessel was preparing for a significant refit to its command and control and combat systems, including the introduction of a modern CMS, upgraded C4I capability and new weapons and sensors.

The KDX-II (*Chungmugong Yi, Sunshin*-class) destroyer as with the KDX-I was indigenously designed and equipped with both Korean and foreign weapons systems, these ships were the first ROKN ships to possess an area/zone air defence capability. Larger than the KDX-I (5,500 tons compared with 3,855 fully loaded); they should not be seen as a direct replacement for any previous platform operated by the ROKN and represent a large increase in firepower, operational range and flexibility.

Initial approval for construction of this vessel was given in 1996, with the first of six platforms laid down in 2001. The central improvement in this class over the KDX-I is the SM-2 (Block IIIA) surface to air missile which has a maximum range of approximately 90 nm. It also possesses strong point defence systems with one RAM launcher for RIM 116 SAM and 1 Goalkeeper CIWS. Other weapons initially fitted to the vessel included eight Harpoon, an ASROC VLS and a 5" gun. The KDX-II is equipped with an upgraded version of the SSCS MK-7 CMS named the KDCOM. The system was jointly developed by British firm BAE-systems and Samsung. This upgrade increased the number of multifunctional combat consoles up to ten.[23] As with the KDX-I, the KDX-II is also fitted with the KNTDS C2 system.

There are, however, weaknesses in the KDX-II sensor to shooter capabilities. The air defence system was based on the US Navy's New Threat Upgrade (NTU) program which began in the 1980s and was designed to upgrade the air defence systems of existing surface ships. However, the ROKN did not fit the required radars to take full advantage of the KDX-II's SM-2 capability. This class of vessel was fitted with virtually the same radar suite as the KDX-I. This includes a Signaal MW-08 3D radar and an AN/SPS-49 (V) 2D air-search radar. While the latter can detect targets at up to 256 nm, the 3D system has a limited range of between 9 and 17 nm depending on the target size.[24] Therefore, for targeting aircraft or missiles beyond this range, the KDX-II is reliant on its two long-range STIR 240 targeting radars. This reduces the number of targets that can be simultaneously engaged at longer ranges.

The KDX-II was upgraded with a 24-cell Korean Vertical Launch System (KVLS) which sits on the bow beside a US-designed 32-cell Mark 41 VLS which carries the SM2 missile. The KVLS allows it to carry the South Korean-designed Hong Sang Eo anti-submarine missile.[25] Each missile carries a K745 Chung Sang Eo torpedo and can engage submerged targets at a range of up to 19 km.[26] The KVLS also accommodates the Hyunmoo-3C land attack cruise missile which has a range of 1500 km.[27]

The KDX-II's complement of Harpoons has been replaced with SSM-700K Haesong AshM. This South Korean-designed subsonic missile has a range of approximately 180 km and carries a single 220 kg warhead.[28] It has advanced targeting, engagement and evasion capabilities. In late 2016, the South Korean Defense Acquisition and Procurement Agency announced a competition to upgrade the KDX-II hull-mounted sonar.[29] There also plans to significantly upgrade the KDX-II's radar, C4I and weapon systems beginning in 2020.

The 10,290 tons KDX-III (*Sejong Daewang*-class) Aegis destroyer is the current culmination of the KDX program. The first of a batch of three was commissioned in 2008 after a 13-year design and construction cycle. The last in this class was commissioned in August 2012. These three vessels, which are close in design to the Arleigh Burke class of the USN, are based around the Aegis combat system and the AN/SPY-1 multifunction radar. They are heavily armed vessels, equipped with two MK 41 VLS, one 48-cell launcher forward and one 32-cell launcher aft which sits in tandem with a 42-cell KVLS. This allows the KDX-III to carry 80 SM-2 (Block IIIA/B) missiles and mix of Hyunmoo-3C and Red Shark ASROC. The KDX-III has the capacity to carry 16 Haesong AshM missiles and has the RAM Block 1 missile system and Goalkeeper CIWS for point defence. In 2016 the Defense Acquisition Program Administration announced that the KDX-III will be upgraded with new a VLS to accommodate the SM-6 and SM-3 missiles systems.[30] This will boost their ability to perform BMD. The Aegis system alongside GCCS-M and SATCOM provide these vessels with a high-degree of C4I capability.

These vessels are to be used as the flag-ships of the ROKN's future mobile fleet concept and currently are tasked to Maritime Task Flotilla 7. The Aegis systems mean that these ships play an important role in monitoring and detecting North Korean ballistic missile launches. This requires that they remain in areas proximate to North Korea. In war these ships are tasked with providing area air defence, performing strategic and tactical strike mission and acting as a Maritime Air Support Operations Centre (MASOC). As with the KDX-II vessels, the size and multifunctionality of these ships have resulted in large increases in ROKN ASW, surface warfare and air defence capabilities. Although these platforms are almost symbolic of the ROKN blue-water modernisation program it is worth highlighting their central role in operations around the peninsula. These powerful vessels provide the ROKN with the multifunctionality it needs to meet the multiple challenges posed by the South Korea's maritime strategic environment.

In 2013, the ROKN received permission to construct three KDX-III Batch-II destroyers.[31] The ROKN had previously requested additional Aegis units but these plans had been cancelled in 2011 in favour of designing a new smaller destroyer designed to complement the KDX-II fleet.[32] The need for additional large Aegis platforms to counter North Korean and regional threats drove the reversal of this decision. These vessels will have upgraded radar and weapons systems and will be fully capable of ballistic missile defence. The first of this new class is expected to be commissioned by 2023. Additionally, preliminary approval has been granted for the development of a new class of destroyer named the KDDX.[33] This vessel be approximately 6,000 tons and construction will likely begin in the mid-2020s.

THE FFX PROGRAM

The FFX program is the name for the next generation frigate programme of the ROKN. These ships are designed to replace the ageing *Ulsan*-class frigates and *Pohang*-class corvettes.[34] When completed, the

FFX program will have massively upgraded the ROKN's littoral combat capabilities and will not only enhance deterrence in a peninsular context but also provide the ROKN with a greater ability to secure South Korean maritime strategic interests in a regional setting.

The first of the class was launched in 2011 and a further 19 are planned in three batches. Each batch allows for the introduction of improvements and design alterations. While in total there will be fewer platforms after the older ships are decommissioned, it is expected that the addition of more capable AAW systems, combined with helicopter capability and advanced ASW/ASUW weapons will ensure that force superiority is maintained.[35]

The first batch of six named the *Incheon*-class have a displacement of 3,251 tons. They lack a VLS and are armed with the RAM Block 1 point defence system complemented by one Phalanx CIWS. They also carry six K745 Chung Sang Eo torpedoes, eight Haesong AShM and eight Haesong-II land attack missiles. The latter has a range of 500 km and can be launched from a VLS or slanted shipboard canisters.[36] All six in this class have now been commissioned into service.

The second batch, named the *Daegu*-class, will consist of the eight vessels and will include a 16-cell KVLS. It will carry a South Korean-designed medium-range air defence missile currently designated as the K-SAAM. Along with the Haesong AShM and land attack missiles and the Red Shark ASROC, each vessel can carry one Super Lynx or AW159 Wildcat. The first of this batch of vessels was commissioned in March 2018. The weapons complement for the third batch of six vessels is currently unknown, but information released by the South Korean government indicates that it will have a phased-array radar, a 360-degree infrared search and track system and improved sonar capabilities.[37] Construction of this class is scheduled to being in 2021.

What is notable about this class is the increasing indigenisation of its systems and the flexibility of its capabilities. The FFX are equipped with Hanwha Naval Shield Combat Management System and LIG Nex1 3D surveillance radar with a range of up to 250 km away. Both systems are derived from European-designed products, the Naval Shield CMS has its roots in Thales TACTICOS CMS, while the radar is a modified version of Thales SMART-S. These vessels have Link-11 and Link-K and are integrated into the KNCCS.

THE PKX PROGRAM

The PKX program began development in 2003 following the discovery of weaknesses in the existing *Chamsuri*-class patrol boats following the sinking of one during the Second Battle of Yeonpyeong.[38] This program has two different classes, the PKG (*Gumdoksuri*-class) and the PKMR. The PKG has 18 vessels in its class, the last of which was commissioned in January 2018.[39] At 579 tons, the PKG carries four Haesong AShM, one 76 mm cannon, one 40 mm cannon, two 12.7 mm machine guns and the Chiron portable SAM system. Each ship is equipped with an SPS-100K surface search radar and an SPS-540K 3D air and surface surveillance radar which also supports gunfire support and is specifically designed to operate in high-clutter littoral environments.[40] The vessel's CMS is a compressed version of the Naval Shield System installed in the *Incheon*- and *Daegu*-class frigates and has Link-K and a Inter Site Data Link (ISDL) connection to the KNCCS.[41] The PKG's top speed is 44 kt which is slower than many of the KPN's faster vessels, however, its superior weapon and fire control systems should mitigate this disadvantage. Although it lacks hard-kill defensive capabilities to protect itself against incoming missiles, the PKG carries chaff dispensers and is equipped with the Korean-designed SONATA electronic warfare system which can detect and jam incoming radar signals.

The PKMR is a 200 tons vessel. It has the same sensor and electronic warfare suite as the PKG but carries a different weapon complement. It has one 76 mm cannon, two 12.7 mm machine guns and a 12-cell launcher for 130 mm guided rockets. The first of this class of vessel was launched in October 2017 and current procurement plans indicate a total class buy of 16 vessels. As was stated earlier, this vessel is specifically designed to counter the threat of KPN high-speed amphibious craft.[42]

AMPHIBIOUS PROGRAM

Commissioned in 2007 the *Dokdo*-class LPD is a significant leap forward for the ROKN. When it was first launched it was one of the largest naval ships in Northeast Asia. It has a 18,800 tons full load displacement and can carry up to 700 troops with 10 main battle tanks (MBT), two air-cushioned landing vehicles (LCAC) and 10 helicopters.[43]

It has a modern surveillance and C4I capabilities. Its combat management system is a derivation of the CMS installed on the

Incheon-class frigates. It is also equipped with the Thales SMART-L 3D long-range surveillance radar, Link-11, Link-16, Link-K and SATCOM and is integrated into the Korean Joint Tactical Data Link System (KJTDLS) which allows it to share tactical information directly with the ROKA and the ROKAF.[44] This provides the *Dokdo* with C4I capabilities allowing it to act as the flag/command ship of any ROKN integrated fleet and amphibious operation. The self-defence weapons systems are 2 *Goalkeeper* CIWS and the RAM 116 missile system.[45] These are adequate for point air defence, but in contested, missile intensive environments, the *Dokdo* class would require support from other ROKN vessels.

This platform represented a major step forward in ROKN amphibious and air operations capability and its proposed mission set reflects this. Its versatility means that the ROKN view it as a platform capable of performing wartime amphibious operations, fleet control and ASW operations and in peacetime, it is tasked with PKO support, humanitarian operations and national prestige enhancement.[46] The latter task is notable as during discussions relating to procuring such a platform the ROKN argued strongly that possession of an LPD/light aircraft carrier was an important symbolic factor in demonstrating South Korea's development as a nation.

Initially planned as a three-ship project, currently only the *Dokdo* is in service. The South Korean government approved the construction of the second in the class, the ROKS *Marado*, in 2014. Construction began in 2017 and it is expected to enter service in 2020. Although the *Marado* will be the same size, some design improvements are expected in this vessel including the ability to carry the V-22 Osprey.[47]

The ROKN is also introducing the *Cheon Wang Bong*-class of landing ship.[48] At 7,140 tons full load, these are capable vessels amphibious vessels. They can carry up to 300 troops, two MBT, eight Amphibious Assault Vehicles (AAV) and have three landing craft (LCM) to transport, men and vehicles to shore.[49] They also have landing facilities but no hangers for two helicopters. This class of ship is armed with a Korean-designed 40 mm dual cannon, a KVLS which can carry air defence missiles and two Rheinmetall MASS naval countermeasure system.[50] The defence capabilities along with heightened ballistic protection in the ship's hull are designed to make this ship more survivable in contested landing situations.[51] Four of these vessels have been constructed with the final vessel expected to be commissioned in 2018. Operating alongside four *Go Jun Bong*-class of LST, the combined ROKN amphibious landing force is designed to be able to perform division-level landings by 2030. The LST-I platform was developed in the late 1980s with the first being commissioned in 1993 and the final in group of four ships in 1999. Equipped with bow and stern ramps, it has a drive-through tank deck and can carry 200 troops, 15–17 MBT or 4 LCVP. They are slow (16 kt top speed) vessels with a limited armament and are potentially vulnerable when landing on opposed shorelines. They have been used in humanitarian relief and other international operations.[52]

MINE WARFARE

The ROKN's minesweeping capabilities are somewhat underdeveloped considering the potential threat posed by the KPN. Publicly available data suggests that the ROKN has sacrificed the procurement of mine warfare capabilities during constrained fiscal periods. The ROKN now operates two large minelaying vessels capable of both defensive and offensive minelaying operations.[53]

Three classes of mine warfare vessel were introduced into between 1986 and 2005. The smallest is the 520-tons *Ganggyeong*-class coastal minehunter. Built in South Korea, it is an unlicensed copy of the Italian-designed *Lerici*-class. Six of this plastic-hulled class are now in operation and each carries two mine-disposal vehicles.[54] In 1999, a new class of minehunter, the *Yangyang*-class entered into service. At 730 tons it is slightly larger than the *Ganggyeong*-class. Three in this class are now in operation.[55] In 1997, a *Wonsan*-class minelayer was commissioned into service. Based on the hull design of the Ulsan-class frigate, it is armed with one 76 mm cannon, twin 40 mm for air defence and two triple 324 mm torpedo tubes. It can up to 500 mines of different variants.[56] The *Wonsan*-class is also equipped to carry out minesweeping operations. Three were of this class were proposed for construction, but only one was completed. Instead, the ROKN introduced a new class, the first of which was delivered in late 2017. The 4,240 tons *Nampo*-class is approximately at 114.3 m is 10 m longer than the *Wonsan*-class and is based on the hull of the *Incheon*-class frigate. It also carries much of the same sensor suite as Incheon class.[57] This is a heavily armed vessel, equipped with cannon, torpedo launchers and a four-cell KVLS which can carry up to 16 K-SAAM anti-air missiles. It has hanger facilities for one medium-sized helicopter and carries up to 500 mines.[58]

AUXILIARIES

The ROKN currently operates three *Chun Jee*-class Fast Combat Support Ships. These vessels can perform at sea replenishment and can carry up to 4,200 tons of fuel and 450 tons of stores. They are, however, slow with a cruising speed of 15 kt and maximum speed of 20 kt. The first of these ships was commissioned in 1990 and the last in the class in 1998. These vessels are not sufficient to fully support the ROKN's mobile flotilla ambitions and consequently a new class of AOE is currently being introduced. The first in this class was launched in 2016 and is intended to enter into service in 2018. Fully laden, it has a displacement of over 21,000 tons and it can carry 250% more stores than the *Chun Jee*-class.[59] At the time of writing it is unknown how many in this class will be constructed, but their superior cargo and fuel capacity will sustain operations away from the Korean Peninsula.

The ROKN also operates one *Cheonghaejin*-class submarine rescue ship (ASR) completed with a deep submergence rescue vehicle (DSRV) and a deep-diving system. This vessel has successfully recovered a North Korean *Yugo*-class submarine and salvaged a North Korean semi-submersible from a depth of 157 metres.[60] A second ASR is currently being designed to ensure that the ROKN has sufficient rescue capabilities for its growing submarine fleet.[61] This vessel is intended to be completed by 2022.[62]

THE SUBMARINE PROGRAM

Much like the KDX program, the ROKN's submarine development plan is characterised by the tiered introduction of more advanced capabilities and the increasing indigenisation of designs, components and construction. At the time of writing three classes of conventional attack submarine are in operation, under construction or being designed.

The initial phase of the program, code-named KSS began in 1987 with the signing of a contract with German company Howaldtswerke Deutsche Werft (HDW) for three *Type 209*-class submarines.[63] The first in the class, the *Chang Bogo*, was constructed in Germany with South Korean engineers working alongside their HDW counterparts to learn construction methods. The following two boats were constructed in kit form in South Korea. Two additional batches of three vessels were ordered in 1989 and 1994. They were commissioned into service between 1993 and 2001. The final three in this class were heavily modified with reports suggesting a lengthened hull and the introduction of Harpoon launching capability. All vessels in this class received an upgrade to their inertial navigation systems sometime after 2011.[64]

Before the final *Chang Bogo*-class entered service, the ROKN had already committed to an upgrade for its next class of submarine. In 2000, the ROKN ordered the equipment and parts to construct three Type 214 submarines from HDW.[65] The Type 214, named *the Sohn Won-il-class* represented a substantial step-up in capabilities. These vessels are 600 tons heavier and equipped with Air Independent Propulsion (AIP) which allows for greater underwater endurance. With eight torpedo tubes, the Type 214 can carry a mix of torpedoes, mines and the Haesong-III anti-ship/land-attack missile. Six more were ordered in 2008 following a decision to delay the construction of an indigenously designed vessel. There have been reports of reliability problems with this class of vessel arising from issues in construction and unexpected noise generation.[66] But the ROKN has reported that these issues have been resolved. The ninth and final vessel in this class was launched in September 2017 with an expected operational date of 2019.[67]

The final phase of the ROKN's current submarine program, named the *Chang Bogo-III* is expected to enter service by the year 2020. This will be an indigenously designed vessel and at 3,000 tons will be 40% larger than the *Sohn Won-il*-class. Initial operating requirements for this boat were created in 2005 and design work began in 2007 with Hyundai Heavy Industries and DSME being jointly contracted to develop the project. The work was delayed for two years in 2009 and in 2014 the steel was cut for the first vessel.[68] It is planned that this boat will have a six-cell VLS alongside its torpedo tubes. Assembly began on the first of the three batch-I class in 2016. It will possess a mix of Korean and foreign warfare and sensor systems with the intention to increase the number of Korean-designed systems in batches II & III.[69] The second batch of three vessels has also been approved for construction. This new batch will include substantial design changes in part in response to North Korea's nuclear program and rumoured construction of a SSB. Reports suggest that the modifications will include the fitting of lithium batteries and a lengthened hull designed to accommodate a heavier weapon load out. It is unclear if the ROKN intends to keep all three classes of vessel in service simultaneously or if the *Chang Bogo-III* will replace the original *Chang Bogo-class*. The first of those vessels entered service in 1993 and should have an expected service life of 30–35 years which suggests that they will be taken out of service as the *Chang Bogo-III* are introduced.[70]

In the context of Northeast Asia, these submarines form the heart of the ROKN's asymmetric deterrent strategy. The capabilities being introduced are a match for any potential competitor. While ageing, the *Chang Bogo*-class remain a potent capability, especially considering their ongoing modernisation, while the Sohn Won-il-class are as capable as any modern conventional submarine operating in the world today. However, in a North Korean context, the anti-submarine capability of these large vessels is questionable given that the KPN's mini and coastal submarines will most likely operate in the cluttered, shallow waters of the near littorals.[71] However, modern passive sonar systems such as those equipped on the Son Won-il-class may overcome this difficulty. By adding land-strike capability later classes of ROKN submarine have greater strategic utility in North Korean war and deterrence scenarios by providing South Korea with the ability to target North Korea from the relative security of the subsurface environment.

AVIATION

Alongside the surface and subsurface elements, the ROKN's air component has undergone substantial force improvement, however, weaknesses are apparent. Maritime surveillance and ASW is currently provided by 16 P-3C and P-3CK Orion aircraft. In 2018 a competition was launched for six modern maritime patrol aircraft with the Boeing P-8 and the SAAB Swordfish emerging as the leading contenders. Unlike in the case of their surface capabilities, there are no indigenous manufactures capable of producing such aircraft, although Korean companies have been involved in upgrading and installing internal equipment and components. These aircraft are all connected to ROKN C4I systems via datalinks.

The ROKN currently operates 22 Westland Lynx MK99/99A ASW helicopters and eight AW159 Wildcat ASW helicopters. A National Assembly audit published the year after the sinking of the *Cheonan* revealed concerns that MK99's sonar and radar capabilities were outdated and insufficient for ASW in littoral waters.[72] This contributed to the purchase of the AW159 helicopters and a competition for a further 12 ASW helicopters is currently underway with the AW159, MH-60R and NH-90 all under consideration.[73]

The ROKN and the ROKMC are weak on amphibious lift capacity. The ROKN currently operates 19 UH 60P Blackhawk helicopters in a utility and lift role. These are not specifically designed for maritime operations and there has been insufficient dedicated helicopter capacity to take full advantage of the *Dokdo's* capabilities. This gap is being rectified with the procurement of 30 Surion amphibious helicopters.[74] These are the maritime variant of a South Korean-designed military helicopter that entered service in 2013. They will be tasked with operating off the *Dokdo* and Marado LPH.

STRUCTURE

Integrating new capabilities into the ROKN's operational structure forms another part of the navy's modernisation plan. Structural changes first suggested in Navy Vision 2020 and included in every MND defence reform plan since 2006 are being slowly implemented as new capabilities come online. These changes are designed to reflect the drive towards NCW and EBO and maximise the operational potential of new platforms.

Naval Headquarters is responsible for the day to day operations of the ROKN. It is headed by the navy's senior officer, the CNO who also sits on the JCS. Naval Headquarters determines naval policy development, education and training and all other matters related to managing the ROKN. Its areas of direct responsibility and structure have altered over the years with adjustments aimed at streamlining command and control and prioritising core elements such as force planning and policy development (Fig. 4.1).[75]

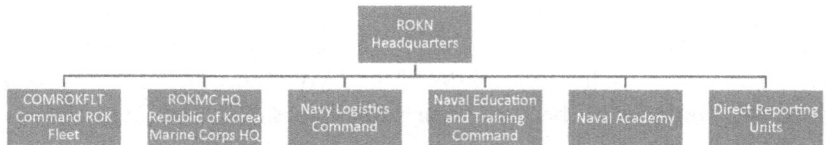

Fig. 4.1 Major commands under ROKN headquarters (*Source* "Organization, Navy Corps Organization," *Republic of Korea Navy Website*, http://www.navy. mil.kr/mbshome/mbs/eng/subview.do?id=eng_010200000000, accessed 13 March 2018)

Command, Republic of Korea Fleet sits under the Naval Headquarters. Based at Busan Naval Base, it is commanded by Commander Republic of Korea Fleet (COMROKFLT) and is responsible for all naval operations.[76] As Fig. 4.2 shows, COMROKFLT overseas three fleet commands alongside several operational commands including Submarine Force Command, Component Flotilla 5 and Maritime Task Flotilla 7. The basis of this structure was first operationalised in 1986, when COMROKFLT was stood-up and the three fleet commands replaced its predecessor, the Naval Sector Command System.

The three fleet commands are individually responsible for geographically defined areas around the peninsula. First Fleet is responsible for operations in the East Sea and has its homeport at Donghae Naval Base. Second Fleet is responsible for the West Sea including the Northern Limit Line and has is headquartered at Pyeongtaek Naval Base and Third Fleet is responsible for the seas to the immediate south of the peninsula and is homeported at Busan Naval Base. Each fleet has three major elements comprised of patrol boats, corvettes (which are now being replaced by the *Incheon*-class frigate) and one KDX-I destroyer.

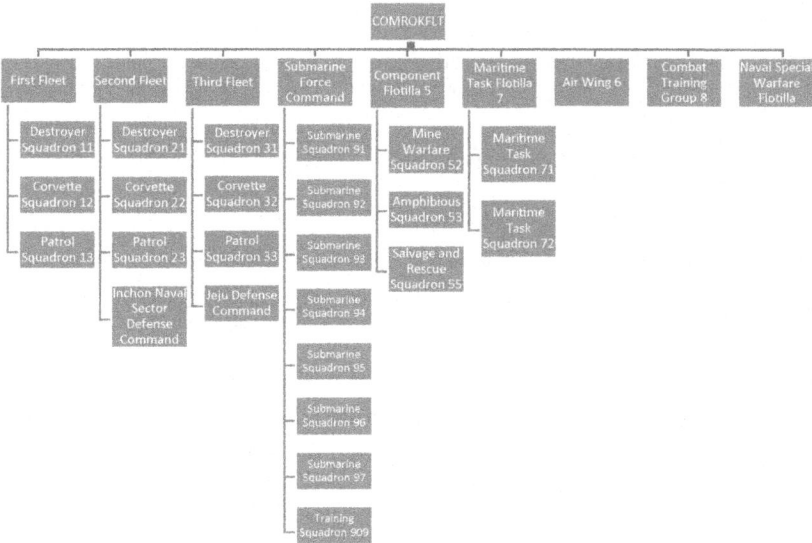

Fig. 4.2 Operational structure of the ROKN (*Source* Various sources compiled by the author)

These fleets form the core of the ROKN's mission to deter North Korea by maintaining a constant presence in the waters around the South Korean coast. Their geographically determined AOE reveals the operational requirements North Korea imposes on the ROKN. But, they also play an important role in supporting the KCG in its efforts to secure the South Korean EEZ and in the case of the First Fleet, protecting the waters around Dokdo. With the introduction of the PKG and PKMR patrol boats and the *Incheon-* and *Daegu*-class frigates, these commands will possess substantially upgraded combat capabilities particularly in ASW, AAW and land attack.

Submarine Force Command is a new unit. Created in 2015 it replaced Submarine Flotilla 9. This alteration was included in Defence Reform plans from 2006 with the intention of being enacted in 2012 but was delayed.[77] The advantage of the new structure is that the all aspects of submarine operations will be placed under one command include training and maintenance and operations.[78] This will allow for the better integration of submarines as the fleet grows. Further, Submarine Force Command is led by a two-star Rear Admiral (Upper Half) who operates out of Jinhae Naval Base. This puts the leader of the ROKN's submarine force at the level as other ROKN commands. A similar alteration has long been proposed for the ROKN's aviation wing, however, delays in the procurement of new aircraft have likely postponed this change. In October 2017, the ROKN informed the National Assembly that a new plan exists to create an Aviation Command by 2023.[79] This command would also have a two-star Admiral in charge and would oversee all ROKN aviation assets.

Likewise, the ROKN intends to upgrade Maritime Task Flotilla 7 to fleet status by 2023. This would mean that the ROKN has finally reached the goal set out under Navy Vision 2020 for a Strategic Mobile Fleet. However, the initial intention was for these fleets to be centred around an aviation asset such as a smaller aircraft carrier or LPH. Currently, the ROKS *Dokdo* and its coming sister ship the ROKS *Marado* are assigned to Amphibious Squadron 53. If this deployment pattern is maintained, the future Maritime Task Fleet will be only comprised of the KDX-II, KDX-III and future KDX-III Batch-II and KDDX destroyers. Other assets will join the fleet on an ad-hoc basis determined by operational requirements.

Linked to the Maritime Task Flotilla is the new naval base on Jeju Island which was formally opened in 2015. Originally conceived by the ROKN in 1993, permission from President Roh, Moo-hyun was granted for its construction in 2007 and building started in 2011 despite widespread protests from residents who complained about the militarisation of an island designated as the Island of World Peace.[80] The base opened for naval operations in 2015 and is now the homeport of Maritime Task Flotilla 7 and Submarine Squadron 93.

The location of Jeju along with its natural harbours will, say the ROKN, allow for speedier access to areas of strategic importance and act as a staging post for future blue-water operations. By basing MTF 7 at Jeju, the ROKN's most advanced naval platforms will able to respond quickly to situations in either side of the peninsula and in South China Sea.[81] As an example, sailing time from Jeju to Ieodo is 4 hours at 20 kt compared to 13 hours if ROKN ships departed from Busan.[82] This base and its faster access is fundamental to the flexible mobility concept of the Mobile Flotilla allowing it to effectively reinforce the Fleet Commands and react to regional threats to South Korea's SLOC.

TRAINING

ROKN training takes place on a service, joint service, US alliance and multinational basis. Within the ROKN and the South Korean military there has been an increasing emphasis on heightening the realism of training, improving joint operations including the use of C4I technologies and developing inter-alliance operating capabilities.

The ROKN has set up an Integrated Maritime Tactical Training Ground and a Guided Weapon Tactical Simulation centre to improve the operating efficiency of ROKN crews in modern warfighting environments.[83] The ROKN has also invested in a new training ship. This vessel will come into service in 2020 and according to media reports, will have six different combat systems to familiarise trainees with various tactical scenarios.[84] Following the sinking of the *Cheonan* the ROKN is introducing disaster control simulators across ROKN fleets to better prepare crews for disaster control scenarios.

Independent training conducted by the ROKN takes two forms, component training and mission-based training. The former is aimed at specific areas of naval warfare, including anti-submarine, mine warfare, amphibious and submarine warfare.[85] Mission-based training is scenario specific and includes the protection of islands, responding to North Korean actions around the NLL and maritime interdiction.[86] This kind of training includes exercising with the ROKMC and ROKAF.

The major interservice exercise is the Hoguk Exercise, which in its current form is a cross-service theatre-level exercise designed to hone the South Korean military's warfighting capacity on the peninsula. It has multiple aims including strengthening operational performance, testing weapons systems, enhancing joint operations and verification of the efficacy of operational plans. This form of joint exercise began in 1988 and it has gradually become more sophisticated and realistic. For example, in 2015, the military combined the Hoguk exercise with other theatre-level rear area and command post exercises. For the ROKN, the exercises have become better integrated with simultaneous training now occurring on both sides of the peninsula. These exercises are also used to practise large-scale amphibious assaults using assets from across the ROKN fleet.[87]

Most USN-ROKN exercises focus on countering North Korea actions around the peninsula. Joint training occurs at regular intervals and includes major exercises such as Combined Landing Operation Training, which focuses on amphibious assault, ground support operations and maritime manoeuvres. The USN also acts as a facilitator for ROKN-JMSDF joint exercises focus on developing interoperability in key areas related to the threat from North Korea including ASW and BMD.[88] Additionally, the United States holds several major combined joint exercises with the South Korean military. The largest one is the Key Resolve/Foal Eagle combined post and field training exercises. These exercises are aimed at an overall response to war on the peninsula, and naval units from the ROKN and the US 7th fleet are heavily involved.[89]

In terms of multinational training, the ROKN's main multinational exercise is participation in the biannual RIMPAC exercise. This is multi-country/multi-mission exercise, involving both offensive and defensive training, SLOC protection and weapons exercises. The ROKN first sent observers in 1988 and participated with vessels in 1990. Since then the ROKN has steadily increased its contribution, for example, deploying one frigate in 1990 to both destroyers and submarines in 2006 and a KDX-III destroyer in 2010 and 2014. In many ways, RIMPAC has been used by the ROKN as indicator of its status among the world's top navies and an arena to build operational expertise, not just with the United States but also other navies including the JMSDF. Other multinational exercises include the tri-annual Pacific Reach submarine rescue exercise, the Western Pacific Mine Countermeasures Exercise and a biannual SAREX exercise with Japan.[90]

CONCLUSION

The fleet modernisation that has occurred since the 1990s has transformed the ROKN. The pursuit and then introduction of a multifunctional, balanced force has created a modern navy capable of independently carrying out a wide range of tasks. This is in stark contrast with the ROKN that came before which was only capable of limited deterrence operations in the littoral of the Korean Peninsula. The ROKN's modernisation program reveals a comprehensive approach to integrating new platforms into existing force structures and there are indications that the ROKN is successfully assimilating its C4I, sensor and weapons into its training programs and operational doctrine. That the ROKN has long-term, concrete plans to modernise existing and introduce new capabilities is an indicator that blue-water modernisation has solid conceptual foundations as it proceeds.

The navy is building a force with a credible surface warfare, ASW and AAW capability. Of course, such credibility is only defined by its effectiveness against potential opponents. Against North Korea, the ROKN's current and future capabilities are most likely sufficient to dominate the waters surrounding the Korean peninsula. The ROKN is gaining the ability to perform effective strike and amphibious operations and to improve its deterrence posture and warfighting capability is addressing its deficiencies in ASW and AAW. These gaps will only fully rectified when the next classes of frigate, destroyer and aircraft come into service in the next ten years.

Within a regional context, the ROKN possesses an increasingly potent deterrent capability centred on its submarine force and bolstered by the surface platforms introduced in recent years. However, despite the modernity of its capabilities, the ROKN is still hampered by a limited number of vessels in relation to the number of potential missions it is required to perform. It remains to be seen if the current force plans will address this weakness in the face of the continued need to maintain deterrence against North Korea. Nevertheless, the extent of the ROKN's fleet modernisation means that it cannot be discounted as a naval force in Northeast Asia.

NOTES

1. Defence documents describe this as having an 'omnidirectional' capability.
2. Republic of Korea Navy Headquarters, *Haegun bijeon 2020* [Navy Vision 2020] (Gyeryong: Republic of Korea Navy Headquarters, 1999), 108–9; Republic of Korea Navy Headquarters, *Haegun bijeon 2030* [Navy Vision 2030] (Gyeryong: Republic of Korea Navy Headquarters, 2008), 33.
3. For a description of the major surface, subsurface and air operations, see: Republic of Korea Navy, *Gandanhago pyeonhage ilgeul su inneun haegungaideubuk* [An Easy and Simple to Read Navy Guide Book] (Gyeryong: Navy Headquarters, 2016), 128–37.
4. ROKN Headquarters, *2008nyeondo haegunjeongchaek bogoseo* [2008 Naval Policy Report] (Gyeryong: ROKN Headquarters), 21; ROKN Headquarters, *Haegun bijeon 2030* [Navy Vision 2030], 24.
5. Sarah Kirchberger, *Assessing China's Naval Power: Technological Innovation, Economic Constraints and Strategic Implications* (Berlin & Heidelberg: Springer, 2015), 5.
6. Ibid.; Republic of Korea Navy Headquarters, *Haegun bijeon 2030*, 24.
7. Chung-inMoon and Jin-young Lee, "The Revolution in Military Affairs and the Defence Industry in South Korea," *Security Challenges* 4, no. 4 (Summer 2008): 121–22.
8. Republic of Korea Ministry of National Defense, *Defense White Paper 2016* (Seoul: Republic of Korea Ministry of National Defense, 2016), 102.
9. Norman Friedman, *The Naval Institute Guide to World Naval Weapons Systems 1997–1998* (Annapolis: Naval Institute Press, 1989), 131.
10. Young-il Kim, "Status of Korean Navy's Tactical C4ISR Systems Acquisition and Issues on Interoperability Between ROK-U.S. Combined Naval Operations," in *Bytes and Bullets: Information Technology Revolution and National Security on the Korean Peninsula*, ed. Alexander Y. Mansourov (Hawaii: Asia Pacific Centre for Security Studies, 2005), 181–82; Republic of Korea Government, *2010nyeondo gukjeong-gamsagyeolgwa sijeong min cheoriyogusahange daehan cheorigyeolgwagoseo (Gukbangbu Sogwan)* [Report on the Completion of the 2010 National Assembly Audit Results and the Completion of the Corrective and Handling Requirements (Ministry of National Defense)], April 2011, 77.
11. Ibid.
12. Republic of Korea Defense Acquisition Program Administration, *HaegunjeonsulC4Ichegye seongneunggaeryangsaeop gaeyo* [Naval Tactical C4I System Performance Improvement Project Summary], 30 November 2016, http://www.dapa.go.kr/user/boardList.action?command=view&page=1&boardId=I_36172&boardSeq=I_38914&id=dapa_kr_030303160000, accessed 20 November 2017.

13. The Link-16 TDL 'allows for real-time transfer of combat data, voice communications, imagery and relative navigation information between dispersed battle elements'. See: "Link 16," The Missile Defense Advocacy Alliance, January 2017, http://missiledefenseadvocacy.org/missile-defense-systems-2/missile-defense-systems/deployed-command-and-control/link-16/, accessed 20 November 2017.

14. John Feffer, "Ploughshares into Swords: Economic Implications of South Korean Military Spending," *Korea Economic Institute Academic Paper Series* 4, no. 2 (February 2009): 6.

15. Richard Bitzinger, *Arming Asia: Technonationalism and Its Impact on Local Defense Industries* (Oxon: Routledge, 2017), 104.

16. Data compiled from Jane's Information Group, *Jane's Fighting Ships 2012–2013* (Coulsdon: Jane's Information Group, 2012).

17. "Gwanggaeto the Great Class/KDX-I Class Destroyer," *Naval Technology*, http://www.naval-technology.com/projects/gwanggaeto-the-great-class-kdx-i-class-destroyer/, accessed 10 March 2018.

18. Eric Wertheim, *Naval Institute Guide to Combat Fleets of the World, 16th Edition* (Annapolis: Naval Institute Press, 2013), 408.

19. Republic of Korea Navy Headquarters, *Daehanminguk haegu = The Republic of Korea Navy* [The Republic of Korea Navy = The Republic of Korea Navy] (Chungnam: Republic of Korea Navy Headquarters, 2008), 173.

20. Norman Friedman, *The Naval Institute Guide to World Naval Weapons Systems 1997–1998* (Annapolis: Naval Institute Press, 1997), 114.

21. The KNTDS was also fitted to three earlier *Ulsan*-class frigates which before the introduction of the KDX-I acted as command and control vessels for smaller patrol boats.

22. Jane's Information Group, *Jane's Fighting Ships 2012–2013*, 469.

23. Jane's Information Group, "South Korean Navy Improves Its Air-Defence Capabilities," *International Defence Review*, 1 November 2004.

24. United States Navy, *MW 08_Multi-Beam Air and Surface Surveillance Radar, Military Applications Summary Bulletin AD-A233 492*, 6 September 1989.

25. This system is also known as Red Shark and K-ASROC.

26. The K745 is also known as Blue Shark.

27. "Haesong I," *Missile Threat, CSIS Missile Defense Project*, 10 November 2017, https://missilethreat.csis.org/missile/haeseong-i/, accessed 4 February 2018.

28. LIG Nex1, *Anti-Ship Missile, C-Star*, https://www.lignex1.com/eng/common/download.jsp?filePath=/upload/2016/09/27/2016092714320532795.pdf&fileName=Cstar.pdf, accessed 20 March 2018.

29. Republic of Korea Defense Acquisition Program Administration, "*Je96hoe bangwisaeopchujinwiwonhoe gyeolgwa* [Results of the 96th DAPA Committee]," *Defense Acquisition Program Administration Press Release*, 30 September 2016.

30. "S. Korean Navy's Aegis Destroyers to Get Upgraded Missile Launch Systems," *Yonhap News Agency*, 29 May 2016, http://english.yonhapnews.co.kr/search1/2603000000.html?cid=AEN20160529004000315, accessed 30 November 2017.

31. Sarah Kim, "Plan to Build Three More Aegis Destroyers Is OKed," *Korea JoongAng Daily*, 11 December 2013, http://koreajoongangdaily.joins.com/news/article/article.aspx?aid=2981846, accessed 20 March 2014.

32. AMI International, *Sejong the Great (KDX-3) Class Destroyer*, 21 November 2017, http://amiinter.com/wnpr/html2pdf/examples/viewproject.php?newcontID=717&countryID=34, accessed 16 December 2017.

33. "S. Korean Navy Seeks Aviation Command, New Task Fleet," *Yonhap News Agency*, 10 October 2017, http://english.yonhapnews.co.kr/northkorea/2017/10/19/98/0401000000AEN20171019004652315F.html, accessed 25 January 2018.

34. At the time of writing (March 2018) 14 Pohang class and six Ulsan class were still in service.

35. 37 vessels down to approximately 24.

36. "Haesong II," *Missile Threat, CSIS Missile Defense Project*, 10 November 2017, https://missilethreat.csis.org/missile/haeseong-ii/, accessed 4 February 2018.

37. Republic of Korea Defense Acquisition Program Administration, "*Bangwisaeopcheong, chagihowiham 3dangye saeop chaksu* [DAPA Launches Third Phase of Next Frigate]," *Defense Acquisition Program Administration Press Release*, 27 December 2016.

38. For lessons learned, see: Republic of Korea Ministry of National Defense, *Defense White Paper 2010* (Seoul: Republic of Korea Ministry of National Defense, 2010), 320.

39. Gabriel Dominguez, "ROKN Commissions 18th and Final PKG-A-Class Patrol Vessel," *IHS Jane's Defence Weekly*, 25 January 2018, http://www.janes.com/article/77348/rokn-commissions-18th-and-final-pkg-a-class-patrol-vessel, accessed 10 February 2018.

40. LIG Nex1, *Air and Surface Short Range Surveillance Radar, SPS-540K*, https://www.lignex1.com/eng/common/download.jsp?filePath=/upload/2016/09/27/20160927150737555221.pdf&fileName=SPS540K.pdf, accessed 3 March 2018.

41. Hanwha Systems, *PKG Combat Management System*, http://www.hanwhasystems.com/views/eng/front/business/biz213.jsp, accessed 3 March 2018.
42. Ridzwan Rahmat, "South Korea to Bolster Northern Limit Line Security with Four More PKX-B Vessels," *Jane's Navy International*, 28 June 2017, http://www.janes.com/article/71874/south-korea-to-bolster-northern-limit-line-security-with-four-more-pkx-b-vessels, accessed 27 December 2017.
43. Janes Information Group, Jane's Fighting Ships, 471.
44. "Dokdo Class LPD—ROK Navy," *Navy Recognition*, https://navyrecognition.com/index.php/134-republic-of-korea-navy-vessels-ships-and-equipment/rok-navy-aircraft-carriers-a-amphibious-vessels/869-dokdo-class-lph-lpx-landing-platform-helicopter-amphibious-assault-ship-lph-6111-roks-marado-baengnyeongdo-ieodo-republic-of-korea-rok-navy-hanjin-heavy-industries-hhi-datasheet-pictures-photos-video-specifications.html, 10 January 2017.
45. Ibid.
46. The anti-submarine role of the *Dokdo* class LPD has not been publicly confirmed, however exercises after the sinking of the Cheonan with the USN suggest that the vessels can used as a launch platform for ASW helicopters.
47. Republic of Korea Defense Acquisition Program Administration, "*Je82hoe bangwisaeopchujinwiwonhoe gyeolgwa* [Results of the 82nd DAPA Committee]," *Defense Acquisition Program Administration Press Release*, 12 August 2014, 2.
48. This program was designated as LST-II, however, due to design changes and budgetary constraints, the final design is for a landing platform dock (LPD).
49. "Cheonwangbong Class Landing Ship Tank," *Naval Technology*, https://www.naval-technology.com/projects/cheonwangbong-class-landing-ship-tank-lst/, accessed 3 March 2018.
50. "ROKN Selects Rheinmetall MASS System for LST-II-Class Ships," *Naval Technology*, 2 May 2012, https://www.naval-technology.com/news/newsrokn-selects-rheinmetall-mass-system-for-lst-ii-class-ships/, accessed 3 March 2018.
51. Republic of Korea Navy, "*Nojeokbongham (LST-II 4Beonham) jinsusik geohaeng* [Warship No Jeok Bong (LST-II 4th Vessel) Launching Ceremony]," *Republic of Korea Navy Press Release*, 2 November 2017.
52. Eric Wertheim, *The Naval Institute Guide to Combat Fleets of the World*, 413.

53. Republic of Korea Navy, "*Chagi giroebuseolham (MLS-II) Nampoham tjinsu* [Next Minelayer (MLS-II), the Warship Nampo Launched]," *Republic of Korea Navy Press Release*, 27 May 2015.

54. Ibid., 412.

55. Ibid.

56. Ibid.

57. "MADEX 2017: Hyundai Heavy Industries HDM-4000 MLS II-Class Minelayer of the ROK Navy," *Navy Recognition*, 25 October 2017, http://www.navyrecognition.com/index.php/news/naval-exhibitions/2017/madex-2017/5656-madex-2017-hyundai-heavy-industries-hdm-4000-mls-ii-class-minelayer-of-the-rok-navy.html, accessed 26 January 2018.

58. Gabriel Dominguez, "South Korean Navy Receives New Minelayer," *IHS Jane's Defence Weekly*, 12 June 2017, http://www.janes.com/article/71328/south-korean-navy-receives-new-minelayer, accessed 10 March 2018.

59. "HHI Launched "Soyang" First 10,000 Tons AOE-II Class Fast Combat Support Ship for ROK Navy," *Navy Recognition*, 29 November 2016, http://www.navyrecognition.com/index.php/news/defence-news/2016/november-2016-navy-naval-forces-defense-industry-technology-maritime-security-global-news/4619-hhi-launched-soyang-first-10-000-tons-aoe-ii-class-fast-combat-support-ship-for-rok-navy.html, accessed 15 March 2018.

60. "Chunghaejin [Cheong-Hae-Jin] ASR," Global Security, https://www.globalsecurity.org/military/world/rok/asr-21.htm, accessed 15 March 2018.

61. "ROK Navy Future ASR-II Submarine Rescue Vessel Passes Capability Test," *Navy Recognition*, 28 December 2017, http://www.navyrecognition.com/index.php/news/defence-news/2017/december-2017-navy-naval-forces-defense-industry-technology-maritime-security-global-news/5829-rok-navy-future-asr-ii-submarine-rescue-vessel-passes-capability-test.html, accessed 15 March 2018.

62. Republic of Korea Defense Acquisition Program Administration, "*Jamsuhamgujoham-II (ASR-II)* [Submarine Rescue Ship-II (ASR-II)]," *Defense Acquisition Program Administration Press Release*, June 2015.

63. Eric Wertheim, *The Naval Institute Guide to Combat Fleets of the World*, 406.

64. "ROKN Chang Bogo Class Submarines," *Naval Technology*, http://www.naval-technology.com/projects/chang-bogo-class-submarine-south-korea-rokn/, accessed 20 March 2018.

65. Jane's Information Group, *Jane's Fighting Ships 2012–2013*, 466.

66. Republic of Korea Government, *2015nyeondo gukjeonggamsagyeolgwa sijeong min cheoriyogusahange daehan cheorigyeolgwagoseo (Gukbangbu Sogwan)* [Report on the Completion of the 2013 National Assembly Audit Results and the Completion of the Corrective and Handling Requirements (Ministry of National Defense)], April 2016, 137.

67. Republic of Korea Navy, "*214Geup Jamsuham (KSS-II) 9Beonham 'sindolseokam' Jinsu* [9th 214 Class Submarine (KSS-II) Shin Dol-Seouk Launch]," *News Release*, 7 September 2017.

68. Republic of Korea Defense Acquisition Promotion Agency, *Jangbogo-III Batch-I saeopchujinsanghwang* [Chang Bogo-III Batch-I Business Situation], 23 December 2016, http://www.dapa.go.kr/user/board-List.action?command=view&page=1&boardId=I_6033&boardSeq=I_40979&id=dapa_kr_030302340000, accessed 20 March 2018.

69. Ridzwan Rahmat, "South Korea to Equip KSS-3 Class with Indigenous Submarine Combat System," *IHS Jane's Defence Weekly*, 10 October 2017, http://www.janes.com/article/74795/south-korea-to-equip-kss-3-class-with-indigenous-submarine-combat-system, accessed 20 March 2018.

70. James Goldrick, "Just How Long Can Submarines Remain Operational," *The Strategist*, 7 March 2016, https://www.aspistrategist.org.au/just-how-long-can-submarines-remain-operational/, accessed 20 March 2018.

71. Jimmy J. Suh, "Effects of the Subsurface Domain on the Security of the Korean Peninsula" (Unpublished MA Thesis, Naval Postgraduate School, 2017), 48.

72. Republic of Korea Government, *2010nyeondo gukjeonggamsagyeolgwa sijeong min cheoriyogusahange daehan cheorigyeolgwagoseo (Gukbangbu Sogwan)*, 75.

73. "Republic of Korea Navy (ROKN) Seeking New Anti-Submarine Warfare (ASW) Helicopter," *Naval News*, 13 November 2017, http://www.navalnews.net/south-koreas-defense-acquisition-program/, accessed 20 March 2018.

74. "Marine Corps to Deploy 30 Amphibious Helicopters by 2023," *Yonhap News Agency*, 28 December 2018, http://english.yonhapnews.co.kr/news/2016/12/28/0200000000AEN20161228004800315.html, accessed 20 March 2018.

75. Legislation on the duties and functions of the ROKN headquarters has been amended 22 times between 1956 and 2017. See *Haegunbonbu jikje* [Navy Headquarters Organisation], *Presidential Decree No. 28425*, 1 November 2017, http://www.law.go.kr/LSW//lsInfoP.do?lsiSeq=198822&chrClsCd=010202&urlMode=lsInfoP&efYd=20171114, accessed 1 March 2018.

76. COMROKFLT moved from Jinhae Naval Base to Busan in 2007 to provide easier access to the waters surrounding the Peninsula. See: Im Jang-hyuk, "Navy Secretly Moves Base to Busan," *Korean JoongAng Daily*, 3 December 2007, http://koreajoongangdaily.joins.com/news/article/Article.aspx?aid=2883441, accessed 5 February 2011.

77. "Navy to Get New Unit for Submarines by 2015," *Korea Herald*, 16 February 2012, http://www.koreaherald.com/view.php?ud=20120216000901, accessed 20 April 2012.

78. Yong-soo Jeong and Myo-ja Ser, "Korea Upgrades Submarine Command Structure," *Korea JoongAng Daily*, 3 February 2015, http://koreajoon-gangdaily.joins.com/news/article/article.aspx?aid=3000459, accessed 10 August 2017.

79. "S. Korean Navy Seeks Aviation Command, New Task Fleet," *Yonhap News Agency*.

80. See Republic of Korea Navy, Jeju Naval Base Website, www.jejunbase.navy.mil.kr (in Korean).

81. "Georeoon-Gil & Bijeon [The Path & Vision]," *Republic of Korea Navy, Jeju Civilian-Military Complex Port*, http://jejunbase.navy.mil.kr/jeju-navy/sp.jsp?p=13, accessed 20 March 2018.

82. Republic of Korea Navy, *Gandanhago pyeonhage ilgeul su inneun haegun-gaideubuk*, 169.

83. Republic of Korea Ministry of National Defense, *Defense White Paper 2016* (Seoul: Republic of Korea Ministry of National Defense, 2016), 91.

84. Gabriel Dominguez, "South Korea to Start Building Training Ship in August," *IHS Jane's Defence Weekly*, 17 July 2017, http://www.janes.com/article/72347/south-korea-to-start-building-training-ship-in-august, accessed 20 November 2017.

85. Republic of Korea Ministry of National Defense, *Defense White Paper 2010*, 196.

86. MND and ROKN documents have previously described this as maritime training and manoeuvre training. It is unclear if the change in name denotes any alteration in training methods.

87. Republic of Korea Ministry of National Defense, *Defense White Paper 2016*, 94.

88. See Chapter 5 for more details on US-ROKN training exercises.

89. Ibid.

90. Republic of Korea Ministry of National Defense, *Defense White Paper 2010*, 196.

The United States and the ROKN

In 2016, the ROKN decommissioned the ROKS *Pyeongtaek*, a salvage and rescue ship, at Jinhae Naval Base.[1] She had been in South Korean service since 1996 and was the last vessel in the ROKN fleet that had seen previous service in the US Navy. In many ways, the decommissioning ceremony signalled the end of an era. The ROKN has successfully transitioned from a force that was wholly dependent on the United States, to one that is now indigenously constructing advanced platforms and weapon systems.

The United States has played a substantial role in how South Korea, its military and its navy has developed. The South Korea–US alliance remains an unusual one. Its origins lie in the aftermath of the Korean War and South Korean dependence on the United States for its security and economic survival. This gave the United States substantial power over the doctrine, developmental direction and priorities of the Korean military. Although South Korea eventually gained economic, political and a level of military independence, the United States, under the auspices of the Combined Forces Command (CFC), still retains wartime operational control (OPCON) over South Korean forces.[2] This level of influence has fundamentally informed the development of the ROKN.

This chapter is divided into four main parts, each of which describes a different period in the US–South Korea alliance relationship and its impact on the ROKN. It begins with the formative period of the ROKN, when South Korea was entirely reliant on the United States for economic and

© The Author(s) 2019
I. Bowers, *The Modernisation of the Republic of Korea Navy*, Critical Studies of the Asia-Pacific,
https://doi.org/10.1007/978-3-319-92291-1_5

military aid and the United States did not embrace the concept of South Korean seapower. Instead, any efforts to modernise the ROKN were framed against the limited naval capabilities of the KPN. Transformative South Korean naval transformation was not a priority as capacity building was focused on the ROKA. ROKN modernisation was slow and even viewed by some within the US administration as a potential strategic risk.

The second and third parts examine the period after 1968 when the alliance relationship began to change as South Korea took more responsibility for its own defence. As South Korea became more independent and under Park Chung-hee developed an industrial capacity to construct its own naval vessels, the ROKN modernised but did not expand its operational remit. The presence of the US 7th Fleet and the ongoing continental threat from North Korea ensured that a limited naval role for the ROKN became imbedded in South Korean strategic thinking. The series of army-dominated governments in Seoul retained the US view of the limited utility of South Korean seapower. US control over procurement may have lessened but Washington's conception of what the ROKN was for remained influential.

This chapter concludes with an examination of the alliance after the end of the Cold war. It argues that the very modernisation that the United States had previously opposed has now facilitated greater operational coordination between the USN and ROKN. As the ROKN gained the ability to operate in more advanced roles, the United States now views the ROKN as an important partner given the threat from North Korea and the changing dynamics of maritime East Asia. The United States role in ROKN modernisation has changed from one of constraint to facilitation.

Post-Korean War and Reliance

In October 1953, two months after the signing of the armistice agreement, the South Korean Minister of Defence Sohn Won-il wrote to his US counterpart Charles Erwin Wilson. Sohn, the founding admiral of the ROKN, outlined his government's assessment of their post-Korean War military requirements. At that time, the ROKN was composed of WWII-era US and Japanese vessels, the largest of which were four 1,400-tons *Tacoma*-class frigates that the United States had loaned the ROKN at the beginning of the war.[3] The South Korean government viewed this force as inadequate and consequently, Admiral Son requested an ambitious naval force improvement plan of six destroyers (DD), 16 destroyer escorts (DE), four minesweepers (AM), two oilers (AO) and three other support vessels.[4]

Although the package requested for the ROKN was relatively small when compared with those for the ROKA and ROKAF, the US JCS rejected South Korea's assessment of their naval requirements. They argued that the United States should provide the ROKN with a substantially weaker force improvement package of two DE, four patrol craft (PCEC), 12 medium landing ships (LSM), four tank landing ships (LST) and five support ships.[5] However, the JCS did recommend increasing the number of ROKN personnel from the 1952 limit of 10,000 up to 15,000.[6] This force level was, the US JCS believed, the maximum the ROKN could efficiently maintain and deploy with US assistance given their limited resources.[7]

These considerations were reflected in the November 1954 *Agreed Minute* signed by the United States and South Korea. This document set out the terms for the future of US-South Korean relations including the level of economic and military aid that the United States would supply to the war-ravaged country.[8] It placed all South Korean armed forces under the command of the US-led UNC and as Washington could set exacting limits on the strength and disposition of the South Korean military, it constrained the South Korean government's control over the modernisation of its armed forces.

The United States committed to allowing the ROKN build towards a maximum future force level of 79 vessels.[9] This figure, based on the US JCS recommendations, was approved by the US Chief of Naval Operations and the terms for the provision of these vessels reflected how the United States used South Korea's economic and industrial weakness to maintain control over the South Korean military.[10] As South Korea could not purchase or construct its own vessels, the ships were to be provided on a five-year loan basis and could be withdrawn if the United States, 'in its own discretion should decide that such vessels are no longer being used to serve the best interests of both the Korean and the United States Governments'.[11]

Despite committing to the 79-ship limit, the US did not provide sufficient assistance to reach that level. In 1955 and 1956, the ROKN received two *Cannon* class DE (which were reclassified as frigates upon entry into Korean service), five LST, 12 LSM, three minesweepers and three support ships, raising the number of ROKN combatant vessels to 61. By 1960, the US National Security Council (NSC) assessed that the ROKN could conduct coastal surveillance but was hindered as they were using radar technology from WWII. They had limited amphibious capabilities and virtually no anti-submarine capacity.[12] By that time the ROKN only had 52 operational ships most which were of WWII vintage. Although the US NSC report recommended that ideally the ROKN would maintain a force of 86 ships including seven destroyers, 19 patrol craft and 24 mine-warfare vessels this level would never be reached.[13] Ultimately, the provision of vessels to the ROKN was not a priority and while funding plans for 1961–1964 called for supplying 23 vessels, only 12 were transferred to the ROKN.[14]

Understanding the US Approach

The limited level of US assistance to the ROKN has a simple primary explanation. As the Korean Peninsula was a continental theatre, the ROKN did not take priority. For policymakers in Washington, the two core objectives of their Korea policy were to ensure that the war did not restart and to reduce the number of US troops deployed in South Korea. Therefore, rebuilding and sustaining the ROKA, and to an extent the ROKAF, took precedence.[15]

South Korea did not have the capacity to support such goals and it was entirely reliant on the United States to provide money, equipment and training.[16] Between 1954 and 1955, the United States withdrew five infantry divisions and one marine division, leaving two infantry divisions deployed on the peninsula. In compensation, the United States transferred the equipment from its departing units to the ROKA and increased funding for South Korea to raise four further divisions.[17] In 1954, the US DOD estimated that the cost of initial equipment for the ROKA would be 750 million USD while the ROKAF required 43.5 million USD to upgrade from propeller to jet-powered aircraft. The peripheral strategic role of the ROKN, the weaknesses of the KPN and the constant presence of the US 7th Fleet in Asian waters ensured the marginalisation of the navy in the allocation of force improvement aid. The cost for the activation and refit of the ROKN's 27 vessels was between 11 and 12 million USD.[18] Further, when the United States struggled to maintain financial support levels in South Korea, the perceived unimportance of the ROKN rendered it vulnerable to further reductions in proposed force modernisation packages.[19]

A 1956 memo from the US JCS to the Secretary of Defense Charles E. Wilson revealed that although 'by US standards the effectiveness and capability of the ROK Navy is limited, it is considered ample for its currently assigned mission'.[20] Discussions at the NSC in 1958 and 1959 about revisions to the 1954 agreement show a commitment to maintaining ROKN levels at approximately 60 vessels.[21] This sentiment persisted in Washington and any further reinforcements to the ROKN reflected Washington's goal of maintaining South Korean naval capabilities at a sufficient level to sustain coastal operations relative to KPN capabilities and support US naval operations when required.[22]

There was also a second explanation for the US reluctance to provide the ROKN with capabilities beyond those required for coastal surveillance and defence. There was a fear within Washington over the loss of control and the potential for South Korea to take actions detrimental to US interests.

The US administration did not trust Syngman Rhee, the South Korean president between 1948 and 1960. They feared that he could unilaterally restart the Korean War with an aim to unify the peninsula by force.[23] Additionally, anti-Japanese sentiment in South Korea was strong and fishing disputes were a constant source of tension.[24] As US Secretary of State John Foster Dulles stated in July of 1954:

> The Koreans were hostile to the Japanese and wished additional naval craft to drive Japanese fishing vessels away from areas that the Koreans claim as theirs...we should not give mobile forces to countries whose interests are not the same as our own, who are hostile to their neighbours and who have a vested interest in starting a third word war.[25]

By curtailing the capabilities of the ROKN, the United States sought to limit South Korea's freedom of action in the maritime sphere. Given that the US did not maintain officers on ROKN vessels this was a particularly important method of control.

A CHANGING RELATIONSHIP?

In 1968, a US' intelligence estimate highlighted a growing disparity between the KPN and the ROKN. While still a coastal force, the KPN, with support from the USSR, had substantially bolstered its offensive capability. It introduced four *W* class submarines and approximately seven *Komar*-class guided missile boats armed with Styx anti-ship missiles (AShM).[26] In comparison, the ROKN's force of approximately 60 vessels lacked the anti-submarine capability to deal with the KPN's new sub-surface vessels and the AShM meant the ROKN would be outranged in any surface combat.

North Korea had also increased its military pressure on the South. It began acting more aggressively when asserting its perceived maritime rights and it sunk the South Korean naval vessel, the ROKS *Dangpo* in 1967. In January 1968, a 31-man North Korean special forces team crossed the DMZ and infiltrated Seoul to attack Cheong Wa Dae (the South Korean presidential compound, also known as the Blue House) to assassinate the President, Park Chung-hee. A few days later, the *USS Pueblo* a US intelligence-gathering ship was captured by KPN vessels in the East Sea. Then in October/November 1968, a 120 strong North Korean SOF team used the sea to infiltrate the west coast of South Korea resulting in a massive manhunt involving 40,000 ROKA and police which lasted several months and resulted in a total of 170 deaths.

Seoul had been increasingly cognizant of the widening gap in naval capabilities between North and South Korea and in 1967 during a conversation with President Lyndon Johnson, South Korean prime minister, Chung Il-kwon emphasised the need for new destroyers for the ROKN arguing:

> the destroyers presently in service in the Korean navy had been in use since 1946 and were the oldest type still in operation. Their speed was only in the 18–24 knot range, and they were simply not competitive as compared with North Korean naval equipment.[27]

Partially because of this plea, two 2,000-tons *Fletcher*-class destroyers were transferred in 1968, one from the active USN fleet and the other from the reserve fleet.[28] For the United States, the desire to assist South Korea in balancing North Korean capabilities was secondary to wider alliance management considerations. The United States approved the transfer of the vessels to assuage the South Korean government, which under the leadership of President Park had contributed substantial Korean forces to the conflict in Vietnam. At that time, sentiment in Seoul was not positive towards the United States. The increased North Korean attacks had led to calls for South Korean troops to be called home from combat in Southeast Asia. There was also a growing perception that Washington's preference for stability on the peninsula meant that it was indifferent to aggressive North Korean actions such as the attack on the Blue House.[29] The two destroyers became part of a broader package of measures designed to reward South Korea for their participation in the Vietnam War and bolster their ability to counter North Korean infiltration.[30]

The United States' broader approach to its allies was to change in 1969 with the declaration of the Nixon Doctrine. This doctrine argued that US allies and security partners 'should supply the bulk of manpower for their own defense while the United States would furnish them with both technical assistant and its nuclear shield where appropriate'.[31] This doctrine accelerated the longer-term plans for South Korea that would see them take more responsibility for their own security. The United States, would, by withdrawing the 7th Infantry Division, reduce its forces on the peninsula by approximately 20,000 men.[32] In compensation, the United States would provide a five-year (1971–1975) Force Modernisation Plan (FMP) that would modernise South Korean forces to the maximum extent possible within the allocated budget of approximately 200 billion USD per year.[33]

Following the announcement, the South Korean government expressed the need to balance military power on the peninsula especially within the context of the ROKAF and ROKN which were both inferior to their North Korean opponents.[34] There is evidence that after some debate military and political leaders in Washington agreed with this sentiment. Initial assessments of what the US FMP would contain excluded aid for the ROKN. Washington judged that 'existing ROKN naval forces were at least minimally adequate to deal with the North Korean naval threat'.[35] However, concerns over North Korea's ability to perform hit and run and infiltration attacks combined with US JCS worries about the material state of the South Korea's ageing equipment resulted in the allocation of 112 million USD to the ROKN for force modernisation.[36] Kissinger in a memorandum to Nixon supported the United States extending aid to South Korea's air and naval forces as it would be cheaper than maintaining equivalent US forces on and around the peninsula.[37]

US estimates as to the ROKN's requirements suggested 48 modernised vessels including eight destroyers and 20 minesweepers alongside 20 smaller fast boats.[38] This number was based on the judgement that 'aside from a large number of small boats, the North Koreans essentially have no offensive naval capability and so the building of any sizeable

ROK navy is a luxury'.[39] US military assessments confirmed that under the conditions set out under the FMP, the ROKN would continue to be only capable of limited independent operations and in wartime would act in a contributory role to US forces.[40]

In peacetime, the new destroyers and patrol boats would maintain surveillance and deterrence in the littoral waters of the peninsula.[41] While in wartime their missions would include coastal patrol, amphibious operations (but reliant on the United States for logistical support) and limited anti-submarine operations.[42] Importantly, the ROKN's mine-sweeping capacity would be vital to keeping South Korean ports open in a time of war, allowing the United States to rush reinforcements and supplies to the Korean theatre.

During discussions over the FMP, an option for a wholly independent ROKN was forwarded but judged too costly. For the United States, the ROKN would still be minimally sufficient to maintain peacetime deterrence and protect the coast. This was economically advantageous as it freed up US naval resources, however funding anything beyond this level of naval power would pull money from the more strategically vital programs that bolstered the ROKA and ROKAF. Debates within the US Army leadership in Korea reveal concern over the provision of the ROKN with missile-armed destroyers. This suggests a persistent fear of giving the ROKN capabilities that could destabilise the region or be used contrary to US interests. A member of the US National Security Council Staff, John H. Holdridge reported General Smith of the 8th Army 'thought the Sea Sparrow was a bad idea, since the ROKN could shoot it at anything they saw on their radar screens and might raise problems for us in that respect'.[43]

Over the course of the modernisation program, South Korea's needs were continuously re-evaluated by the United States and it is evident that assessments of the ROKA were increasingly positive as to their ability to independently defend against a North Korean assault. Concern in Washington was increasingly focused on the ROKAF and South Korea's air-defence capacity. In 1973, Kissinger wrote to Nixon stating that 'South Korean air defences were seriously deficient, and it is recommended that this area receive greater emphasis'.[44] It is apparent that the ROKN did not prominently feature as a force improvement priority in this period.

This was crucial for the ROKN as the FMP became under-funded and delayed due to opposition in the US Congress; scheduled to end in

1975, it was pushed to 1977. Over the period of the FMP, the ROKN received six *Gearing* and *Sumner*-class destroyers, all of which were fitted with the FRAM upgrade package, which significantly improved their anti-submarine capabilities.[45] They also received nine ex-US Coast Guard *Cape*-class cutters that would be deployed to counter seaborne infiltrations and two new minesweepers.[46] Taken together this was a substantially reduced number of vessels when compared with was proposed only six years previously.

In 1975, the Bureau of Intelligence Research for the State Department wrote that the ROKN remained the weakest of the services when compared with their North Korean adversaries.[47] It argued that the ROKN remained out-gunned and out-ranged by the KPN's missile and submarine capabilities.[48] A similar report in 1978 echoed this finding but highlighted that such an imbalance would not have a material effect on the outcome of combat operations as neither navy would play a decisive role in a wartime scenario.[49] The efforts to create naval balance in the waters surrounding the peninsula through the FMP were only moderately successful and while the ROKA and ROKAF were gaining the ability for independent operations, even in wartime, the ROKN was still fully reliant on the support of the USN.

THE YULGOK PROGRAM

Despite US' efforts to build-up South Korea's military, President Park's government believed that South Korea had become far too reliant on the United States. Seoul was concerned about the political situation in Washington and the seemingly wavering US commitment to South Korean security. Consequently, in 1971 Park ordered the South Korean government to begin a long-term industrial and military project to develop a self-reliant defence capability.[50]

In 1974, the *Yulgok* program was initiated. Named after a sixteenth-century Korean scholar who advocated improving the Joseon Kingdom's defence capabilities, this self-reliance defence initiative sought to develop South Korea's military while at the same time building an indigenous defence industry. These developments were to be funded by South Korea but would still rely heavily on the United States for access to advanced weapons technology and manufacturing know how. While increasing South Korea's own military capability and providing long-term insurance against the possibility of US withdrawal, the *Yulgok* program did not include altering the command structure on the peninsula nor did it call for a change in the doctrine of deterrence.

The *Yulgok* program extended past Park's rule (he was assassinated in 1979) and lasted until 1981. It was then replaced with two further Force Improvement Plans (FIP), the first from 1982–'86 and the second from 1987–'92. Each of these plans was designed to improve specific aspects of South Korea's defence-industrial complex. The *Yulgok* phase focused on the development of a basic military-industrial capacity, the replacement of old equipment, new military infrastructure and specific improvements in the ROKN and the ROKAF to match developments across the DMZ. The second phase aimed at developing qualitative superiority over North Korea. This too was a cross-service development plan that focused on the pursuit of indigenous R&D capability to reduce further South Korea's reliance on the United States and other foreign powers. The final plan was dedicated to building upon the advances made since 1974. The focus was the development of high-tech weaponry and improvements in South Korea's indigenous defence capabilities through the mass production of ground vehicles and weaponry and through the licensed production of aircraft and naval vessels.[51]

Funding

The *Yulgok* period saw a progressive change in the US provision of military financial support. Between 1950 and 1970, South Korea was almost entirely reliant on the United States to fund its military. The majority of assistance was funnelled through Military Assistance Program (MAP) grants and the International Military Education and Training Program (IMET). Through the MAP and IMET, the United States provided South Korea with just under $4 billion in military grant aid and it proved difficult to wean South Korea off such support.[52] Even by the late 1960s, South Korea's contribution to its own defence budget was less than 25%.[53] This allowed the United States to control and manage South Korean procurement practices.

During the 1971–1977 FIP, South Korea was gradually shifted away from this type of assistance and was moved on to the Foreign Military Sales (FMS) system where credit would be in part provided to assist South Korea in its own force development, while the rest of procurement would be paid for directly by South Korea under the FMS scheme.[54]

This alteration of funding shifted the burden of defence spending onto South Korea and Seoul responded to the reduction in direct financing by increasing its own proportion of defence spending.[55] By 1976, South Korea paid 90% of its military costs and in the same year raised taxes to support an increase in defence spending.[56] This was an indicator of the country's rapidly developing economy, in that it could match the reduction in US funding through its own finances. By 1986, South Korea had stopped receiving military grants and had fully transferred to FMS and direct commercial sales for its procurement needs.[57] This was significant in that financial independence matched the self-reliant defence goals of South Korea, but it also contributed to reducing the level of US influence over South Korea's procurement decisions.

Despite this reduction of US influence, the ROKN remained a lesser priority for funding. As President Park stated during a meeting with President Jimmy Carter in 1979, 'Our priorities are ground forces, air forces and the navy in that order'.[58] As long as North Korea posed a substantial land-based threat and the South Korean government could rely on the US Navy and its 7th Fleet to intervene in the event of a serious incident the ROKN would not receive a substantial share of the available funds. During the *Yulgok* program the navy share of the defence budget was 15%.[59] As the threat from North Korea altered, this increased to approximately 20% in the subsequent FIP.[60]

The ROKN and the Yulgok Program

The relative paucity of funding for the ROKN should not, however, be confused for neglect. President Park and his government's goal was to acquire new and more powerful vessels to match KPN capabilities. Ultimately, the *Yulgok* Program was a boon for the ROKN. While initially reliant on the United States for technical assistance, licensed production and funding, this dependence began to shift as US support for wide-ranging development lessened and South Korea's increasing purchasing power gave it more scope to procure the capabilities it wanted.

Between 1974 and 1992 the ROKN's capabilities saw substantial improvement. It went from a force of approximately 20,000 men to one that was over 45,000 strong (not including the ROKMC). Its platform numbers also increased, going from 63 surface platforms (including patrol craft) and 80 assorted landing craft to a force with 40 destroyers and frigates, 122 patrol and coastal vessels, 51 landing and amphibious craft and submarines with modern frigates and logistics support ships on order.[61]

As previously highlighted, between 1971 and 1977, the ROKN received several vessels from the United States however, South Korea's increasing financial independence altered the terms of future procurement from the United States. Despite gaining seven destroyers, South Korea deemed it necessary to procure a further two *Gearing*-class vessels. Unlike previous transfers of equipment, these were not loaned but paid for directly by Seoul.[62] They were delivered in 1981 and replaced the ageing *Fletcher*-class vessels which were increasingly costly to maintain. South Korea did not have the ability to manufacture or procure new vessels of that size and with such capabilities, but the purchase of these vessels indicated a shift in the relationship between the two allies. Indeed, as loan agreements expired, the United States encouraged South Korea to purchase vessels outright, advising that loans would not be extended.[63] The United States, while losing a measure of control over the ROKN, had gradually succeeded in weaning them off financial and material support.

The *Yulgok* program also developed the industrial capability to allow for the indigenous production of ROKN vessels. While this had a political and strategic rationale, there was also strong economic incentives. As South Korea began to self-fund its military procurement, price became an increasingly important consideration. Between 1972 and 1979, the ROKN began development work on two classes of patrol boat, an 80 tons Patrol Killer (PK) and a 150 tons Patrol Killer Missile (PKM). These vessels were closely based on US designs which had been loaned to the ROKN in 1972 and again later in 1975. The craft loaned in 1975 was the Coastal Patrol Interdiction Craft (CPIC) which was designed specifically for coastal operations and was marketed to South Korea and Taiwan. The procurement of this class of vessel was not covered by grant aid and would needed to have been purchased under the FMS program.[64] Hence, South Korea chose to pursue indigenous production as it was considerably less expensive with ROKN estimates suggesting that indigenous construction would be 50% cheaper than purchasing craft from the United States.[65]

South Korea still required US assistance in developing technical competence. In 1975 South Korean and US shipbuilding industries began more formal cooperation. This took the form of licenced production agreement of the US-designed 250 tons *Asheville*-class gunboat. South

Korea gained experience in operating this class of vessel when one, the *USS Benicia*, was transferred to the ROKN in 1971 (renamed *ROKS Paeku*). The ROKN ordered eight more of these vessels. Three of which were built in the United States and five were built under licence by Korea Tacoma, a South Korean-owned subsidiary of Tacoma industries.

South Korea's pursuit of an indigenous naval capability raised some concerns in Washington regarding the direction of Seoul's procurement and the potential loss of control over South Korea's FIP. The *Yulgok* program, as it was being funded internally, allowed South Korea to look to other countries to supply weapons. Something European defence manufacturers took notice of. This, argued Assistant Secretary of State for East Asian Affairs Philip Habib, caused both a political and potential strategic problem. With South Korea able to acquire weapons from third parties, the United States feared that 'priority requirements that have been set jointly between ourselves [the US] and the Koreans as to what arms they need' could be disregarded.[66] Politically, Habib feared that if South Korea were to buy weapons from other countries, the US Congress would reduce already pressured military assistance programs, stating that:

> If I were a congressman and I discovered that I appropriated 145 million dollars to a country which spent another hundred million dollars for weaponry from another country, I don't think I'd appropriate 145 million dollars.[67]

A 1975 meeting at the State Department revealed that South Korea had requested to buy the Harpoon AShM.[68] A subsequent cable from the US embassy in Seoul revealed that due to production-line problems the United States could not supply the Harpoon immediately and that the South Korean government was willing to risk the anger of Congress and procure the French-made Exocet missile, as it was necessary to maintain deterrence at sea.[69] By 1978, the United States had decided to provide South Korea with the *Harpoon* system, however, this followed the purchase of *Exocet* missiles.[70] South Korea seemed to prefer using US systems and wanted to retain interoperability, but if these were not available they were willing and able to look elsewhere. Although the purchase of *Exocet* was quite small, in total 24 missiles were bought in two tranches, it was indicative of a future where South Korea could ignore US objections to the procurement of non-US military equipment.

This was a substantial shift in the US-South Korea relationship as it provided Seoul with some leverage over Washington to obtain the arms they desired. The ability to procure from other sources raised concerns regarding the potential for South Korean purchases to destabilise the military balance on the peninsula. If the United States was no longer the sole-supplier of South Korean weapons, their ability to influence the South Korean government would be reduced.[71] Nevertheless, the US embassy in Seoul seemed confident that 'continued Korean dependence on US security guarantees and desire for close ties with the US should provide considerable leverage in areas of major concern to the US'.[72]

This diversification, driven by necessity but also by commercial and political demands, became more apparent in the building of three new classes of surface ship. The 1,070 tons *Donghae* and 1,200 tons *Pohang*-class corvettes and the 2,350 tons *Ulsan*-class frigate. All three of these ships were indigenously constructed and used mostly non-US weapon and command and control systems. The first of these classes, the *Ulsan*-class frigate, was first proposed in 1975 when President Park looked at the need to mass produce heavier vessels to counter the KPN.[73] It was decided to pursue domestic construction as foreign purchases were deemed to be too costly.

The construction of the *Ulsan*-class frigate reflected an increasing commercialisation of the alliance procurement relationship. US embassy cables written during the initial tender and design phase of the frigate portray a fierce competition between a US and a UK firm for the design contract.[74] This was ultimately awarded to the US firm John J. McMullen. However, the vessel's weapons systems which were chosen by the ROKN reveal a diverse array of suppliers. The US firm Emerson Electric supplied the Emerlec 30 mm cannon and US-made Harpoon missiles and Type-40 torpedoes formed part of the weapons complement. However, Italy, Germany and the Netherlands supplied weapons (guns), engines and the sensor suite.

Although billed as an indigenous frigate, the ROKN still relied on external suppliers and assistance. Nevertheless, the successful completion of the project with the first in the class launched in 1980 demonstrated that that South Korea was (a) capable of building ships but lacked the technological skill in developing more complex items, (b) capable of funding its own large shipbuilding program, and (c) the reliance on the US in the naval sphere was diminishing. The same indications come from the *Donghae*-class and *Pohang*-class corvettes, which were first launched in 1982 and 1984, respectively. These ships, carried similarly diverse load-outs to the *Ulsan*-class, in that they carried weapons, sensor and propulsion systems from several countries including the US.

The ROKN's pursuit of submarines tested the limits of its *Yulgok* resources and ultimately reflected the altered relationship with the United States in terms of procurement control and direction. As South Korea's economy grew so did their ability to pursue their own independent procurement objectives. In 1975, President Park outlined his reasoning for purchasing submarines during a meeting with then US Secretary of Defense James R. Schlesinger. He argued that as North Korea possessed submarines (*Whiskey* & *Romeo* classes from the Soviet Union and China respectively), South Korea required an equivalent capability to deter their use.[75] At that meeting, Schlesinger expressed US opposition citing more efficient methods of countering the threat such as P-3 Orion aircraft and mines.[76] As the United States were unwilling and unable to assist in the provision of small submarines, South Korea looked further afield and in sign of their economic weakness briefly considered British WWII-era vessels.[77]

This procurement plan fell through and in 1979 a US Navy study, while not advocating the South Korean purchase of submarines, did acknowledge their military utility in the West Sea.[78] Discussions with the US embassy in Korea revealed the potential purchase of two *Tang*-class submarines which had been previously destined for Iran. This plan also did not proceed but South Korea continued to pursue a subsurface capability, attempting to negotiate with several European countries in the early 1980s despite some US opposition.[79] It wasn't until 1987, after a failed competition in 1984–1986 that an agreement was reached with HDW of Germany to supply nine *Type-209* submarines, the first of which would be built in Germany and the remaining eight to be constructed in kit form in South Korea. This type of contract provided South Korea with the technical expertise to pursue a fully indigenous submarine construction capability. It was also the first major ROKN project with a non-US contractor. In that respect, the submarine programme is symbolic of the ROKN's hard-won ability to procure and develop its forces without the United States.

A New Relationship

The end of the Cold War saw the growth of a new and still evolving relationship between the ROKN and the United States. The US connection with the ROKN has changed from one of South Korean dependence and US disregard to one of cooperation and ever-increasing operational coordination. Perhaps ironically given the previous resistance from US stakeholders, it is the ROKN's modernization that in part facilitates this greater level of collaboration. The US influence over ROKN modernisation has, since the 1990s, gradually become more indirect. South Korea has slowly taken more responsibility in the alliance and is working towards the transfer of OPCON. There is recognition across the South Korean military that the requirements of modern war as first demonstrated in the 1990–1991 Gulf War and the vital need to maintain interoperability with the US means embracing RMA style technologies and warfighting techniques. Consequently, US technology, capabilities and tactics now shape the ROKN's, procurement and operations. Further, as the ROKN has modernised it has looked to the United States for guidance. Although the development of an independent operational capability is a core element of the ROKN's modernisation goal, South Korean naval planners have recognised the operational and strategic benefits of closer coordination with their US counterparts.[80]

Despite some concern particularly within the US Congress that South Korea was investing in naval capabilities and not in the ROKA, thus requiring US troops to stay longer on the peninsula, the US has become broadly supportive of South Korean naval modernisation.[81] This stems from several factors. In the 1990s, the USN began to take more of an interest in littoral operations and the navies that could carry them out.[82] The evolution of the strategic environment in East Asia including the continued threat from North Korea, which was placed in focus with the sinking of the *Cheonan*, and the rise of China has placed an added emphasis on the role of seapower. The so-called US rebalance to Asia under the Obama administration saw the commitment of 60% of US naval forces to the Asian area of operations.[83] However, the US Navy remains overstretched as budget constraints and a high operational tempo across the world has tested USN platforms and personnel to their limit.[84] Consequently, the US naval leadership, through initiatives such as the Global Maritime Partnership, has put increasing emphasis on developing maritime partnerships and strengthening allied naval cooperation. A powerful, interoperable ROKN can assist in burden sharing and contribute to US security in the waters of Northeast Asia and beyond.

For much of the post-Korean War period, the USN has had comparatively little operational experience with the ROKN. Retired US admiral and naval analyst Michael McDevitt argues that for naval planners in United States, the ROKN was a secondary priority to the JMSDF.[85] The reasons for this were multiple; the low technological ability of the ROKN meant that the USN had little interest in cooperating with the ROKN.[86] Divergent mission sets also played a prominent role. During the Cold War, the overwhelming operational focus for the USN was blue-water operations and it increasingly eschewed the littoral theatre. As the ROKN was a primarily littoral force, there were reduced opportunities for joint training and operations. Further, unlike much of the Pacific theatre, which for the United States is organizationally dominated by the USN, South Korea is primarily an US Army command. The USN has traditionally had a very small presence on the peninsula. There are no US ships home-ported in South Korea and Command, US Naval Forces Korea has traditionally been a shore-based command with a small number of personnel. When compared with the USN presence in Japan, the difference is notable and the lack of operational US naval personnel on the peninsula has had an impact on the natural development of closer ties.[87]

Although, since the end of the Korean War, there had been consistent interaction in terms of staff talks, personnel exchanges and some exercises, this did not translate into efficient interoperability between the two forces.[88] This was made evident during the 1991 Ulchi Focus Lens and Team Spirit exercises. The USN identified significant problems in operational coordination, tactics, communications and the ROKN's lack of experience in working with other navies.[89] Importantly, both the USN and ROKN worked to rectify these issues. The first step was the clarification of the naval chain of command in wartime.

In 1994, the United States reorganised the commands responsible for Korean Peninsular naval operations in times of war. If war on the peninsula began and the CFC implemented the OPLAN, the deployment of substantial US naval forces is to be expected. Once this occurs, the Commander of the US 7th Fleet, on arrival in the area of operations will become Commander, Combined Naval Component Command (CNCC) with a ROKN admiral acting as his deputy. Under armistice conditions, as Command US Naval Forces Korea has no ships, the ROKN three star Commander Republic of Korea Fleet is dual-hatted as CNCC.[90] This arrangement resolved a significant previous issue where in wartime the ROKN would report to the CFC, but the US naval forces would report to Pacific Command in Hawaii. It also tied the 7th Fleet to ROKN operations and created some momentum behind efforts to increase cooperation. The momentum was bolstered on US side by the nascent North Korean nuclear crisis, which altered the USN thinking about their immediate role in the waters around the Korean Peninsula. Suddenly, cooperation and operational coordination with the ROKN became a higher policy priority. Prior to the 1995 Ulchi Focus Lens exercise, the staffs of the ROKN and the 7th fleet held talks to improve joint readiness.[91] During the exercise itself, the command of the 7th Fleet, Vice Admiral Archie Clemmens served as the Commander of Combined Naval Component Command. The lessons learned from this exercise indicated an improvement in operational coordination between both navies.[92]

In the early 1990s, some in the ROKN felt that the procurement of larger more powerful platforms and the consequent change in operational capabilities would automatically lead to greater interoperability between it and the USN.[93] However, the US side emphasised the development of interoperable C4I capabilities, without which the ROKN would fall behind the trend of other close US naval partners.[94] This mirrored a concern that has been frequently highlighted by successive US commanders in Korea. The United States believes that the procurement of command can control communications, computer and intelligence (C4I) capabilities is the key to making modern South Korean forces interoperable with the United States and creating the foundation for the eventual transfer of OPCON.[95]

It is evident that the ROKN quickly came around to this way of thinking. Since the 1990s, the ROKN has begun to build a command and control (C2) and later a C4I capability. There was also an emphasis on integrating these systems with US ones. This fits within a broader trend in South Korean defence procurement in the age of RMA where the US influence over the nature of South Korean military procurement is more indirect. As Michael Raska highlights, the US adoption of the Revolution in Military Affairs and network-centric warfare greatly influenced how South Korea developed its own RMA inspired technologies and tactics.[96]

The ROKN first discussed its C2 system the KNTDS with the United States in 1993 at the US-South Korea Command and Control Interoperability Board. However, it was not until 2006 that the United States validated it as a secure platform for the creation of a common operational picture. Data can be shared between KNTDS and US forces via Link-14 and Link-11.[97] For better interoperability with the United

States, the ROKN has procured the Global Command and Control System-Maritime (GCCS-M) and SATCOM system through the FMS program.[98] This came about as a result of USN recommendations following a number of exercises to better operational coordination.[99] The ROKN built upon these capabilities with the addition of the Common Datalink Management System (CDLMS) for its KDX-III-class and the upgrade of its KDX-I-class with the Maritime Datalink Management System (MDLMS), which includes Link-11 and Link-16 datalinks.[100] New classes of the ROKN vessel including the *Incheon* and *Daegu*-class frigates will be equipped with similar interoperable datalinks including Link-K.

For systems the ROKN cannot procure indigenously it has continued to view the US as the preferred partner. For example, the ROKN decided to procure a US-made 5″ gun for ROKN ships even though South Korea has a long history of purchasing such systems from Italian companies. The shift in supplier was primarily because the ROKN deemed that in a time of emergency such as war the US and its manufacturers would be potentially more reliable in supplying spare parts and other equipment than foreign manufacturers.[101]

Aside from the slow technological convergence between the two navies, several forums now exist to translate this long relationship into substantial operational cooperation. An early example is the Submarine Warfare Committee Meeting that first met in 1994 and facilitates navy-to-navy discussion on submarine operations, tactics and exercises.[102] Since 2013, the ROKN and USN have held an Aegis development seminar to focus on the future of BMD and the Aegis system.[103] A year later, an ASW charter was signed between the two navies.[104] This charter is designed to increase cooperation and enhance the coordinated development of ASW capabilities and skills. Part of this new effort is the ASW Cooperation Committee which is chaired by the commanders of the ROKN and US 7th Fleet and 'synchronizes the activities of all ROK and U.S. Navy commands dedicated to improving anti-submarine warfare in Korea'.[105] There has also been an increased emphasis on mine-warfare cooperation though the UNC Naval Component Mine Countermeasures Symposium and the long-held mine-countermeasures exercise Clear Horizon. These two events were initially held separately but were combined in 2016 to facilitate the participation of personnel from UN sending states. In the same year, the two navies began sharing data on the underwater environment around the Korean Peninsula.[106]

Again in 2016, CNFK opened a new headquarters within the ROKN's base at Busan.[107] This was first planned in 2011 and is indicative of a desire to tighten the relationship between the two navies.[108] It is also the only US installation on a Korean military base and likely facilitated the opening of a combined maritime operations centre in January 2017.[109]

In his 2017 statement to the House Appropriations Committee, General Vincent Brooks, the Commander CFC, highlighted the increased number of combined naval exercises and their role in improving interoperability.[110] Currently, the two navies hold approximately 20 combined exercises per year in the waters around the Korean Peninsula. These include the two naval components of the two major South Korea–US exercises; Key Resolve/Foal Eagle which is usually held each year in February and March and a command post exercise called Ulchi Guardian Freedom which is held in August/September. The former is often used by both navies to test new concepts, introduce new assets into the theatre and iron-out interoperability issues. It usually has a substantial USN and ROKN presence often including a US carrier strike group and numerous other major platforms such as USN and ROKN destroyers and submarines. Other exercises held throughout the year include a biannual ASW exercise, submarine exercises, BMD exercises and an annual large-scale amphibious exercise.

Exercises are also held in response to real-world events such as the sinking of the *Cheonan*. That the ROKN has become increasingly involved in such exercises indicates their developing ability to operate alongside the most advanced US platforms. In 2010, the US and South Korean militaries quickly organised the Invincible Spirit exercise which involved the USS George Washington and approximately 20 other ships. A second Invincible Spirit exercise was held in 2016 and included seven US vessels led by the USS Ronald Reagan and over 40 ROKN ships. In June 2012, a combined exercise involving the USS George Washington was held in the West Sea to commemorate the Second Battle of Yeonpyeong. The stand-off over North Korea's nuclear program has also resulted in further operational coordination in the form of exercises designed to demonstrate capabilities and increase pressure on the North Korean regime. An October 2017 exercise called the Maritime Counter Special Operations Exercise (MCSOFEX) involved the USS Ronald Reagan, US destroyers and over 30 ROKN vessels.[111] A month later seven ROKN vessels were involved in four days of exercises which included three US aircraft carriers.[112]

The developing ROKN-US relationship also has implications for ROKN cooperation with the JMSDF. The outstanding strategic, political and historical issues between Seoul and Tokyo serve to drastically limit bilateral operational cooperation between the ROKN and JMSDF. The role of the US and its navy is to act at as facilitator and go-between, providing political cover for both sides to work in a trilateral setting. Naval exercises take place away from the public gaze making it easier for the three services and the ROKN to avoid potentially damaging public opinion regarding such cooperation. The ability to do this is also facilitated by the ROKN's interoperable capabilities without which useful cooperation would not be possible.

The United States was instrumental in developing an intelligence-sharing agreement between South Korea and Japan. The new agreement which came into effect in December 2014 places focus on the threat from North Korea centred on its nuclear weapon and missile capabilities. It also allows for the exchange of information on 'the protection requirements contained within the U.S.—ROK agreement and the U.S.-Japan agreement'.[113] This opens the door for intelligence sharing on a wider range of issues related to Northeast Asia security within the context of previously signed mutual defense treaties. The United States acted as a hub through which this intelligence was shared, therefore direct contact between the security establishments of South Korea and Japan was avoided.[114] In 2016, Japan and South Korea signed a bilateral General Security of Military Information Agreement to facilitate direct information sharing on North Korea.[115]

Operationally, the United States has initiated a series of trilateral naval exercises. Between 2012 and 2017, the three countries' naval forces held twelve trilateral exercises. These exercises have focused on developing key interoperable disciplines and standard operating procedures. For example, the first of these exercises in 2012 sought to improve tactical coordination in BMD scenarios.[116] Later exercises have tested joint capabilities in ASW, maritime interdiction and BMD.[117]

CONCLUSION

Since the end of the Korean War, there has been a substantial change in South Korea's relationship with the United States. South Korea has ended its economic reliance on the United States and is gradually taking greater responsibility for its own security. This chapter has shown that

US control over the South Korea military at the end of the Korean war had a vital foundational impact on the ROKN.

The United States did not view South Korean naval power as a priority and only conceived of its necessity within the context of the KPN. This consideration was first determined in 1954 but continued well into the 1980s. The United States had set the developmental path for the ROKN and even more South Korean independence in terms of procurement during the Yulgok period and after did not change this. The constant presence of the US 7th Fleet and the continental mindset of the South Korean government ensured that the ROKN would remain rooted to the littoral.[118] When it did occur, modernisation was focused on meeting the increasing capabilities of the KPN. What changed was the ROKN's ability to look to foreign suppliers. The United States could no longer restrict South Korean weapons procurement.

Ironically a change was to occur as, South Korea gained increasingly operational autonomy and the nature of warfare began to change with the onset of the RMA, interoperability became more important. As the ROKN became more advanced and developed a blue-water capability, it was of more utility to the United States. It was these two factors which drove the ROKN back towards the USN, a service which in the past had view its South Korean counterpart as largely inconsequential. For the majority of the ROKN's history, the United States has constrained its operational scope. The USN has now embraced the concept of an interoperable and capable ROKN and views it as an important element within their maritime security network in the Asia-Pacific.

One large question remains. What will happen when OPCON is eventually transferred to South Korea. In 2009, when preparing for the proposed OPCON transfer in 2012, the two navies agreed that the ROKN would take the lead and the USN would act in support during wartime. This reversal in operational roles was postponed following the delay in OPCON. But many outstanding issues exist regarding the future chain of command for both USN and ROKN and the ability of the ROKN to take a lead role in any wartime scenario. The closer interoperability and operational cooperation which is evident since the 1990s will serve to mitigate some of these problems. Even after OPCON, the US Navy is unlikely to leave Asia and their technological, tactical and operational development will continue to influence ROKN modernisation well into the future. They challenge for the ROKN, as for all of US allies, will be to keep pace as the US introduces new technologies into its fleet.

NOTES

1. "Last US Ship Transferred to ROK Navy Decommissioned in Ceremony Highlighting Naval Partnership," *Commander, US Naval Forces Korea Public Affairs*, 29 December 2016, http://www.navy.mil/submit/display.asp?story_id=98304, accessed 3 March 2017.
2. South Korea regained peacetime OPCON in 1994. Transfer of OPCON has been delayed twice due to reluctance from both sides to upset the balance of power and stability on the Peninsula. It was first delayed in 2010 following the sinking of the Cheonan and again in 2014 due to the North Korean nuclear crisis.
3. Gordon L. Rottman, *Korean War Order of Battle: United States, United Nations, and Communist Ground, Naval, and Air Forces, 1950–1953* (Westport: Praeger, 2002), 159–60.
4. "Memorandum by the Joint Chiefs of Staff to the Secretary of Defense (Wilson)," 31 March 1954, *Foreign Relations of the United States (FRUS), 1952–1954, Vol. XV, Korea Part 2* (Washington, DC: Government Printing Office, 1984), 1781.
5. "Memorandum by the Joint Chiefs of Staff to the Secretary of Defense (Wilson)," 1783.
6. Ibid., 1782; Robert J. Watson, *History of the Joint Chiefs of Staff, Vol V: The Joint Chiefs of Staff and National Policy 1953–1954* (Washington, DC: Office of Joint History, 1998), 233.
7. "Memorandum by the Joint Chiefs of Staff to the Secretary of Defense (Wilson)," 1783.
8. "Text of Agreed Minute," 19 November 1954, *The Department of State Bulletin*, 31/805 (Washington, DC: Government Printing Office 1954), 810–11.
9. The force level of 79 vessels was included in a September 1954 memo to General Hull the UNC Commander differs from a maximum force level of 83 vessels that was in a March 1954 memo to Secretary of Defence Wilson. The author can find no reason for this discrepancy. See: "Memorandum by the Joint Chiefs of Staff to the Secretary of Defense (Wilson)," 1782; "The Department of the Army to the Commander in Chief, United Nations Command Hull," 15 September 1954, *FRUS, 1952–1954, Vol. XV, Korea Part 2*, 1880.
10. "The Department of the Army to the Commander in Chief, United Nations Command Hull," 1880.
11. Ibid.
12. US National Security Council, *NSC 6018: U.S. Policy Toward Korea*, 28 November 1960, 22.
13. Ibid., 35.

14. Ibid., 37.
15. James S. Lay, NSC 170/1, *A Report to the National Security Council by the Executive Secretary on US Objectives and Courses of Action in Korea*, 20 November 1953, 5.
16. "Memorandum by the Secretary of Defense (Wilson) to the Executive Secretary of the National Security Council (Lay)," 2 April 1954, *FRUS, 1952–1954, Vol. XV, Korea Part 2*, 1778.
17. Jung-ik Kim*The Future of the U.S.-ROK Military Relationship* (London: Macmillan Press, 1996), 34.
18. "Memorandum Distributed by the Secretary of Defense (Wilson) at the 193d Meeting of the National Security Council," 13 April 1954, *FRUS, 1952–1954, Vol. XV, Korea Part 2*, 1788.
19. "Telegram from the Embassy in Korea to the Department of State," 5 September 1959, *FRUS, 1958–1960, Japan; Korea, Vol. XVIII*, Doc. 281.
20. "Memorandum from the Joint Chiefs of Staff to the Secretary of Defense (Wilson)," 11 October 1956, *FRUS, 1955–1957, Korea, Vol. XXIII, Part 2* (Washington, DC: Government Printing Office 1992), Doc. 172.
21. "Memorandum of Discussion at the 411th Meeting of the National Security Council," 25 June 1959, *FRUS, 1958–1960, Japan; Korea, Vol. XVIII* (Washington, DC: Government Printing Office 1994), Doc. 277.
22. "Telegram from the Commander in Chief, United Nations Command (Lemnitzer) to the Department of the Army," 30 January 1956, *FRUS, 1955–1957, Korea, Vol. XXIII, Part 2*, Doc. 113.
23. "Progress Report on NSC 170/1, 'US Objectives and Courses of Actions in Korea'," 26 March 1954, *FRUS, 1952–1954, VXV, Korea Part 2*, 1767.
24. "The President of the Republic of Korea (Rhee) to President Eisenhower," 29 December 1954, *FRUS, 1952–1954, VXV, Korea Part 2*, 1937.
25. "Memorandum of Discussion at the 208th Meeting of the National Security Council," 29 July 1954, *FRUS, 1952–1954, VXV, Korea Part 2*, 1854.
26. "Special National Intelligence Estimate: The Likelihood of Major Hostilities in Korea," 16 May 1968, *FRUS, 1964–1968, Vol. XXIX, Part 1 Korea* (Washington, DC: U.S. Government Printing Office, 2000), 2000.
27. "Memorandum of Conversation, 14 March 1967," *FRUS, 1964–1968, Vol. XXIX, Part 1 Korea*, Doc. 237.

28. "Telegram from the Department of State to the Embassy in Korea," 7 February 1968, *FRUS, 1964–1968, Vol. XXIX, Part 1 Korea*, Doc. 159.
29. "Notes on Conversation Between President Johnson and President Park," 21 December 1967, *FRUS, 1964–1968, Vol. XXIX, Part 1 Korea*, Doc. 140.
30. Included in the package was the provision of helicopters, finance for eight new infantry battalions, equipment for a counter-infiltration battalion, new F-4 Phantom aircraft and a counter-infiltration package worth $32 million. See: "Memorandum from Under Secretary of State (Katzenbach) to President Johnson," 5 February 1968, *FRUS, 1964–1968, Vol. XXIX, Part 1 Korea*, 327.
31. Melvin R. Laird, "A Strong Start in a Difficult Decade: Defense Policy in the Nixon—Ford Years," *International Security* 10, no. 2 (Fall 1985): 7.
32. Henry A. Kissinger, *Memorandum from the President, U.S. Programs in Korea*, 14 March 1970.
33. US National Security Council, *National Security Memorandum No. 48, U.S. Programs in Korea*, 20 March 1970.
34. "Memorandum of Conversation," 1 April 1969, *Foreign Relations of the United States, 1969–1972, Vol. XIX, Part 1, Korea* (Washington, DC: U.S. Government Printing Office, 2010), 9.
35. NSC Under Secretaries Committee, *Memorandum for the President, Subject: Modernization of the Republic of Korea Armed Forces*, 2 September 1970, 3, https://search.proquest.com/dnsa/docview/1679053123/AD7354928B4A4244PQ/1?accountid=8017, accessed 3 March 2018.
36. Ibid.; "Memorandum from the President's Assistant for National Security Affairs (Kissinger) to the Chairman of the NSSM 27 Steering Group (Brown)," 16 September 1969, *FRUS, 1969–1972, Vol. XIX, Part 1, Korea*, 106; "Memorandum from the Joint Chiefs of Staff Representative to the National Security Council Review Group (Unger) to the Chairman of the Review Group (Kissinger)," *FRUS, 1969–1972, Vol. XIX, Part 1, Korea*, 133; "Draft Minutes of a National Security Council Meeting," 4 March 1970, *Foreign Relations of the United States, 1969–1972, Vol. XIX, Part 1, Korea* (Washington, DC: U.S. Government Printing Office, 2010), 145.
37. "Memorandum from the President's Assistant for National Security Affairs (Kissinger) to President Nixon," 22 August 1970, *FRUS, 1969–1972, Vol. XIX, Part 1, Korea* (Washington, DC: U.S. Government Printing Office, 2010), 181.
38. National Security Council, Memorandum for Dr. Kissinger, Subject: Five-Year Korea Program, 30 July 1971, 2.

39. Ibid.
40. United States Joint Chiefs of Staff, *Joint Intelligence Estimate for Planning, Vol. II, FY 1973 through FY 1980, Book VII East Asia and The Western Pacific* (Washington, DC: US Department of Defense, 1970), VII-G-4.
41. "Report by John H. Holdridge of the National Security Council Staff," 16 April 1971, *FRUS, 1969–1972, Vol. XIX, Part 1, Korea*, 233.
42. United States Joint Chiefs of Staff, *Joint Strategic Objective Plan for FY 1973 Through FY 1980, Vol II Analyses and Force Tabulations, Book VII Free World Forces, Part II Major Objectives for Free World Countries, Section 3, The Pacific/Asia Area* (Washington, DC: US DOD, 1970), 3-G-5;
43. Ibid.
44. *Memorandum for the President, Subject: Korean Force Modernisation*, 25 July 1973, Korea-NSDM 48, NSC East Asian and Pacific Affairs Staff: File, 1969–1977, Gerald R. Ford Presidential Library.
45. A further *Gearing*-class was delivered in 1978.
46. "Memorandum from Secretary of Defense Laird to President Nixon," 19 July 1971, *FRUS, 1969–1972, Vol. XIX, Part 1, Korea*, 255.
47. Bureau of Intelligence and Research, *North and South Korea: The Military Balance*, 23 June 1975, 1.
48. Ibid., 7.
49. Central Intelligence Agency, *Military Balance on the Korean Peninsula*, 10 May 1978, 3.
50. "Memorandum of Conversation," 27 August 1975, *Foreign Relations of the United States, 1969–1976, Vol. E-12, Documents on East and Southeast Asia* (Washington, DC: Government Printing Office 2013), Doc. 271.
51. Republic of Korea Ministry of National Defense, *Jajugukbanggwa Uriui Anbo* [Self-Reliant National Defense Capability and Our Security] (Seoul: ROK MND, 2003), 21–23.
52. Jung-ik Kim *The Future of the U.S.-ROK Military Relationship*, 35.
53. Ibid.
54. NSC Under Secretaries Committee, *Memorandum for the President, Re-examination of the Korea Force Modernization Plan*, 30 May 1973.
55. Between 1971 and 1977 the ROK went from paying for only 42.5% of its defence burden to 87.4%. See: Jung-ik Kim, *The Future of the U.S.-ROK Military Relationship*, 40.
56. Department of State, *Policy Problems in Korea*, January 1976; Joo-hong Kim "The Armed Forces," in *The Park Chung Hee Era: The Transformation of South Korea*, ed. Kim Byung-kook and Ezra F. Vogel (Cambridge: Harvard University Press, 2011), 178.

57. Defense Security Cooperation Agency, *Fiscal Year Series as of 30 September 2015* (Washington, DC: Department of Defense, 2010), 77–80.
58. The White House, "Memorandum of Conversation," 5 July 1979, Memorandum 4112-X.
59. Young-joo Cho "The Naval Policy of the Republic of Korea: From the Beginnings to the Twenty-First Century" (Unpublished PhD Dissertation, University of Hull, 2003), 136.
60. Ibid., 168.
61. International Institute of Strategic Studies, *The Military Balance 1975–1976* (London: International Institute of Strategic Studies, 1975); International Institute of Strategic Studies, *The Military Balance 1992–1993* (London: Brassey's, 1992).
62. South Korea, Seoul, *ROK Government's Request for Two Destroyers*, 5 January 1978, ID1978SEOUL00054_d.
63. Department of State, *Sale of Ships on Loan/Lease*, 21 April 1973, ID 1973STATE075795.
64. American Embassy Seoul, *CPIC Production Funding*, 21 July 1974. 1974SEOUL04544_b.
65. ROKN Headquarters, *Daehanminguk haegu = The Republic of Korea Navy* [The Republic of Korea Navy = The Republic of Korea Navy] (Chungnam: ROKN Headquarters, 2008), 211.
66. Ibid., 35.
67. Ibid., 39.
68. "Minutes of the Secretary of State's Staff Meeting," 6 January 1975, *Foreign Relations of the United States, 1969–1976, Vol. E-12, Documents on East Asia, 1973–1976* (Washington, DC: US Government Printing Office, 2013), 34.
69. US Embassy Seoul, *Possible ROK Third Party Procurement of Major Military Items*, 17 January 1975, https://wikileaks.org/plusd/cables/1975SEOUL00329_b.html, accessed 3 March 2018.
70. SIPRI, *SIPRI Arms Transfers Database*, www.sipri.org/contents/armstrad/as_data.html, accessed 21 February 2018.
71. American Embassy Seoul, *Assessment of US Security Assistance Programs for FY 1979*, 11 August 1977, https://wikileaks.org/plusd/cables/1977SEOUL06708_c.html, accessed 3 March 2018.
72. Ibid.
73. Young-joo Cho *The Naval Policy of the Republic of Korea*, 138,
74. American Embassy Seoul, *Korean Frigate Project*, 2 July 1976, https://wikileaks.org/plusd/cables/1976SEOUL05107_b.html, accessed 3 March 2018.

75. "Memorandum of Conversation," 27 August 1975, *FRUS, 1969–1976, Vol. E-12, Documents on East and Southeast Asia, 1973–1976*, Doc. 270.
76. Ibid.
77. "Minutes of the Secretary of State's Staff Meeting," 6 January 1975, *Foreign Relations of the United States, 1969–1976, Vol. E-12, Documents on East Asia, 1973–1976* (Washington, DC: US Government Printing Office, 2013), 36.
78. US Embassy Seoul, *ROK Interest in the Purchase of Submarines*, 30 March 1979, https://wikileaks.org/plusd/cables/1979SEOUL04656_e.html, accessed 3 March 2018.
79. Eui-sung Chung *Ultramodern Conventional Submarine KSX as a Leverage for the Future Defense of the Korean Peninsula* (Seoul: Korea Institute of Maritime Studies, 2007), 141–42; Interview with Admiral An Byeong-tae, April 2011.
80. Michael McDevitt, "Final Report," in *Workshop Report: The Future of ROK Navy-US Navy Cooperation*, ed. Michael McDevitt (Alexandria: Centre for Naval Analyses, 2007), 5–6.
81. Robert Karniol, "Acquiring a Global Viewpoint," *Jane's Defence Weekly* 22, no. 18, 5 November 2004.
82. Geoffrey Till, "Editorial Introduction," in *Seapower: Theory and Practice*, ed. Geoffrey Till (Essex: Frank Cass, 1994), 1–6, 5.
83. United States Department of Defense, *Asia-Pacific Maritime Security Strategy* (Washington, DC: United States Department of Defense, 2016), 22.
84. Bryan Clark, Peter Haynes, Jesse Sloman, and Timothy Walton, *Restoring American Seapower: A New Fleet Architecture for the United States Navy* (Washington, DC: Centre for Strategic and Budgetary Assessments, 2017), 45–46.
85. Michael McDevitt, "The Maritime Relationship," in *The U.S.-South Korea Alliance Meeting New Security Challenges*, ed. Scott Snyder (London: Lynne Reinner, 2012), 23.
86. Christopher Yung et al., *Trilateral Naval Cooperation: Japan, US, Korea—A Workshop Report* (Virginia: Centre of Naval Analyses, 1996), 18–19.
87. Ibid.
88. Sung Hwan Wie et al., *Prospects for U.S.-Korean Naval Relations in the 21st Century* (Virginia: Centre for Naval Analyses, 1994), 19.
89. Robert T. Collins, "Commander Combined Naval Component Command; A Significant Change in a Command Relationship" (Unpublished MA Dissertation, US Naval War College, 1996), 10–11.
90. Ibid., 12; ROK-US Combined Forces Command, *Air-Ground Operations-Korea, CFC PUB 3-2.2*, 15 June 2002, 4.

91. Edward J. Marolda, *Ready Seapower: A History of the U.S. Seventh Fleet* (Washington, DC: Naval History and Heritage Command, 2011), 120–21.
92. Robert T. Collins, *Commander Combined Naval Component Command*, 13.
93. Sung Hwan Wie et al., *Prospects for U.S.-Korean Naval Relations*, 21.
94. Ibid.
95. Senate Armed Services Committee, *Statement of General Thomas A. Schwartz, Commander in Chief United Nations Command/Combined Forces Command & Command United States Forces Korea Before the 107th Congress Senate Armed Service Committee*, 5 March 2002, 17.
96. Michael Raska, *Military Innovation in Small States: Creating a Reverse Asymmetry* (Oxon: Routledge 2016), 107.
97. Harry H. Blanke III, "Korea Theatre Command and Control Enhancements Support Decisive Actions," *Signal*, November 2006, https://www.afcea.org/content/korea-theater-command-and-control-enhancements-support-decisive-actions, accessed 4 February 2018.
98. The US Navy describes the GCCS-M system as one that 'supports decision making at all echelons of command with a single, integrated, scalable C4I system that fuses, correlates, filters, maintains, and displays location and attribute information on friendly, hostile, and neutral land, sea, and air forces, integrated with available intelligence and environmental information'. See: United States Navy, *Program Guide 2013* (Washington, DC: Department of the Navy, 2013), 147.
99. Young-il Kim "Status of Korean Navy's Tactical C4ISR Systems Acquisition and Issues on Interoperability between ROK-U.S. Combined Naval Operations," in *Bytes and Bullets: Information Technology Revolution and National Security on the Korean Peninsula*, ed. Alexander Y. Mansourov (Hawaii: Asia Pacific Centre for Security Studies, 2005), 183; Republic of Korea Navy, *Haegun haeoemugi doip gwallyeon* [Naval Overseas Weapons Acquisitions] (Seoul: Republic of Korea Navy, 2005).
100. The KDX-II is scheduled to receive the MDLMS in the future. See: Ultra Electronics, *MDLMS, Multi Data Link Management System: Ultra Electronics Advanced Tactical Systems* (PPT Presentation, 2017), http://www.ultra-ats.com/files/mdlmspresentation17-s-0382.pdf, accessed 1 February 2018.
101. Author conducted Interview with Admiral An Byeong-tae, April, 2011.
102. Brian G. Reynolds, "USN Hosts ROKN 45th Submarine Warfare Committee Meeting," *Commander, US Pacific Fleet*, 12 May 2017, http://www.cpf.navy.mil/news.aspx/140017, accessed 15 November 2017.

103. Duk-ki Kim "ROKN's Requirements for Countering North Korea's Potential Nuclear and Ballistic Missile Threats," in *The Evolution of the Maritime Security Environment in Northeast Asia and ROKN-USN Cooperation* (Seoul: Korea Institute for Maritime Studies, 2016), 171.

104. Abraham Essenmacher, "US, ROK Navies Strengthen Partnership Through ASW Cooperation," *Commander, US Pacific Fleet*, 27 April 2015, http://www.cpf.navy.mil/news.aspx/030536, accessed 15 November 2017.

105. "Naval Forces Korea Commander Highlights US, ROK Cooperation at Symposium," *Commander, US Naval Forces Korea Public Affairs*, 6 June 2016, http://www.pacom.mil/Media/News/News-Article-View/Article/792527/naval-forces-korea-commander-highlights-us-rok-cooperation-at-symposium/, accessed 15 November 2017.

106. "S. Korea, US to Share Underwater Data on N. Korean Waters," *KBS World Radio*, 28 August 2016, http://world.kbs.co.kr/english/news/news_Po_detail.htm?No=121419&id=Po, accessed 15 November 2017.

107. Park, Bo-ram, "USFK's Naval Forces Move Headquarters to S. Korean Base in Busan," *Yonhap News Agency*, 19 February 2016, http://english.yonhapnews.co.kr/news/2016/02/19/0200000000AEN20160219009000315.html, accessed 15 November 2017.

108. House Appropriations Committee, *Statement of General Curtis M. Scaparrotti Commander, United Nations Command; Republic of Korea and United States Combined Forces Command; And United States Forces Korea in Support of U.S. Pacific Command's Testimony Before the House Appropriations Committee-Defense Subcommittee*, 26 April 2017, 08.

109. "Allies' Navy Forces Launch Combined Maritime Operations Center in Jan.," *Yonhap News Agency*, 21 May 2017. http://english.yonhapnews.co.kr/search1/2603000000.html?cid=AEN20170520001600315, accessed 15 November 2017.

110. Senate Armed Services Committee, *Statement of General Vincent K. Brooks, Commander, United Nations Command; Commander United States-Republic of Korea Combined Forces Command; And Commander, United States Forces Korea before the Senate Armed Services Committee*, 23 February 2016, 10.

111. Franz-Stefan Gady, "US, ROK Navies Hold Military Drill off Korean Peninsula," *The Diplomat*, 16 October 2017, https://thediplomat.com/2017/10/us-rok-navies-hold-military-drill-off-korean-peninsula/, accessed 03 March 2018.

112. Brad Lendon, "North Korea: 3 US Aircraft Carriers Creating 'Worst Ever' Situation," *CNN*, 20 November 2017, https://edition.cnn.

com/2017/11/12/politics/us-navy-three-carrier-exercise-pacific/ index.html, accessed 1 March 2018.

113. *Trilateral Information Sharing Arrangement Concerning the Nuclear and Missile Threats Posed by North Korea among the Ministry of National Defense of The Republic of Korea, The Ministry of Defense of Japan, and the Department of Defense of the United States of America*, http://www. defense.gov/pubs/Trilateral-Information-Sharing-Arrangement.pdf?-source=GovDelivery, accessed 1 February 2015.

114. Ibid.

115. "South Korea, Japan Agree Intelligence-Sharing on North Korea Threat," *Reuters*, 23 November 2016, https://www.reuters.com/article/us-southkorea-japan-military/south-korea-japan-agree-intelligence-sharing-on-north-korea-threat-idUSKBN13I068.

116. United States Senate, Committee on Armed Services, *Department of Defense Authorization of Appropriations for Fiscal Year 2014 and the Future Years Defense Program: U.S. Pacific Command*, 9 April 2014, 425–26, http://www.armed-services.senate.gov/imo/media/doc/DODauthorizationFY2014_fullcommittee_hearings_2013.pdf, accessed 14 January 2015.

117. Ministry of Defense of Japan, *Defense of Japan 2017* (Tokyo: Ministry of Defense of Japan, 2017), 500.

118. Republic of Korea Navy Headquarters, *Haegun bijeon 2020* [Navy vision 2020] (Gyeryong: Republic of Korea Navy Headquarters, 1999), 80.

CHAPTER 6

Creating a Naval Identity

South Korea, being a country created out of the geopolitical competition in Asia following WWII, has a strategic culture which is informed by the historical memory of Japanese invasion and Chinese suzerainty but is ultimately driven by the trenchant division of the peninsula and the need to manage the US alliance.[1] This reality plays a substantial role in determining how elites in South Korea understand and set security policy. It also restricts their ability to make changes to South Korea's strategic outlook if such changes conflict with deep-rooted public expectations of its orientation.[2]

Although South Korea is a country that uses that sea for economic advantage, the history of the Korean peninsula and South Korea itself reveals only a fleeting interest in the military elements of seapower. Any form of naval identity has only been briefly embraced and for most of Korea's history, the ruling elites on the peninsula have not maintained any sense of a formal relationship with the sea nor have they demonstrated any interest in the long-term development of naval power. Writing in 1981, seventeen years before he became president, Kim Dae-jung argued that South Korea had no sense of a naval identity, stating:

> In spite of the fact that our country faces the ocean on three sides, we have refused completely to recognise this reality. This is why we have been bothered so persistently by the Japanese. If we were to try to identify the

© The Author(s) 2019
I. Bowers, *The Modernisation of the Republic of Korea Navy*, Critical Studies of the Asia-Pacific, https://doi.org/10.1007/978-3-319-92291-1_6

great navigators or others engaged in maritime activities, Chang Po-go from the late Silla period is about the only one that comes to mind.[3]

This bold thesis summed up the difficulty the ROKN would face in its efforts to embed the importance of seapower into South Korea's political and public consciousness. The ROKN has recognised that without a sustained alteration in South Korea's internal strategic perception, long-term ROKN blue-water transformation would not be politically or financially sustainable. It would need to foster a changed understanding in South Korea of the strategic importance of seapower and imbed this new naval identity in the minds of the public and political elite. This new identity would place naval power at the heart of a transformed South Korean strategic consciousness and ensure that future security planning would have a maritime orientation.

This chapter explores how the ROKN has gone about its task of creating a new South Korean naval identity. It argues that the ROKN has looked to link itself to Korean and South Korean history to create an ideational narrative where the navy is the natural successor to great Korean historical figures. In doing so it is attempting to position itself as the service which protects South Korea against all future threats. Its campaign includes public engagement to sell the ROKN to the general populace and leveraging a growing academic interest in seapower to persuade policymakers of the navy's importance to South Korean security. However, this project is long-term and has been fraught with difficulties. The continental threat from North Korea and the sinking of the *Cheonan* forced the ROKN to suspend but not stop its naval identity-building efforts. A new opportunity has now presented itself as the strategic situation both in North Korea and in maritime Northeast Asia has provided the ROKN with a space to justify continued naval expansion. It remains to be seen if its efforts to foster a South Korean naval identity will be successful or if South Korea's current embrace of an expanded naval role is merely a repetition of history and a temporary reaction to strategic circumstance.

NAVAL IDENTITY AND WHY IT MATTERS

Historians and political scientists alike have acknowledged the difficulties states face in building and then sustaining seapower. Some states have a natural geographic, strategic and cultural inclination towards the sea. In these cases, such as the United Kingdom, the Netherlands and even present-day Japan, seapower develops organically over a long period.[4] The role of the sea in national security and economic development becomes part of a state's strategic culture and identity. Essentially, the maritime and naval traditions of a country are an ever-present factor in the political and public mindset and this informs the strategic decisions of the ruling elites. In other cases, seapower is developed artificially as consequence of government directives.[5] States such as Russia and Imperial Germany have sought to force the development of seapower to meet certain strategic or political goals. In this latter case, competing strategic issues on land, changed political circumstances or the reprioritisation of state resources often interrupts the long-term momentum that seapower development requires.[6]

Even in the former case, the strategic and cultural rationale for substantial investment in a naval capability that is often out of sight and out of mind of the general populace must be continuously advocated. If not, as in the case of the United Kingdom, a state may suffer sea blindness as the public and political elites alike may lose their strategic understanding of, and emotional connection to the sea.[7] This can result in a navy losing its place in a state's strategic narrative with a consequent reduction in capabilities and funding.

The cementing of democracy in the early 1993, together with the potential for improved ties with North Korea, a growing political recognition of the economic importance of the sea and ambitions to be a globalised power all combined to provide naval leaders in South Korea with an opportunity to create a new naval identity. This is not an easy task, as late as 1999 the ROKN acknowledged that public support was needed to legitimise its modernisation goals and that previous efforts to engage with the populace had proven insufficient.[8]

The ROKN understood that South Korea's form of sea blindness restricted their ability to grow into a substantial blue-water force. Unlike in China where naval modernisation had the full support of political elites who successfully convinced the public of its importance, in South Korea the ROKN has to continuously convince both the public and the politicians in charge as to necessity of seapower development.[9] If successful, the ROKN can lay the groundwork for a sustainable and strategic approach to seapower in South Korea. However, if it fails, the ROKN's long-term ambitions for an advanced naval operational capability may be thwarted, as naval capacity will not have primacy of place in strategic, economic or political decision-making.

HISTORY AND IDENTITY: PLACING THE ROKN

The ROKN has sought to utilise history to bolster its security credentials within South Korea. A rich national naval history replete with victories and defeats can provide strategic guidance to contemporary planners and may provide a navy with a strategic language with which to 'articulate its role in the context of defence policy and the development of its fleet and capabilities'.[10] At the same time, history can both provide a navy with traditions from which it can project an image to the public and political elites and build an internal operational ethos.[11]

The problem the ROKN faces in using history is the relative paucity of South Korean naval traditions. Unlike, the JMSDF, which built its identity and strategic approach on the rich operational history of the Imperial Navy that preceded it, the ROKN has no such immediate antecedents.[12]

Korean history reveals an intermittent relationship with its surrounding waters. While historical evidence demonstrates that people living on the Korean peninsula have long utilised the sea for sustenance and trade, Korea arguably reached its maritime zenith in the ninth century. This success was down to one figure. Chang Bo-go (790–856 AD) was a merchant turned naval officer during the Silla dynasty. He exploited Korean maritime superiority to crush the threat of Japanese and Chinese piracy in the waters of Northeast Asia and for a brief period Korea dominated the trade links of the region.[13] After his death, Korean maritime activity slowly declined as the ruling elites once again turned inward and Korea's control of the sea ended by the end of the ninth century.[14]

While maritime activity did continue in coastal communities around the peninsula, it was only in the sixteenth century that the sea and the importance of naval power became a matter of immediate national security. The Japanese attack on the Korean Peninsula in 1592 sparked the six-year long Imjin Wars. The Joseon Kingdom's inability to control the waters around Korea left the country exposed to Japanese power projection. However, as much as the water is a medium for attack it is also something that can be defended. When Admiral Yi Sun-shin took control of the Korean fleet, he changed the course of the invasion. He married advanced naval technology to innovative naval tactics and managed to defeat the numerically superior Japanese forces in a succession of naval battles. This allowed the Korean navy to cut Japanese supply lines and thereby assist ground forces in containing the Japanese advance.[15]

Much of his success was linked to the Turtle Ship or *Geobukseon*. This was the world's first iron-plated vessel. Its covered deck, which protected its sailors, was most likely studded with spikes and armoured with iron plates making boarding very difficult. It also possessed a powerful broadside of up to 10 cannon. As historian Jeremy Black argues, the Turtle Ship was one of the most 'impressive warships of the age' and Yi Sun-shin's inventiveness in integrating the Turtle Ship with cannon 'demonstrated the role of a gunned warship off East Asia' for the first time.[16] Following Yi Sun-shin's death in battle in 1598 and the Japanese withdrawal from the Korean Peninsula, Korean seapower once again began a slow decline.

Despite maintaining a naval fleet in the seventeenth and eighteenth centuries, Korean elites essentially neglected the sea due to a combination of political infighting, socio-cultural opposition and eventual inward looking isolationist policies.[17] Maritime trade was confined to a limited interaction with Japan that was as much diplomatic as it was commercial.[18] Korea, while successful in achieving internal social stability, fell victim to the rise of western powers in the region and the expansion of Japanese interests on mainland Asia. By the end of the nineteenth century, Korean naval power was unable to resist the advanced capabilities of the Imperial Japanese Navy that facilitated Tokyo's increasing control over the peninsula. With the formal colonisation of Korea in 1910, Imperial Japan ended an independent Korean maritime or naval presence until after the Second World War.

Exploiting History

Drawing upon this history, the ROKN and advocates of South Korean seapower have sought link contemporary naval modernisation to the famed figures of Yi Sun-shin and Chang Bo-go and have frequently emphasised the disastrous security consequences when Korea does not possess naval power to protect its interests.

The ROKN has made a substantial effort to position itself as the successor to the legacy and competency of Yi Sun-shin and reclaim him as a naval figure. In many ways Admiral Yi Sun-shin towers above other Korean historical figures and is a prominent element in South Korea's broader historical identity. In recent South Korean history his legacy has been used in numerous ways, from the promotion of nationalist ideals to the embodiment of the perfect Korean character. In 2014, a movie about

Yi Sun-shin broke all South Korean box office records indicating how he remains a central figure in South Korean identity.[19]

His statue stands tall in the centre of Seoul. Built in 1968, it portrays Yi Sun-shin wearing armour and holding a sword and Park Chung-hee commissioned it to symbolise Korean resistance and independence from the Japanese.[20] Park Chung-hee looked to use Korean history to bolster certain elements of his policies and to provide commentary on the state of the nation; Yi Sun-shin was central to this approach.[21] His characterisations progressed from a national hero in the early 1960's to someone who had been at the cutting edge of military technology. He also came to symbolise the perfect Korean, loyal and willing to serve the nation. This came at a time when national security was a major concern in South Korea and issues such as conscription and the use of reserve forces were at the forefront of the national debate.[22]

Because of this broad ideological positioning of Admiral Yi, he was not consistently portrayed within a predominantly naval context and as such has not entered the public's mind as primarily a naval figure. However, the naval community has made significant efforts to reclaim Yi's legacy. As Yi Sun-shin was primarily a coastal admiral, his ideational utility in promoting an expanded blue-water capability is a little problematic for the ROKN.[23] Using lectures, imagery and publications, the ROKN and naval institutes have sought to position Yi Sun-shin as a defender of Korean sovereignty on the seas around the peninsula and the navy as his natural successor. This is an explicit effort to ideationally and strategically link the ROKN to the current and future protection of South Korea.

The ROKN, through Yi Sun-shin is attempting to remind the South Korean public and political elites of the necessity of seapower and the highlight narrative that it was Korean naval forces that saved the country from Japanese invasion. The ROKN named two vessels in honour of the admiral and built a replica of a turtle ship that is on display at the Korean Naval Academy.[24] The turtle-ship itself features prominently in the insignia of many of the ROKN's commands including those of the First, Second and Third Fleets. Admirals, supportive academics and even politicians have all stated that South Korea should not forget the mistakes of the past and ignore the strategic importance of the sea. For example, in his 2008 inauguration speech, the 27th ROKN CNO Admiral Jung Ok-Keun, talked about the need for advanced naval forces, stating:

Nations who fail to learn from history have retrogressed or perished...if future vision does not exist, neither will development nor hope...we must take deeply into heart [sic] the historical facts and grim reality.[25]

To create an ideational basis for an expanded, blue-water naval role the ROKN has also looked to exploit the legacy of Chang Bo-go. Although his position within the Korean historical narrative is difficult to judge, he is certainly representative of an ongoing effort to publicise Silla maritime history and his public portrayal is that of an archetypal Korean legendary figure.

There is some indication that his profile is rising within South Korea with the making of a TV drama about his life in 2004 and a museum dedicated to his control of the Northeast Asian maritime sphere opened near his traditional base on Wando in 2008. Alongside Yi Sun-shin, he provides the historical linkage between Korea's past maritime supremacy (no matter how brief) and its potential naval power. Kim Young-sam was the first president to link Chang Bo-go to the future of the ROKN in a speech made to the Korean Naval Academy in 1994, saying:

We are surrounded by the ocean on three sides but have never uti-lised the sea well. The great achievements of Admiral Chang Bo-go and Chungmugong were not properly followed. However now, in terms of change and revolution we are heading to the Pacific Ocean with confi-dence based on change and reform.[26]

In 1996, the ROKN began a formal campaign to inform the public about Chang Bo-go's career and legacy.[27] His control of Northeast Asian waters and the economic benefits it brought provide the ROKN with a slim but nonetheless important historical link between national prosper-ity and naval power. The ROKN named its counter-piracy mission in the Gulf of Aden *Cheonghae*. This name was chosen to honour Chang Bo-go whose headquarters was called *Chonghaejin* and was of central impor-tance to his operations against piracy in Northeast Asia.[28]

Both Yi Sun-shin and Chang Bo-go feature prominently in political speeches made at naval academy commencement ceremonies, it is impor-tant to note these occasions are the primary arena for the announcement of naval policy and as such, through media reporting find wider audi-ence than the ROKN and assembled guests. Excerpts of these speeches demonstrate a deliberate attempt to foster a naval identity through linking current and future roles of the ROKN to these significant figures of the past.

> The Navy has a duty of guaranteeing the safety of all ships and tankers going far and near in the glorious tradition of Admirals Yi, Sun-shin and Chang, Po-go. (Kim Dae-jung 2000)[29]

> Our navy has a brilliant legacy, indeed. Four hundred years ago, the navy of the Joseon Kingdom, under the command of Yi, Sun-shin, saved the nation that was like a flickering candle before the storming invaders...You are the true descendants of Chang, Bo-go, the great commissioner of the Cheonghae garrison, and Yi, Sun-shin. Your heartbeat is powered by the spirit of Chang, Bo-go who once had absolute control over all East Asian seas. (Roh Moo-hyun 2003)[30]

> You will be the core members to staff the major task fleet the Korean Navy will be building up. You are the descendants of Commissioner Chang, Bo-go who controlled the East Asian sea routes and Admiral Yi, Sun-shin who saved the country from foreign invaders. (Roh Moo-hyun 2007)[31]

The ROKN and Ship Names

In 1993, the ROKN christened the first of its new *Type 209* submarines, the *Chang Bogo*. Naming a vessel after an historical figure, even one so closely associated to Korean seapower was a substantial departure for the ROKN as previously the navy had named its vessels after geographic features. This first use of an historical figure connected the ROKN to a long tradition of navies across the world using ships names for political or ideational ends.

In its formative years, the Imperial German Navy named its ships after towns and cities across the newly unified country to develop a cohesive sense of national identity. They also drew upon famous German military leaders, mostly from the land in order to provide the navy with a type of artificial martial tradition. As noted historian Jan Rüger states, 'the military past was to offer the navy an Ersatz tradition, it served as a source of national identification'.[32] Germany was not alone in utilising such tools; the Royal Navy too drew upon the names of cities and great military leaders as a method of solidifying a somewhat divided United Kingdom under the concept of a great maritime tradition.[33] The use of cities as ship names provided the Royal Navy with the opportunity to put on events in these cities and create a sense unity between the ship, its crew and the populace of its namesake.

With the introduction of new classes of vessel and the espousal of the blue-water concept, the ROKN formally expanded its naming conventions in order to achieve similar effects. As Table 6.1 shows, the navy has now spread a wide net for its ship names, linking itself directly to Korean and South Korean historical figures and military heroes. In doing so, the ROKN has seized the opportunity to create a more advanced naval identity for itself, one that is directly linked to Korean history.

Ships names are now a tool for the ROKN to instil within its officers, sailors and the public a sense of a naval identity and tradition, one that embodies the spirit of these Korean heroes.[34] The names of the KDX series of destroyers encapsulates this ideational approach. As Table 6.2 shows, each of these names are related to either nation building or national protection efforts and promote the image of the navy as a service that is natural successor to those who had protected Korea and South Korea in the past. The ROKN is placing itself at the forefront of national security and state development.

The ROKN's naming policy also reveals a move to utilise their own recent history to develop its own service traditions. Sohn Won-il the

Table 6.1 ROKN naming conventions

Type	Naming convention
DDG/DDH	Person who has contributed greatly to national affairs
FFG/FF	Special, metropolitan cities, provincial capitals
PCC	Middle and small sized cities
PKG	Heroes who have died in battle since the founding of the ROKN
PKM	Birds
LPH	Outermost Islands
LST	Mountains
MLS	Mine warfare campaigns during the Korean War
MHC/MSH	Towns/Areas near naval bases
AOE	Large bodies of water (lakes/rivers)
ASR	Region with strong maritime connection
ATS	Coastal industrial cities
SS (209)	Historical figures with a connection to the sea
SS (214)	Independence Movement figures

Taken from ROKN Headquarters, *Gandanhago pyeonhage ilgeul su issneun haegungaideubug* [A simple and easy to read naval guidebook] (Gyeryong: ROKN Headquarters, 2016), 57

Table 6.2 Ship names of the KDX-I, KDX-II and KDX-III classes of destroyer

Hull number	Name	Notes
DDG 991	Sejong Daewang	Ruled during the Joseon Dynasty between 1418 and 1450; he is credited with inventing Hangul, upgrading the military and defeating Japanese raiding
DDG 992	Yulgok Yi L	Sixteenth century scholar who advocated the training of a large army to fight of the Japanese
DDG 993	Seoae Yu Seong-ryong	Korean scholar and prime minister who was in office at the time of the sixteenth century Japanese invasion of Korea
DDH 975	Chungmugong Yi Sun-Shin	One of the most prominent figures in Korean history. As an admiral, he defeated the Japanese on numerous occasions
DDH 976	Munmu the Great	A seventh century Silla King credited with defeating the Tang invasion of Korea and unifying the peninsula
DDH 977	Dae Jo-yeong	An eighth century king who created the Balhae and defeated a Chinese Tang invasion
DDH 978	Wang Geon	A tenth century King who founded the Goryeo dynasty
DDH 979	Gang Gam-chan	A Goryeo general, credited with defeating the Mongolian Khitan invasion in the eleventh century
DDH 981	Choi Young	A Goryeo general of the twelfth century, among his many victories was the defeat of the Japanese Wokou pirates
DDH 971	Gwanggaeto Daewang	A King of Goguryeo credited with greatly expanding the power and influence of his dynasty
DDH 972	Eulji Mundeok	A seventh century Goguryeo general, he defeated a Sui Chinese invasion. He is one of the earliest symbols of Korean nationalism
DDH 973	Yang Manchun	A seventh century military commander, Yang is famous for refusing to surrender a fortress and thus delaying and eventually defeating a Tang invasion

ROKN's founder looms large in its historical identity. The ROKN typically places him, alongside Chang Bo-go and Yi Sun-shin in its literature and identifies him as both a patriot and Korean War hero. Unlike the ROKA whose founding leaders served under the Japanese military during the WWII and the Japanese occupation, Admiral Sohn did not; indeed, he had to leave Korea because of his anti-Japanese activities.[35] This has allowed the ROKN to imply that they are not tainted by the Japanese occupation; as a result they named the lead ship of their *Type 214* class of submarines in his honour (the rest of this class are named after figures from the Korean Independence Movement during the Japanese occupation).

The ROKN has also sought to honour the sailors who have fought or died in historical and contemporary combat against North Korea. The first six ships in the new class of PKG (*Gumdoksuri*-class) are named after the sailors who died at the Second Battle of Yeonpyeong. At the time, the South Korean press noted that this was an unusual more given the potential for inflaming relations with North Korea.[36] However, for the ROKN it has allowed them to honour its fallen sailors and link their legacy to ongoing operations.

This contextual emphasis on the historical record has naturally pushed the ROKN towards leaning on Korea's past history with Japan to draw ideational inspiration. Some have misconstrued this as a deliberate signal that the ROKN viewed or views the Japanese as a potential threat. While Japan forms part of South Korea's security calculus, the use of figures related to independence from Japan equally reflects the reality that the major seaborne threats to Korea have come from across the East Sea.

The relationship between the two countries now forms part of the ideological bedrock with which the ROKN's has formed is naval identity. While such names may resonate with the general nationalist inclinations of the South Korean public when it comes to South Korea–Japan relations, they are not a signal of future intent but rather are attempts by the ROKN to link itself with the strongest possible historical identifiers of Korean independence and nationalism.

An example of this is the naming in 2007 of the ROKN's new LPH class of ship as the *Dokdo*-class. The use of this name caused a minor diplomatic spat with the Japanese government lodging an official protest.[37] Yet, from the ROKN's perspective, it served a dual purpose. Naming the vessel after the disputed territory provided the public with a direct linkage between the ROKN and the protection of South Korean interests. This was made clear at the ship's launch when Admiral Ahn Ki-seok the then CNO said:

> The Dokdo ship reflects the Korean people's desire for the Navy to faith-
> fully carry out its mission of protecting the national interest in oceans, as
> well as guarding out territorial sovereignty.[38]

The name also served an important political purpose. In using Dokdo
as a ship name, the ROKN took advantage of particularly tense time in
South Korea–Japan relations to remind political elites of a naval role that
was separate from the dominant North Korean threat.[39]

PUBLIC PRESENTATION

Persuading the public as to the benefits of naval power can be problematic. Naval vessels operate out of sight and much of their strategic value
goes unseen. The ROKN pursues various methods to alter the public's
image of the navy and cement its importance within the public perception of South Korean security.

One of their primary methods is the production of publicity booklets aimed at explaining not only the roles and duties of the ROKN, but
also the importance of seapower and naval power to South Korean security and development. To explain blue-water modernisation, the ROKN
published a volume in 1995 and again in 1998 titled *The Navy Heading
Toward the 21st Century*. This was the first attempt to explain to the
public the importance of South Korean seapower in relation to South
Korea's security, economic development and place on the world stage.[40]
Since then the ROKN has produced a number of booklets that provide
information about ROKN culture, traditions and operations. Many of
these now explain in some detail how the ROKN deters North Korea
and is pursuing future operational roles.[41]

The publication of these books occurs within the context of a military culture that has always been reluctant to provide any information
about its operations or capabilities. However, it is evident that the navy
has become more accustomed to releasing information about its operations and intentions. *Navy Vision 2020* was a classified document when
it was released in 1998 and therefore not available to the public. When
the ROKN produced *Navy Vision 2030*, it published an abridged version
for public consumption. While this gradual loosening of military censor-
ship has allowed for a more detailed public examination of naval policy,
reflecting the growing importance of influencing the electorate, publicly
available data remains limited. In comparison with the US Navy or other

western navies, the ROKN's publications are sparse on detail especially regarding doctrine and core operational concepts. There is for comparison purposes no ROKN version of the US Navy's *Navy Operational Concept* or *Cooperative Strategy for the 21st Century* in terms of breadth of detail.[42]

The ROKN has also invested in information technology to connect to the wider South Korean public. This should not be a surprise given that South Korean is one of the most connected and tech-savvy states in the world.[43] This embrace of IT is a key element in the ROKN's public engagement strategy to create a naval culture in South Korea.[44] It maintains a useful website that has an average hit rate of approximately 12,000 visits per day; creates its own on-line content including a monthly magazine and videos, and it disseminates information through a variety of social networking platforms.[45]

A concerted effort is made to project a more modern and independent image of the service. This includes the development and use of a corporate image concept in the early 2000s.[46] As part of this approach, the ROKN produced a new logo based on the shape of an aircraft carrier. The ROKN states that this logo promotes the image, ideals and ambition of a twenty-first century blue-water navy.[47] Some versions of the logo also included the use of English alongside the Korean alphabet, Hangul. Much like the inclusion of an aircraft carrier, this mixed linguistic construction highlights modernity and a forward-looking service.[48]

In 1992, the ROKN began using the slogan, *to the sea, to the world*. The slogan espoused the concept that the sea was the gateway through which South Korea could enter the developed world. As with the logo, the slogan adorned the majority of ROKN publications, was prominent in social and traditional media. In 2008 a new slogan was introduced which the ROKN would use alongside *to the sea, to the world*. This slogan, *the power of the navy, the future of Korea*, in the navies words was designed to signal that 'naval strength is the most efficient means to secure the future of the Republic of Korea'.[49]

These efforts to engage the public run through various media run hand in hand with a number of other initiatives designed to increase the ROKN's visibility and persuade the South Korean populace of its value. They include ship open-days, naval ceremonies, naval band performances and events that link specific ships to their namesakes.[50] Since 1999, the ROKN has run a Navy Camp for teenagers interested in the navy.[51] The ROKN also seeks to engage younger generations through picture and essay writing contests, navy sponsored sports events and the use of well-known celebrities and sports stars to act as naval ambassadors.[52] During the popular annual cherry blossom festival at Jinhae, the ROKN opens its naval base and academy to the public putting on public displays and allowing visitors aboard ROKN ships. In 1998, the ROKN held a Fleet Review to commemorate the 50th anniversary of the Korean Government. This was the first of three such events, the next in 2008 and the third in 2015. The Fleet Reviews aim to engage with the public and in the words of one ROKN document create 'a maritime ideology'.[53] In 2015 over 30 vessels were involved as were ROKN aircraft. There was also a week of events in the city of Busan designed to present the ROKN in a favourable light. Also, in 2017 a 'battleship park' opened on the Han River in central Seoul; this permanent exhibition includes three decommissioned ROKN vessels including ROKS *Seoul* and is designed to educate the public about the role of the navy in South Korean security.

Capturing the Debate

Heightened efforts to engage the public in the traditions and concepts of the ROKN are not alone sufficient to develop the permanent naval identity that the navy desires. The reality is that although South Korea has extensive civil seapower interests, its politicians and bureaucrats do not naturally understand the connection between the state's seapower, naval power and national security.[54] This maritime interaction is not at the heart of South Korea's defence planning and policymakers have little experience in viewing South Korean security through a maritime lens. Early in its blue-water initiative the ROKN identified the need to not only gain public support but also convince politicians, rival services and civilian defence employees of the need to pursue a wider operational remit.[55] This necessarily involved the consistent diffusion of the strategic rationales for South Korean seapower and their connection to state security and development.

One of the solutions the ROKN hit upon was a series of on-board debates. First started in 1992, these debates target a South Korean audience of defence officials, academics, military officers and graduate students.[56] The ROKN used these events to promote core concepts of naval power and its connection to South Korean security. To increase their impact, the debates often include demonstrations of naval power and the ships that host the debates have sailed around well-known South Korean maritime landmarks including Dokdo, Marado and Jeju Island. This provides the guests with a visceral connection to the sea and South Korean sovereignty. Speakers included academics, policy analysts and naval officers. As an indicator of their importance, the ROKN CNO has often given the keynote opening address.

Seventeen of these debates have been held between 1992 and 2016. Participation has expanded to include foreign speakers, including representatives from the US, Japan and other Asian countries.[57] The utility of these debates lies in the ROKN's ability to give targeted messages on issues of maritime importance. The inaugural debate examined the ROKN's role after unification and the strategic situation in maritime Northeast Asia and was one of the ROKN's opening shots in justifying a future change in South Korean naval posture.[58] Since then, the debates have explored themes of immediate strategic or political importance such as the construction of Jeju naval base, the ROKN's position within the Defence Reform 2020 initiative or emphasising the importance of seapower and blue-water modernisation following the sinking of the *Cheonan*.

As part of the shipboard debate program, the ROKN embraced a formative academic debate within South Korea regarding the nature of the state's seapower. Writing in 1989, Edward Olsen argued that there had been a 'major if diffuse effort to expand the horizons of naval thinking in South Korea'.[59] A small number of research groups, institutes and interest groups formed around this time and they joined with the ROKN to form a core research and public presentation program aimed at promoting naval matters and a new future for the ROKN.

Significant areas of cooperation include joint seminars (including the on-board debates), public presentations and the production of seapower related academic work. Retired naval officers often play an important role in bridging the civil-military divide regarding the promotion of seapower thinking. This is particularly important as retired military officers, particularly of flag rank, are a powerful defence lobby and play a critical role in determining the nature of the security debate in the South Korean media and government.[60]

The SLOC Study Group-Korea performed much of the initial public work on South Korean seapower. Based in Yonsei University, it began operations in 1981 and comprised a mix of academics and executives with an interest in South Korean maritime affairs.[61] This was not a solely

Korean initiative, but it was born out of two international conferences held in 1979 in Taipei and then 1980 in Washington DC. Four groups were set up in Japan, Taiwan, the US and South Korea. The group developed close ties with the ROKN and in 1989, together with the navy, held the first International Sea Power Symposium. Much like the shipboard debate series, this biannual conference covers concepts that reflect the strategic concerns and proposed responses of the ROKN and other seapower advocates. These include the twenty-first century maritime security environment, naval cooperation and following the sinking of the *Cheonan*, the changing nature of the threat from North Korea.[62] These symposia have heightened in profile in recent years. In 2017, Admiral Scott Swift, the US Pacific Fleet Commander was one of the speakers, where he addressed the challenges facing the East Asian maritime region.[63] The SLOC Study Group also participates in the shipboard conference series and in a number of international events.

In 1997 a maritime research institute was formed called the Korean Institute for Maritime Strategy (KIMS). Its role is to conduct and promote research into seapower and South Korean naval operations. Comprised of academics, policymakers and retired naval officers, it works closely with the ROKN and the SLOC Study Group to organise conferences and it gives frequent lectures on issues of maritime security to a variety of audiences. It also publishes a large number of indigenous and translated works on seapower and the ROKN.[64] Other maritime-related institutes and organisations include the Korean Maritime Institute (KMI) founded in 1984 that has a greater focus on the civilian elements of South Korean seapower and the Sea Power League of the Republic of Korea founded in 1997. These institutes work alongside the ROKN to forward the central themes of South Korean seapower and inculcate them into South Korean strategic discourse.

CONCLUSION

The efforts to create a South Korea naval identity demonstrate that the ROKN recognises the delicate position it is in within South Korea's strategic hierarchy and that the inherent difficulties it faces in sustaining naval force development outside of a North Korean context. Decades of army dominance and the influence of the US left the ROKN in a weak position to develop as independent entity. The strategic paradigm that focused on North Korea resulted in a failure to develop a South Korean naval identity and a consequent lack of understanding in public and policy circles of the importance of naval power to a country that is essentially an island.

The advent of democracy in 1988 and the election of the first civilian president five years later resulted in a weakening of army dominance, which provided the space for the ROKN to argue that seapower, was essential to a country striving to become a modern twenty-first century middle power. What has occurred in the intervening years is multi-track approach to inculcating a naval identity in the consciousness of the body politic and political elites. The importance of this effort cannot be underestimated. The long-term nature of naval force development, the required capital expenditure and the shifting sands of peninsular security means that the ROKN needs to secure a permanent place for naval strategy within South Korea's strategic thinking. A failure to do so endangers the sustained modernisation and operational freedom that is required for blue-water operations.

The sustained efforts of the ROKN to persuade the public of its utility through events, image projection and other media is vital to maintain the navy in the minds of the populace. The use of historical figures is a time-honoured method to provide the public with a sense of a naval identity and connect the past with current strategic requirements. Efforts to persuade politicians and other security stakeholders through constant engagement and the diffusion of seapower and maritime strategic concepts are important to provide an alternative narrative to the continental-focused strategy that dominates South Korea security discourse.

The success of these efforts remain difficult to judge. Certainly, the current achievements in terms of blue-water development suggest that the ROKN has created a nascent South Korean naval identity. Successive governments have put resources into naval modernisation and given the ROKN the freedom to develop new operational concepts. However, the sinking of the *Cheonan* raised some significant questions. The tragedy clearly had a significant impact on the ROKN's public reputation and led to calls for it to maintain a singular focus on North Korea. The public reaction was one of anger of confusion. Polls showed a lack of trust towards the military over its handling of the situation and confusion over why the ROKN failed to detect a North Korean submarine.[65] The ROKN's reaction was to temporarily pull its slogan *to the sea, to the world*, and it publically stated that it would reorient itself back towards peninsular operations.[66] The political and public environment required a public shift away from the rhetoric of blue-water operations and therefore the ROKN obliged despite never truly giving up on its long-term blue-water modernisation program.

Since then the National Assembly and the Blue House have once again given financial and political support to the development of large platforms including the KDX-III Batch-II and the KDDX destroyers and in 2012, the ROKN revived the *to the sea, to the world* slogan.[67] Publicly, this reversion has been justified by the continued threat of North Korea and the changing strategic environment in maritime Northeast Asia. This suggests that the ROKN has at least been partially successful in embedding the importance of the naval power into the South Korean strategic identity. Nevertheless, one question remains, if the strategic environment alters, will seapower continue to receive funding as it considered core to South Korea's well-being or will it be left to diminish as it did so many years previously after the death of Yi Sun-shin?

Notes

1. Chung-in Moon, "South Korea Recasting Security Paradigms," in *Asian Security Practice Material and Ideational Influence*, ed. Muthiah Alagappa (Stanford: Stanford University Press, 1988), 267; Victor D. Cha, "Strategic Culture and the Military Modernization of South Korea," *Armed Forces and Society* 28, no. 1 (Fall 2011): 116.
2. James R. Holmes, "China Fashions a Maritime Identity," *Issues and Studies* 42, no. 3 (September 2006): 97.
3. Quotation taken from: Michael J. Seth, *A History of Korea from Antiquity to the Present* (Plymouth: Rowman & Littlefield, 2011), 495.
4. Geoffrey Till, *Seapower a Guide for the Twenty-First Century*, 2nd ed. (Oxon: Routledge, 2009), 83.
5. Ibid.
6. Robert S. Ross, "China's Naval Nationalism: Sources, Prospects, and the U.S. Response," *International Security* 34, no. 2 (Fall 2009): 48–50.
7. Duncan Redford, "Introduction," in *Maritime History and Identity: The Sea and Culture in the Modern World*, ed. Duncan Redford (London: I.B. Tauris, 2014), 1–10, 6.
8. ROKN Headquarters, *Haegun Bijeon 2020* [Navy Vision 2020] (Gyeryong: ROKN Headquarters, 1999), 79.
9. Robert S. Ross, "China's Naval Nationalism: Sources, Prospects, and the U.S. Response," 48–50.

10. Alessio Patalano, *Post-War Japan as a Sea Power: Imperial Legacy, Wartime Experiences and the Making of a Navy* (London: Bloomsbury, 2015), 10.
11. Ibid., 11.
12. Ibid.
13. Lincoln Paine, *The Sea and Civilisation: A Maritime History of the World* (London: Atlantic Books, 2013), 299.
14. Seth, *A History of Korea*, 67.
15. Stephen Turnbull, *The Samurai Invasion of Korea, 1592–1598* (Oxford: Osprey Publishing, 2008), 18.
16. Jeremy Black, *Naval Power: A History of Warfare and the Sea from 1500 Onwards* (Basingstoke: Palgrave Macmillan, 2009), 18.
17. Seong-yeong Park, "The Development of the Republic of Korea Navy in a Changing National Defense and Northeast Asian Security Environment" (Doctoral Thesis, University of Salford, 2009), 2.
18. Angela Schottenhammer, "The East Asian Maritime World, c. 1400–1800: Its Fabrics of Power and Dynamics of Exchanges—China and Her Neigbours," in *The East Asian Maritime World 1400–1800: Its Fabrics of Power and Dynamics of Exchange*s, ed. Angela Shottenhammer (Weisbaden: Harrassowitz Berlag, 2007), 53.
19. The movie's English title is The Admiral Roaring Currents, in Korean its was *Myeongryang*. For box office data see: Lee Hyo-won, "2014 South Korean Box Office: 'Roaring Currents' Takes All-Time Record, Stellar Year for Hollywood," *The Hollywood Reporter*, 21 December 2014, https://www.hollywoodreporter.com/news/2014-south-korean-box-office-759768, accessed 13 March 2018.
20. Young-gi Chun and Bong-moon Kim, "Korea's Statues Without Limitations: Kim Jong-pil Remembers: 70," *Korea Joongang Daily*, 6 October 2015, http://mengnews.joins.com/view.aspx?aId=3009977, accessed 10 November 2017.
21. Young-koo Roh, "Yi Sun-shin, an Admiral Who Became a Myth," *The Review of Korean Studies 7*, no. 3 (2004): 29–31.
22. Young-koo Roh, "Yi Sun-shin, An Admiral who Became a Myth," 29–31.
23. Edward Olsen, "Prospects for an Increased Naval Role for the Republic of Korea in Northeast Asian Security" (Unpublished MA Thesis, US Naval War College, 1989), 10.
24. Based on the author's visit to Jinhae Naval Base (April 2011). Turtle ships are also on display in other major South Korean cultural sites including the War Memorial of Korea and the Sejong Centre in Seoul. Prior to its disbandment, the ROKN Naval War College's logo most prominent feature was the bow of a Turtle Ship.

161

25. "Chief of Naval Operations Change of Command Ceremony (26th & 27th)," *Navy News*, 21 March 2008. Link no longer available.

26. Young-sam Kim, *Address by President Kim, Young-sam at the 48th Graduation and Commissioning Ceremony of the Korean Naval Academy*, 4 March 1994, http://14cwd.pa.go.kr/president/1bm/1b-29m/1b29i012.asp, accessed 5 January 2016.

27. Sang-yup Lee, "Ships, Security, and Symbols: A Constructivist Explanation of South Korea's Naval Build-Up" (Unpublished PhD Dissertation, Rutgers University, 2013), 251.

28. Sung-ki Jung, "Anti-piracy Naval Unit Inaugurated," *The Korea Times*, 3 March 2009, http://www.koreatimes.co.kr/www/nation/2017/08/205_40629.html, accessed 27 April 2016.

29. Dae-jung Kim, "In the Glorious Traditions of Admirals Yi Sun-shin and Chang-Po-go: At the 54th Commencement Ceremony of the Korean Naval Academy," 16 March 2000, in *Government of the People: Selected Speeches of Kim, Dae-jung Vol. III* (Seoul: Office of the President of the Republic of Korea, 2001), 73–74.

30. Moo-hyun Roh, *Address by President Roh Moo-hyun at the 57th Graduation and Commissioning Ceremony of the Korean Naval Academy*, 13 March 2003, http://pa.go.kr/research/contents/speech/index.jsp?spMode=view&artid=1309355&catid=c_pa02062, accessed 5 January 2016.

31. Moo-hyun Roh, *Address by the President Roh, Moo-hyun at the 61st Graduation and Commissioning Ceremony of the Korean Naval Academy*, 2 March 2007, http://pa.go.kr/research/contents/speech/index.jsp?spMode=view&artid=1310000&catid=c_pa02062, accessed 5 January 2016.

32. Jan Rüger, *The Great Naval Game Britain and Germany in the Age of Empire* (Cambridge: Cambridge University Press, 2007), 159.

33. Ibid., 166.

34. Interview with Admiral An Byeong-tae (April 2011) & Admiral Song, Keun-ho (April 2011).

35. Republic of Korea Navy, *Haegun* [Navy] (Gyeryong: ROKN Troop Information and Public Relations Office, 2011), 16–17.

36. "New Patrol Boat to Be Named After Killed Soldier," *The Korea Times*, 15 June 2007, https://www.koreatimes.co.kr/www/common/printpreview.asp?categoryCode=205&newsIdx=4797, accessed 3 March 2017.

37. "The Dokdo Class: An LHD for the ROK," *Defence Industry Daily*, https://www.defenseindustrydaily.com/aegis-awd-lhd-for-rok-03431/, accessed 1 February 2016.

38. Sung-ki Jung, "Navy Commissions Large Landing Ship," *The Korea Times*, 3 July 2007, http://www.koreatimes.co.kr/www/news/nation/2007/07/113_5869.html, accessed 1 February 2016.

39. The ROKN frequently uses the island of Dokdo as a backdrop in many of its publicity photographs. They understand that this easily identifiable landmark, which is central to South Korean identity, can serve remind the people that the ROKN is central to South Korea's security.

40. Republic of Korea Navy Headquarters, *21 Segireul hyanghan haegun* [The Navy Heading Toward the 21st Century] (Nonsan: Republic of Korea Navy Headquarters, 1998).

41. For a selection see: Republic of Korea Navy, *Haegun* [Navy] (Seoul: Republic of Korea Navy, 1998); Republic of Korea Navy, *Haegun* [Navy] (Gyeryong: ROKN Troop Information and Public Relations Office, 2011); ROKN Headquarters, *Gandanhago pyeonhage ilgeul su issneun haegungaideubug* [A Simple and Easy to Read Naval Guidebook] (Gyeryong-dae: ROKN Headquarters, 2016).

42. See: US Department of the Navy, *Naval Operations Concept 2010: Implementing the Maritime Strategy* (Washington, DC: US Department of the Navy); US Department of the Navy, *Forward, Engaged Ready: A Cooperative Strategy for 21st Century Seapower* (Washington, DC: US Department of the Navy).

43. Silja Baller, Soumitra Dutta, and Bruno Lanvin, eds., *The Global Information Technology Report 2016: Innovating in the Digital Economy* (Geneva: World Economic Forum, 2016), 26.

44. Republic of Korea Navy, *Haegun Bijeon 2030* [Navy Vision 2030] (Gyerong: ROKN Headquarters, 2008), 63.

45. Data on hit rates for websites is an estimate only. This data is taken from www.siterankdata.com/navy.mil.kr, accessed 12 March 2018. These platforms include Youtube and Facebook where ROKN-curated pages had 2958 and 134,134 followers respectively (as of 12 March 2018). See: https://www.youtube.com/user/MsRoknavy/videos; https://www.facebook.com/ilovenavy/.

46. Sang-yup Lee, *Ships, Security, and Symbols*, 246.

47. "ROKN Mark," *Republic of Korea Navy PR*, http://www.navy.mil.kr/mbshome/mbs/eng/subview.do?id=eng_040100000000, accessed 11 March 2018.

48. Korean advertising often uses English to project an image of modernity. See: Jamie Shinhee Lee, "Linguistic Constructions of Modernity: English Mixing in Korean Television Commercials," *Language in Society* 35 (2006): 59–91.

49. "Navy Introduces New Slogan, Marching Song to Mark 63rd Anniversary," *Ministry of National Defence News*, 21 November 2008, http://www.mnd.go.kr/user/boardList.action?command=view&page=1&boardId=O_47261&boardSeq=o_1000000010030&titleId=&siteId=mndEN&id=mndEN_020100000000, accessed 2 August 2010.

50. ROKN Headquarters, *Gandanhago pyeonhage ilgeul su issneun haegun-gaideubug* [A Simple and Easy to Read Naval Guidebook] (Gyeryong-dae: ROKN Headquarters, 2016), 57.

51. Republic of Korea Navy, *Haegun*, (2011), 63.

52. "Badaui wangja marinboi Park Taehwan seonsu, haegun hongbodaesaro wichok [Prince of the Sea, Marine Boy Park Tae-hwan Appointed Navy PR Ambassador]," *Republic of Korea Navy News Release*, 31 May 2013.

53. Republic of Korea Navy, *Haegun* [Navy] (1998), 43.

54. Michael McDevitt, "Final Report," in *Workshop Report: The Future of ROK Navy-US Navy Cooperation*, ed. Michael McDevitt (Alexandria: Centre for Naval Analysis, 2007), 6–7; Bae Sang-yoon, "Maritime Developments in South Korea," in *Maritime Power in the China Seas: Capabilities and Rationale*, ed. Dominic Sherwood (Canberra: Australian Defence Studies Centre, 1994), 54.

55. Interview with Admiral An Byeong-tae, April 2011.

56. "Dongbuga haeyanganbohwangyeong byeonhwae ttareun hangukae-gunui dojeongwa gwaje [Challenges and Tasks of the Republic of Korea Navy Due to Changes in the Northeast Asia Maritime Security Environment]," *Korea Institute for Maritime Strategy*, http://www.kims.or.kr/%EC%A0%9C41%ED%9A%8C-%EA%B5%AD%EC%A0%9C/, accessed 12 November 2017.

57. "je17hoe hamsangtoronhoe gongdong gaechoe gyeolgwa [Results of the 17th Shipboard Co-Hosted Debate]," *Korea Institute for Maritime Strategy*, http://www.kims.or.kr/notice_16_6_7/, accessed 12 November 2017.

58. Kwang-sup Oh, "*Dongbugajiyueogui gunsajeongse gwallyeon haegun hamsangtoronhoe yeollyeo* [Opening Navy Shipboard Debate on Military Affairs in Northeast Asia]," *MBC News*, 1 November 1992, http://imnews.imbc.com/20dbnews/history/1992/1918429_19402.html, accessed 1 March 2014.

59. Edward Olsen, *Prospects for an Increased Naval Role for the Republic of Korea*, 9.

60. This was particularly evident in the debate surrounding the reorganisation of the South Korean JCS in 2011. Senior retired naval and air force officers put up substantial opposition to the proposed reforms as they threatened to weaken the power of the two services relative to the army. See: "Renewed Calls by Minister for Reforms in the Military," *Korea JoongAng Daily*, 2, June 2011, http://koreajoongangdaily.joins.com/news/article/article.aspx?aid=2937039, accessed 16 November 2012; Su-jeong Kim and Gwang-lip Moon, "With Reforms It's Blue House Versus the Generals," *Korea JoongAng Daily*, 30 March 2011. http://

koreajoongangdaily.joins.com/news/article/article.aspx?aid=2934132, accessed 16 November 2012.

61. "Seollipbaegyeonggwa yeonguhoe bijeon [Establishment Background and Vision]," *The SLOC Study Group—Korea*, http://www.sloc. co.kr/%EC%84%A4%EB%A6%BD%EB%B0%B0%EA%B2%BD%EA%B3% BC-%EC%97%B0%EA%B5%AC%ED%9A%8C-%EB%B9%84%EC%A0%84 /?ckattempt=1, accessed 19 February 2018.

62. "The Security Environment of the Korean Peninsula and Direction for Development of ROK Navy," *Academic Conference, Korea Institute for Maritime Strategy*, http://www.kims.or.kr/en/the-36th-international/, accessed 3 March 2018.

63. Admiral Scott H. Swift, *Republic of Korea Navy International Seapower Symposium Seoul, Republic of Korea September 5, 2017 as Prepared for Delivery*, http://www.cpf.navy.mil/leaders/scott-swift/speeches/2017/09/rok-seapower-symposium.pdf, accessed 3 March 2018.

64. "KIMS Founding Purpose," *Korea Institute for Maritime Strategy*, http://www.kims.or.kr/en/history/, accessed 19 February 2018.

65. Lee Sang-ho, "Issue of Oceanic Navy and Complement of Naval Force After Warship Cheonan-Ham Incident," *Sejong Commentary 181* (29 April 2010); "Public's Faith in Military Authorities Shaken After Cheonan Sinking," *Hankyoreh*, 12 April 2010, http://herstory.hani. co.kr/arti/english_edition/e_national/415603.html, accessed 4 August 2011.

66. IHS Jane's, "Ambitions for a Blue Water Fleet Tempered by Stark Realities," *Jane's Navy International*, 20 April 2011, https://janes.ihs. com/Janes/Display/jni74397-jin-2011, accessed 21 February 2012.

67. "Navy Revives 'Ocean-Going' Slogan," *The Korea Times*, 17 February 2012, http://koreatimes.co.kr/www/news/nation/2012/02/113_105079. html, accessed 10 November 2017.

CHAPTER 7

Politics, Strategy and Naval Modernisation

The pathway for Republic of Korea Navy (ROKN) modernisation is of course shaped by the external strategic environment, but it is ultimately determined internally. Domestic political and bureaucratic structures combined with strategic culture determine the direction of naval innovation, strategic development and operations.[1] The threat of North Korea has dominated South Korean strategic culture and the Republic of Korea Army (ROKA)'s long-term control over the levers of power, bolstered by alliance requirements reinforced the strategic proclivity towards the continent. Consequently, for a sustained period following the end of the Korean War, South Korea was missing what Alfred Thayer Mahan described as the national and governmental character to support the development of a comprehensive naval strategy that looked beyond the littoral waters of the Peninsula.[2]

This chapter examines how the ROKN took advantage of changed political circumstances following the democratisation of South Korea to win presidential support for blue-water modernisation.[3] It starts with the Presidency of Kim Young-sam who took office in 1993 and was the first elected civilian head of state in over 30 years. The chapter then proceeds to examine the relationship between the three subsequent administrations and ROKN modernisation. By covering a period of 20 years, the chapter demonstrates that internal naval goals for blue-water modernisation coincided with a political environment that was increasingly open to such concepts. Following the election of Kim Young-sam, successive

© The Author(s) 2019

I. Bowers, *The Modernisation of the Republic of Korea Navy*, Critical Studies of the Asia-Pacific, https://doi.org/10.1007/978-3-319-92291-1_7

administrations sought to expand South Korea's security agenda, thereby providing the ROKN with a window to modify its operational posture. The ROKN gained the sustained political backing and budgetary support needed to develop new capabilities which could be used to advance South Korea's geostrategic agenda both around and beyond the Korean peninsula. However, the nature of the political system in South Korea combined with the threat from North Korea exposes the ROKN to sudden shifts in administration policy and as political priorities in Seoul changed the ROKN's desire for a wider operational role has proven to be somewhat vulnerable. A broader concept of South Korean security beyond the Peninsula became a battleground issue in the political debate between the conservative and liberal parties in the mid to late 2000s and as the conservative President Lee Myung-bak took office, the ROKN's drive for blue-water operations fell afoul of political and economic reprioritisation. The chapter concludes by arguing that political support for the ROKN blue-water modernisation is still not a given but has been helped by a strategic environment which can now justify such expenditure.

THE ROLE OF THE EXECUTIVE

In South Korea, the imperial-like nature of the presidency ensures that the holder of the office plays the primary role in determining the strategic direction of the armed forces and the allocation of funds for major force improvement projects.[4] For the military therefore, the policies of the sitting president have substantial implications for their strategic priorities, operations and future force development. Therefore, over the long-term, consistent future force planning can prove problematic in South Korea given that each president is term-limited to five years. Changing administrations with different priorities can push South Korean defence reform in numerous directions often resulting in inconsistent and inefficient force transformation efforts. For successful long-term force development, policy consistency across administrations in combination with concerted political efforts to push through reform is required.[5]

Since democratisation, other bureaucratic actors, particularly the National Assembly have slowly gained some influence in South Korea's defence decision-making process.[6] While its role remains limited, it does have some oversight over the defence budget and assembly members can use their power to reprioritise the division of funds proposed by each administration.[7] The impact of divergent Presidential and National Assembly views on defence matters is usually contingent on whether the ruling party also has a majority in the National Assembly.[8] By using its control over the budget, the National Assembly has the power to delay the introduction of new capabilities or prioritise specific projects and in this regard it has shown to be influenced by external lobbying particularly by service branches set for relative losses arising from defence reform efforts.[9]

THE TRANSFORMATIVE EFFECT OF KIM YOUNG-SAM (1993–1998)

The ascension of President Kim Young-sam to power in 1993 heralded a sea change in South Korean politics. The first elected civilian leader since 1962, he came to power with an ambitious agenda to transform the social, economic, political and military structures of a country that for 30 years had been dominated by successive security-centric, military-led governments. Kim's reform of South Korean civil-military relations had three core objectives; to remove the political influence of the military, assert civilian control over the country's defence apparatus and eliminate corruption within the upper echelons of the military's command structure. Consequently, the military and particularly the ROKA underwent a dramatic depoliticisation, lost a substantial proportion of its political power and surrendered its total control over the country's defence and security institutions.

The Kim Young-sam government provided the initial political impetus for ROKN development as its efforts to decouple the ROKA from the reins of power allowed for a reconsideration of South Korean foreign and security policy. The ROKN's desire to build a more advanced regional-operational capability matched the administration's goal of making South Korea a responsible normalised international stakeholder.

The Control of the Generals

Thirty years before Kim Young-sam entered the Blue House, retired general Park Chung-hee won election as President of South Korea. Park was the leader of the 1961 military coup which had overthrown the civilian Second Republic Government of Chang Myon. His election, which had taken place following US pressure, heralded the beginning of a sustained period of military and ROKA dominance over the reins of government.

Effectively, despite constitutionally enforced neutrality, the military developed and then held a controlling interest across all levels of South Korean politics.[10] Many of President Park's fellow officers also resigned from the ROKA and were inserted into various government agencies and departments thereby formalising the army's influence across the country's administration. Graduates of the Korean Military Academy (KMA), who upon leaving the military would be appointed to top positions within government, tightly controlled access to the inner circle of power in successive regimes.[11] What followed was a series of quasi-civilian governments led by retired generals, supported by the military and a network of retired officers who had been strategically placed in positions of influence and were vested in sustaining this structure.[12]

This domination resulted in an extremely narrow strategic view within the Ministry of National Defense (MND) and the military. Their security policies, which were determined by the Blue House reflected an inherent conservative anti-communist ideology, one in which the security of the regime, the state and the nation were paramount.[13] While the threat from North Korea was the primary strategic priority, the ROKA's political influence in combination with the US military's preference for the development of land forces resulted in a marginalisation of the ROKN. There was little to no consistent strategic thinking regarding naval power and the role of the ROKN beyond the littorals of peninsula and the threat posed by North Korea.[14]

Depoliticisation

To regain civilian command of South Korea's military and defence sectors, Kim Young-sam adopted a top-down approach. He named a comparatively junior two-star general as Minister of National Defense and a civilian from the Ministry of Finance as his deputy, two positions that were normally held by senior 4-star generals. He increased civilian control over strategic departments such as the Ministry for Foreign Affairs and Trade and the Ministry for Unification and appointed civilians to the posts of National Security Advisor and the Director of the Agency for

National Security Planning.[15] For the first time since the creation of the South Korean JCS, the ROKA lost the position of Chairman with Air Force General Lee Yang-ho assuming the role.[16] The Defense Security Command (The ROKA's counter-intelligence service), which had been instrumental in monitoring political opposition and ensuring regime security was reorganised and placed under civilian control.[17]

Importantly, the *Hanahoe*, a semi-secret faction of Korean Military Academy (KMA) graduates who held the most powerful positions in the army and across the administration was abolished. They had played an instrumental role in assisting both Park Chung-hee and his successor Chun Doo-hwan in gaining and then maintaining power.[18] Kim encouraged the promotion of officers who had no connection with the *Hanahoe* or who had been trained through the university-based ROTC program. The MND also actively discriminated against former members of the group by limiting their opportunities for promotion.[19] These newly promoted officers, by gaining positions of authority and power, supported and bolstered the civil-military reforms instituted by the Kim government.[20]

Large-scale corruption was uncovered in two areas; the endemic issue of bribes for promotions and corruption in the arms procurement process. This was found across all three services, with the ROKN's CNO and eight other flag officers being implicated. Thus, the post of CNO was given to two-star Admiral Kim Hong-yeul. This forced the retirement of a further seven flag officers who had been bi-passed for promotion and put in place a younger generation of senior officers who were sympathetic to the civilian-led government.[21]

This campaign of reform had several wider effects within South Korean society. The military was effectively removed from the political sphere as evidenced by the arrest, trial and punishment of the two previous presidents; Roh Tae-woo and Chun Doo-hwan (both former ROKA generals) and a number of their close aids including 13 senior officers on charges of rebellion, conspiracy and corruption.[22] In addition, the imbalance within the defence establishment between the army, airforce and navy was partially rectified as the two smaller services gained in relative influence. The civilianisation of the defence and foreign affairs related ministries resulted in an increase in cross-departmental working groups and a decrease in the over-arching power and influence of the army-dominated MND over foreign and security policy.[23]

Globalisation and the ROKN

These reforms created an administrative and command environment which allowed the ROKN to undertake a comprehensive review of its strategic planning and modernisation goals. This review maintained the centrality of North Korea in current and future ROKN operations. But as it was performed independent of the ROKA and MND, it could better address weaknesses in the navy's force structure and future operational thinking. Consequently, the ROKN's nascent blue-water agenda was factored into its planning and was allowed to gain traction as its ambition matched the foreign and security policy of Kim Young-sam.[24]

In his seminal 1994 Sydney Declaration, Kim Young-sam announced that South Korea would follow the policy of *Segyehwa* or globalisation. It called for a large-scale societal embrace of internationalism in order to meet the economic and political challenges that globalisation would inevitably bring.[25] It was, as described by prominent academic Samuel S. Kim, an attempt to recast South Korea's national identity as a 'newly industrialized and democratized country deserving membership in the Organization for Economic Cooperation and Development (OECD) and the United Nations Security Council'.[26] It was premised on the concept that South Korea needed to move away from its traditional cultural, economic and political ideas and embrace international norms to become an independent and advanced nation.[27] While of debatable success, the policy laid the bedrock for further attempts at internationalisation under subsequent administrations.

For the ROKN, *Segyehwa* was the transformational policy opportunity that it had been waiting for. Kim Young-sam believed that if South Korea was to pursue a more globalised foreign policy a naval force that could operate in the region and beyond was required. Naval power was understood by the administration to be an expression of national status and therefore a regional naval capability comparable with South Korea's growing international presence was crucial.[28]

When Admiral An Byeong-tae was appointed to CNO in 1995, he came into the position in a period when there was fertile ground for transforming the future ROKN. In the face of some opposition within the MND, he presented Kim Young-sam with his plan to turn the ROKN into a blue-water navy.[29] At this point, internal naval goals to develop blue-water capability matched the ambitions of the most powerful politician in the land. Moving away from the singular operational construct driven by North Korea, the ROKN would now aim to build a future force capable of meeting the operational challenges posed by South Korea's growing international interests and desired global footprint. Following a 15-minute meeting the plan was approved.[30]

In speeches made at the Korean Naval Academy by the president, the ROKN's role within South Korea's new foreign policy was made clearer with distinct linkages made between naval power, globalisation and economic development.[31] There was an acknowledgement of the centrality of the sea to South Korea's economy and the need for the state to have an ability to protect its own interests in an area that was of growing geostrategic importance following the end of the Cold War.[32] This was reflected in South Korean defense policy. For the first time, the 1994–1995 Defense White Paper explicitly stated that surface combat capability would be pursued 'beyond the current role of anti-North defense'.[33] The ROKN would transform itself into a 'regional navy through the balanced improvement of surface-underwater-air capabilities and the acquisition of a strike capability'.[34] A year later in 1996, the ROKN submitted a requirement for the development of the *Dokdo* class LPD. In the same year, initial approval was given for the construction of the KDX-II class destroyers.

The Kim Young-sam government provided the initial political impetus for ROKN reform through its efforts to alter South Korea's internal conception of its place in the world and through the reforms it carried out in bringing the military under civilian control, but it would require others to advance ROKN development further. In this vein this administration also provides a key lesson, Kim supported ROKN reform because it matched a central foreign policy objective; that of *Segyehwa*, the future of ROKN ambitions would too depend on their goals matching those of successive leaders.

Change and Continuity Under Kim Dae-jung (1998–2003)

Kim Dae-jung's election victory in 1998 was a further significant milestone in South Korean politics. Arrested and forced into exile when South Korea was under military rule he was the first left-wing politician to become president. His election not only consolidated South Korea's move towards a fully representative democracy, but also resulted in a radical shift in South Korea's policy towards North Korea. For the ROKN, the Kim Dae-jung administration proved to be a perfect bed-fellow in its pursuit of a blue-water capability.

This shift in policy towards North Korea was known as the Sunshine Policy.[35] It was aimed at breaking what Kim Dae-jung believed to be an unsuccessful and unproductive policy of containment. Long-term engagement through economic incentives and political reciprocity backed by what was described during the administration as a 'firm defence posture' was central to the new policy.[36] This was the flagship policy of the administration and set the tone of the internal and international policy debate regarding North Korean relations for the next ten years. While South Korea's land-centric defense posture did not significantly change during this period of his administration, the Sunshine Policy indicated the administration's openness to new and radical policy initiatives and its desire for long-term change in South Korea's security posture.[37]

The administration's wider foreign and security policy was predicated on the ultimate success of the Sunshine Policy and South Korea's continued embrace of globalisation would enable the country to become an independent political and economic medium power.[38] Kim Dae-jung believed that this would require a long-term shift in the mindset of the South Korea's ruling elites. They would have to adjust the dominant Cold War mentality which had focused South Korean foreign and security policy on containing North Korea, opposing communism and allowing the US to set South Korea's foreign policy agenda. Instead, South Korea would operate as a responsible international actor in-line with established economic and political norms. This would include dropping protectionist economic policies and trading on the open market, contributing to international security in areas such as peacekeeping and providing increased aid and capacity building to less developed countries.[39]

Defence Policy

For the military, these policies would alter their geostrategic priorities and operational scope. While North Korea remained the primary strategic determinant, Kim Dae-jung required the military to develop a concurrent ability to act within the wider region.[40] Regionalism was a key element in the administration's pursuit of independent middle power

status and Kim Dae-jung viewed regional strategic and economic stability as a prerequisite for Korean Unification. A strong military capable of
operating within this regional context, would ensure that South Korea
could resist the proclivities of the larger powers and would provide Seoul
with the ability to drive and influence the regional agenda. Kim Dae-
jung's belief that the military would have to reform to meet these new
goals was articulated in his Armed Forces Day speech where he stated:

> The environment of our national security is also changing as the new cen-
> tury is approaching. Our armed forces have to be reborn to adapt to the
> new situation and come out even stronger.[41]

In its thinking at least, the MND began to demonstrate that this shift was
altering its future strategic planning. The first defence policy document
of his administration spelled out the concept that national security was
no longer solely defined by the priority of preventing war on the Korean
Peninsula. Rather, the administration chose to emphasise that South
Korea must develop a comprehensive security approach which would
include 'political, military and economic spheres'.[42] The Defense White
Paper of 2000 continued the themes set two years previously. But what
is significant was the declarative statement that to achieve such objectives
'the current defense policy, centred on preparing for North Koran threats,
will be transformed into one that prepares for future threats as well'.[43]

The culmination of defence policy alteration under the Kim administration was spelled out in greater detail in the 2001 publication of
Defence Data Statistics. Under a plan entitled *New Defense for the 21st
Century*, the military would alter its previous strategic focus and embrace
the uncertainty of what was termed a changing security environment.
This resulted in a four-point conceptualisation of what 'New Defense'
would entail.[44]

The first: 'Adherence to Basics' focused on maintaining the military's
ability to respond to both military and non-military threats, regardless
of the diplomatic and security relations on the peninsula. The second:
'Management of Change' called on the defence establishment to be pro-
active within the peninsular and regional security environments in order
to shape security changes in line with South Korean interests. This theme
focused on the management of South Korea–US relations, improving
regional military cooperation and cooperating with confidence-building
measures between North and South Korea. The third: 'Preparation for

the Future' related to the creation of armed forces capable of responding to future threats through the construction of an 'Advanced information and technology force of the 21st century'. Finally, the plan called for winning the approval of the populace to support these changes.[45]

In the spirit of these policies, the administration launched a five-year defense reform initiative. This was undertaken by a newly created body, the National Defense Reform Committee (NDRC), which was based in the MND.[46] The NDRC was tasked with exploiting advances in military technology and particularly the RMA and according to Michael Raska was designed to 'provide a comprehensive strategic blueprint to transform the ROK military into a "high-technology defense force"'.[47] The NDRC laid the groundwork for the long-term transformation of the South Korean military.[48] It also provided the three services with a conceptual framework to explore their future roles within the context of the RMA and the administration's future-looking defence transformation policy.[49]

A New ROKN

The ROKN's extant plans to develop a modern blue-water capable force complete with modern weapons technology sat nicely with the Kim Dae-jung foreign and security policy agenda. As with the previous administration; the desire for South Korea to have regional strategic, political and economic leverage required a strong navy given the maritime geostrategic environment of Northeast Asia. In addition, the underlying focus on more positive relations with North Korea and the beginnings, no matter how hesitant, of a recasting of South Korean security thinking away from the peninsular dynamic allowed the ROKN's development goals to prosper under Kim Dae-jung administration. Thus, the creation of a blue-water capable navy, approved by the previous right-wing administration saw partial fruition under the succeeding left-wing one, ensuring the political and policy continuity so vital for long-term force development.

As Table 7.1 shows, the administration's approval for the ROKN's continued development of advanced capabilities led to some of the most significant force improvements being approved or coming to fruition under Kim Dae-jung's term.

The level of naval procurement under the Kimd Dae-jung administration is made more significant by the financial circumstances under which it took place. The 1998 Asian financial crisis severely damaged the South

Table 7.1   Status of ROKN projects under the Kim Dae-jung administration

Type 214	Three Type 214 submarines were ordered in 2000 with the first being laid down in 2003 at the end of the Kim Dae-jung government's term.
KDX-II	Final decision for the KDX-II destroyer was made in late 1998 (although initial approval had been given in 1996). The contract was awarded in 1999 and the first of the class was laid down in 2001.
KDX-III	The KDX-III was delayed due to budget issues related to the Asian financial crisis, while initial Operational Requirements (ROC) were set out in 1996, funding and design approval was given under the Kim Dae-jung administration.
FFX	ROC for FFX Project were laid out in 1998, but the project was delayed due to the Asian Financial Crisis.
Dokdo	An order was placed for one *Dokdo* Class LPD in 2002.

Korean economy and saw the International Monetary Fund place harsh restrictions on government spending. The administration had the power to pull funding for many of the ROKN's more expensive projects, however while some were delayed, they were maintained over the long-term through the introduction of supplementary budgets.[50] Considering, that one KDX-III destroyer cost approximately one billion USD and each KDX-II approximately 385 million USD this represented a substantial financial outlay for the Blue House and was indicative of the priority the administration placed on naval development.

In his speech at the 1998 Korean Naval Academy commencement ceremony, Kim while acknowledging the ROKN's role in maintaining peninsular deterrence specifically linked economic prosperity and globalisation with naval strength.[51]

> The 21st century will be an age of globalization as well as an age of the sea…There is a saying that only those who conquer the sea can conquer the world. I believe that only a nation that can make the best use of the sea will be a victor on the world stage.[52]

The theme of advancing into the world and the economic importance of the sea was further emphasised in his speech to the Naval Academy the following year. He acknowledged that South Korea as medium power in Northeast Asia must have the ability to defend its own interests within Northeast Asian maritime environment.[53] A position that was expanded upon in the following year when his policy goal of making South Korea a regional hub was explicitly linked to the protection of maritime trade and South Korea's potential as a maritime power.[54]

The strength of his support for naval development reached its peak in 2001, when again he promoted South Korea as a regional hub in Northeast Asia and the necessity of a powerful ROKN to support this goal. His connection between national interests and the ROKN is central to the development of blue-water naval development as seen in the first mention of a strategic mobile fleet which would become the centre of ROKN planning for the next ten years. This speech highlighted the growing awareness in the South Korean administration of the danger of armed conflict over contested maritime resources in East Asia. The Kim Dae-jung administration believed that South Korea's position and rights must be maintained within this context. For the first time a non-North Korea focused mission was explicitly provided, not only to the ROKN but also to the wider public.

> The navy has strenuously prepared to build an ocean-going force without a hitch (sic)...In the not too distant future, our navy will have a strategic fleet with the purpose of protecting the national interests and international peace. The government will not spare any effort to help the navy grow into a substantial ocean going force...The 21st century is being touted as the age of the ocean. All countries are heavily bent on securing marine resources, it is also a reality that various conflicts and confrontations between nations have already surfaced. The Northeast Asian waters are no exception. We cannot emphasize too strongly the importance of securing safe seas. The seas too are our sovereign space. The safety of the homeland depends on our protection of the seas.[55]

ROH MOO-HYUN AND DEFENSE REFORM 2020 (2003–2008)

When Roh Moo-hyun came into power in 2003, his administration attempted the biggest shake-up in South Korean defence policy since the Korean War. Winning election with the support of a younger generation of voters and successfully taking advantage of growing anti-US feeling in South Korea he promised to create a more balanced partnership between South Korea and the US.[56]

The Roh administration retained the Sunshine Policy of the previous government. But its views on South Korea's future role in regional security, the need for an independent defence posture and the shape of a restructured US-South Korea alliance were better articulated and more radical than any preceding government. Roh's vision for the country's armed forces was encapsulated in the ambitious Defence Reform 2020 initiative which sought to wholly restructure South Korea's security architecture. The ROKN found substantial support within the administration as their own long-term force development ambitions conformed to Roh's vision of the future structure, capabilities and missions of the South Korean military.

An Independent Approach

Roh's central foreign and security policy agenda focused on South Korea creating its own path by independently determining and achieving its policy goals.[57] South Korea would continue to pursue improved relations with North Korea while at the same time transforming its relationship with the US. The alliance, instead of being the central foundation of South Korean defence policy, would become one pillar alongside an independent defence capability.[58] This was driven by a belief held by Roh and a coterie of his younger advisors that South Korea's material and psychological dependency on the US was severely detrimental to South Korea's future security on the peninsula and in the region.[59] A fact Roh emphasised in his first Armed Forces Day speech as president when he stated:

> The time has come for us to assume the core responsibility for our national defense...Up until now, we have not been able to assume the role of main actor in our own security matter and instead were swayed by developments in the external environment...Self-reliant national defense aims at resolving this kind of problem and raising our national security capacity and stability'.[60]

The Roh government is often viewed as anti-American, mainly by those who focused on the difficulties of the relationship caused by Seoul's North Korea and China policies plus Roh's anti-American rhetoric during his election campaign.[61] Roh's time in office coincided with Donald Rumsfeld's tenure as US Secretary of Defense and South Korea was directly affected by the US policy of strategic flexibility. Roh feared South Korea being dragged into an Asian conflict, particularly over Taiwan and entered into negotiations with the US regarding this doctrine, publicly stating in 2005 that South Korea would 'not be embroiled in any conflict in Northeast Asia against our will'.[62] While Seoul and Washington ultimately reached an agreement, Roh's unwillingness to accommodate the US soured relations with the US and exposed him to vitriolic internal and some external accusations of his desire to end the alliance.[63]

However, this argument does not stand-up to scrutiny when Roh's deployment of troops to Iraq and his support of the domestically unpopular US-South Korea Free Trade Agreement are considered.[64] While the administration did not embrace the US alliance to same degree as its predecessors and under Roh's administration ties between the two countries were strained, on an operational level the alliance retained its solidity. Roh's ultimate ambition was to gradually increase South Korea's own independence while simultaneously modernising but not ending the alliance.

The administration viewed South Korea's geostrategic environment both as an opportunity and as a potential threat. Roh believed that South Korea had the ability to take advantage of regional economic development and act as a hub once security conditions on the peninsula permitted.[65] At the same time, the administration emphasised the potential for increased great power competition as China's rise would force a reaction from the US and Japan.[66] Under such circumstances, Roh believed, South Korea would require an independent defence capability to ensure its interests were protected.[67] More ambitiously, Roh saw South Korea as a balancer between China and Japan in a Northeast Asian future where the US was less engaged.[68] Through the possession of a strong independent military, Seoul would be able to mediate or take a neutral role in future regional conflict while at the same time maintaining South Korea's foreign and security interests.[69]

Roh from the start of his administration embraced the ROKN's growing blue-water capability. Using a speech in 2003 at the Korean Naval Academy, he made the ROKN a central pillar to delivering his plan for regional cooperation while at the same time protecting South Korea from potential regional conflict.[70] The ROKN was in Roh's view, the military branch charged with protecting South Korea's growing regional and global interests and representing South Korea as a sovereign nation.

As many of the major platforms came online during Roh's tenure, he used ship launches as platforms to espouse his foreign policies and assert South Korea's regional role. At the launch of the first KDX-III destroyer, Roh used the opportunity to emphasise the role of the ROKN in regional security and his views on the security situation in Northeast Asian, stating:

> As you know well, South and North Korea will not keep picking quarrels with each other forever. I believe that in the foreseeable future, Northeast Asia will move toward an order of reconciliation, cooperation and integration. It is my firm belief that just as the global international order is moving in that direction, Northeast Asia will have no choice but to follow suit. But at the present time, Northeast Asia is still in an arms race, and we cannot just sit back and watch.[71]

This statement sums ups Roh's policies and the role the ROKN played in his vision of South Korean security. The view of a regional arms race was hyperbolic, but it does reinforce his perception of an Asia that was competitive and of a South Korea that needed to match developments in the region for its own security.

In one statement at the launch of one, albeit significant vessel, the president linked his view of South Korean security with the ROKN. While his policy was radical it was essential for the navy as it allowed the ROKN to maintain consistency in its development plan. As Roh himself stated:

> The Participatory Government intends to support the construction of an "advanced navy" ...The nation is about to open the age of an ocean-going Korean Navy that can manoeuvre the five great oceans and around the six continents in the interest of world peace.[72]

Defence Reform 2020 and the ROKN

The drive for increased South Korean security autonomy fell under the moniker of cooperative self-reliant defense and was aimed at achieving an independent operational capability within ten years. At its heart was the transfer of operational control (OPCON) from the US to South Korea, which was to be achieved after the end of Roh's tenure between 2009 and 2012.

To meet this objective, the administration created a plan to restructure the armed forces and give fresh impetus to its modernisation efforts. Under a plan named Defense Reform 2020, the South Korean military would develop the required command and control, intelligence and strike capabilities to replace/augment those provided by the US. At the end of the program, South Korea would have a force capable of coping both with the threat from North Korea and regional security environment (including the changes in US alliance) and exploiting the technological developments in warfighting.[73] This was, as Roh stated, a necessary step for South Korea to maintain an international presence which reflected the country's economic standing.[74]

This reform plan called to a substantial restructuring of the military. To rebalance the armed forces and deal with South Korea's changing demographics, manpower would be reduced from 680,000 to 500,000 with the ROKA suffering most of the cuts.[75] This reduction in manning levels would be compensated by the introduction of high-technology equipment.[76] The Joint Chiefs of Staff would be strengthened, and the three services would be represented on a more equal footing. This was to increase the military's ability to undertake joint-service operations.[77]

For the ROKN, the objectives laid out in Defense Reform 2020, were not as radical as those proposed for the ROKA. The document conformed to the modernisation plans set out under the two previous administrations. It called for a naval force capable of safeguarding South Korea's 'national interests and oversee the entire sea area surrounding the peninsula'.[78] At Table 7.2 shows several ROKN projects continued or were initiated under Roh's administration. However, budgetary constraints resulted in a reduced class buy for the KDX-III and *Dokdo*-class projects. Permission was given for three rather than six KDX-III

Table 7.2 Status of ROKN projects under the Roh Moo-hyun administration

Operational structure	Creation of a submarine and aviation command by 2020.
	Formal integration of the mobile flotilla into ROKN structure.
Bases	Final approval of and construction of Jeju Naval Base.
	Final approval for and construction of KDX-III.
	Funding continued for entire class of KDX-II.
Vessels	Funding continued for and construction of one *Dokdo* class vessel.
	Design and construction of PKX[a].
	Project development: FFX & LST-II programs[b].

[a]"Gumdoksuri Class," *Naval-Technology*. http://www.naval-technology.com/projects/pxk-gumdoksuri/, 19 February 2018
[b]"Korea's New Coastal Frigates: The FFX Incheon Class," *Defense Industry Daily*, 23 August 2016, http://www.defenseindustrydaily.com/ffx-koreas-new-frigates-05239/, accessed 19 February 2018

destroyers as they were deemed too expensive. Similarly, the administration only provided immediate funding for one *Dokdo*-class vessel. Combined both decisions resulted in the ROKN receiving the go-ahead for two, rather than three mobile task groups.[79]

An independent operating capability as called for by the Roh administration did not have the same impact on the ROKN as did on the other services. The ROKN was already the leading deterrent force at sea, while the USN provided back-up at times of heightened tension or war. This would not change under the self-reliant concept. What Defense Reform 2020 did for the ROKN was place its regional blue-water ambitions within a structured national security developmental framework. It also clarified the command structure for integrating these new capabilities, thereby facilitating the transition from a purely coastal force to one which could operate effectively around the peninsula and in blue-waters of the region and beyond.

LEE MYUNG-BAK AND A CHANGE IN DIRECTION (2008–2013)

The election of conservative Lee Myung-bak in 2008 marked the end of ten years of liberal rule. His government published a comprehensive security document linking foreign affairs, defence and the economy. Under the banner of *Global Korea*, it provided a broad concept of South Korea's place in the international community and could have been a natural expansion in many of the areas that previous administrations espoused.[80] However, the Lee administration reoriented South Korean security policy back towards the traditional focus on North Korea and concentrated on revitalising the US alliance. The ROKN under the Lee administration for the first time in 15 years faced significant challenges to sustain modernisation and its blue-water project stalled under the pressure of political opposition and renewed provocations from North Korea.

Lee's North Korea policy was in effect a rejection of the accommodating sunshine initiative of the previous ten years. His *Mutual Benefits and Common Prosperity* policy called for denuclearisation and a resultant effort to increase the economic well-being of North Korea and its citizens. Operationalised, this was a tough regime where concessions and assistance to North Korea would be given if they gave up their nuclear program and opened their political system.[81] This was a return to the more defensive policies of the governments before Kim, Dae-jung and reflected the belief held on the conservative side of South Korean politics that Seoul had stopped taking the North Korea threat seriously and had been giving aid and financial inducements for very little return.[82]

The second major policy shift was US alliance management. Prior to the election, Lee had described US-South Korea relations under Roh as ill-managed and he intended to reset the alliance by making it central to the security of South Korea and at the same time cooperating with the US on the global stage.[83] While accepting the agreements and alliance transformation initiatives which had been agreed between the Roh-Bush governments, his re-aligned North Korea policy fit closely with that of the Obama administration. Under a 2009 initiative agreed by the two leaders, the US restated its support for South Korea and the Mutual Defense Treaty, while at the same time extending the alliance so that it would operate on a cooperative regional and global basis.[84] A fact confirmed by the deployment of troops and a Provincial Reconstruction Team (PRT) to Afghanistan and South Korea's joining of the Proliferation Security initiative.[85]

These developments reflected not only Lee's belief in the necessity of the security alliance but also his understanding that South Korea needed to expand its reciprocal commitment to the US. Additionally, it reflected his conviction that for South Korea to operate in global environment it would need the support of the US, particularly in the face of the rising power of China in East Asia. While Kim Dae-jung and Roh Moo-hyun sought active engagement and in the process often risked Washington's ire for being too close to China, Lee while continuing and developing economic engagement distanced himself politically Beijing, thus effectively ending the balancing role that Roh had attempted to create for South Korea.

Lee and his advisors criticised the Defense Reform 2020 plan, believing that it did not consider the worsening relationship with North Korea, that it was too expensive and that downsizing the army to such an extent was not advisable or politically advantageous.[86] However, once in office this position changed and limited amendments to the plan were proposed instead of a full-scale revision. The revisions reduced the rate of increase in military spending, largely because of the 2008 financial crisis and made efforts to refocus the military back to the threat from the North. This was reflected in the proposed reinforcement of the ROKMC through providing them with a rapid response capability and alterations to the restructuring of the ROKA.[87] However, importantly, despite committing to most of the troop reductions set out in the original plan, the amendments stated that maintaining a defensive capability against North Korea would take precedence.

For the ROKN the amendments did not make any reference to altering the missions and force improvement projects set out over the previous years.[88] But, the administration's position towards ROKN modernisation and its blue-water ambition was much opaquer. The 2008 Defense White Paper did include measures to continue building blue-water capable vessels and the *Global Korea* Policy Initiative suggested that SLOC protection and energy security were particularly important.[89] However, procurement policies during his term suggested otherwise. The reorienting of the military and its force improvement programs back towards North Korea was particularly problematic for the ROKN. With shrinking defence budgets and an altered security focus, new procurement for the ROKN in terms of fresh platform development dried up despite commitments to the contrary. This was particularly apparent in the freezing of the 3,000-tons submarine program and while the PKX and FFX projects continued, (the contract for the first batch of Incheon class frigates was signed in December 2008) they were slowed down.[90] The *2010–14 Mid-term Defense Plan* which was written in 2009, failed to mention any significant new force improvements for the ROKN, instead focusing on developing technologies designed to counter North Korea and improve South Korea's deterrence capabilities on land.[91]

This reduction in support for naval modernisation came in the face of ROKN's first blue-water deployment to the Gulf of Aden, such a deployment met the aims of the administration's policies and demonstrated the advantages of having a blue-water capable navy, yet Lee's overall naval policies provided very little new in the way of continuing platform development.

This would change following the sinking of the *Cheonan* and the shelling of Yeonpyeong-do. The first significant political consequence was a national security review launched in May 2010 which pointed to several weaknesses in the ability to defend and respond to limited attacks. The review resulted in a new defence reform titled *Defence Reform 307*, later renamed *Defense Reform 11–30*. This defence plan reoriented South Korean defence planning away from future threats and towards meeting the current threat from North Korea.

In doing so it ranked operational priorities: (1) Regional provocations and asymmetric threats (for regional read North Korea), (2) all-out war, and (3) potential threats.[92] In order to meet such priorities, the plan advocated *active deterrence* which was designed to counter the threat of North Korean provocations. What this meant in practice was initially not explicitly defined, yet the focus of future procurement would be on technologies that would not only prevent Pyongyang from undertaking a provocation but would punish them if they did so suggesting South Korean retaliation following future incidents.[93]

These changes had significant short-term implications for the blue-water project and the ROKN. The ROKN now had to be able to better respond to limited provocations as well as the threat of all-out war in both the East and West Seas.[94] The ambition to develop forces and an operational posture which included managing future threats seemed to be moribund. Indeed, within the ROKN itself there was considerable concern that the sinking of the *Cheonan* would have a significant impact on political support for the blue-water concept, a fear which in the aftermath of the sinking was somewhat justified.[95] The effect on procurement was dramatic with the PKX and FFX programs being accelerated, ostensibly to increase the ROKN's ability to counter the KPN's submarine capability. A fact confirmed by the *2012–2016 Midterm-Defense Plan* which emphasised the need to develop sea control around the peninsula and protect maritime traffic within this area of operations.[96] The only major new procurement program which went ahead was a class of four *Cheon Wang Bong* class LST.

CONCLUSION

By the time Lee Myung-bak left office in February 2013, the ROKN's blue-water modernisation plans had suffered the twin blows of a lack of administrative support and the sinking of the *Cheonan*. However, this period proved to be only a temporary set back for the ROKN long-term plans. Even though Lee Myung-bak did not fully fund the ROKN and the sinking of the *Cheonan* exposed the navy to criticism, the ROKN did not abandon its plans and the prior modernisation of the navy soon proved its strategic value. North Korea's nuclear program, South Korea's increasing emphasis on deterrence by punishment and the development of strike capabilities coupled with the increasing regional tension at sea between China and Japan all brought into focus the requirements of a modern naval force. The ROKN's existing capabilities that had been introduced under its blue-water modernisation program provided solutions to many of these strategic issues and therefore won political and financial support. The subsequent administration of Park Geun-hye supported the ROKN's force modernisation goals and the decision to construct a second *Dokdo* class LPH and new KDX-III Batch-II destroyers were made under her tenure.

This chapter has shown that ROKN blue-water modernisation matched the political ambitions and strategic policies of three successive administrations across the political spectrum. The ROKN's ambition for a wider operational role coincided with democratisation and subsequent changes in South Korea's foreign and security policy ambitions. However, once an administration came to power that did not support such goals, the ROKN struggled to maintain the momentum of its modernisation. That blue-water modernisation has current political support lies in the relationship between the contemporary strategic environment and the advantages a powerful, multifunctional navy can provide. The idea of a powerful, independent blue-water navy has once again won political support but has not yet fully embedded itself into South Korean political thinking. If the ROKN can continue to demonstrate strategic value, something that will become apparent as it becomes more powerful, and matches the ambitions of political elites in Seoul, blue-water modernisation will likely continue.

NOTES

1. Using Johnston's definition, strategic culture is an 'ideational milieu' which influences strategic choices. See: Alastair Iain Johnston, "Thinking about Strategic Culture," *International Security* 19, no. 4 (1995): 46. It can be determined by examining both core beliefs about the nature of warfare and 'preferences about security planning and conflict resolution'. See: Victor Cha, "Strategic Culture and the Military Modernization of South Korea," *Armed Forces and Society* 28, no. 1 (2001): 115.
2. Alfred T. Mahan, *The Influence of Sea Power Upon History 1660–1783*, 12th ed. (Boston: Little Brown and Company 1947), 58.
3. Eric Heginbotham has demonstrated that democratic rulers with liberal economic policies are more likely to support naval expansion, however this work does not explain the influence of external threats on continental borders on the policies of naval expansion. See: Eric Heginbotham, "The Fall and Rise of Navies in East Asia: Military Organisations, Domestic

Politics and Grand Strategy," *International Security* 27, no. 2 (2002): 86–125.

4. Jiyul Kim, "Strategic Culture of the Republic of Korea," *Contemporary Security Policy* 35, no. 2 (2014): 270–89, 280.

5. Hwee-rhak Park "South Korea's Failure to Implement 'Defence Reform 2020'," *The Korean Journal of International Studies* 12, no. 2 (2014): 379–401, 392–93.

6. Zoltan Barany, *The Soldier and the Changing State* (Princeton: Princeton University Press, 2012), 190.

7. Takeshi Watanabe, "Reform of South Korea's Defense Acquisition Program Administration," *NIDS Commentary No. 41*, 25 December 2014. http://www.nids.mod.go.jp/english/publication/commentary/pdf/commentary041e.pdf, accessed 5 May 2016.

8. Guen Lee, "Strengthening the National Assembly's Influence on South Korean Foreign Policy," in *Domestic Constraints on South Korean Foreign Policy*, ed. Scott A Snyder, Guen Lee, Young Ho-kim, and Jiyoon Kim (Washington, DC: Council on Foreign Relations, 2018), 6–7.

9. Myo-ja Ser and Yong-soo Jeong "Assembly Increases Defense Budget for 2016," *Korea Joongang Ilbo*, 4 December 2015. http://mengnews.joins.com/view.aspx?aId=3012354, accessed 21 March 2018.

10. Joo-hong Kim "The Armed Forces," *The Park Chung Hee Ere: The Transformation of South Korea*, ed. Kim Byung-kook and Ezra F. Vogel (Cambridge: Harvard University Press, 2011), 168–99, 168–71.

11. Carl J. Saxer, "Generals and Presidents: Establishing Civilian and Democratic Control in South Korea," *Armed Forces & Society* 3, no. 3 (2004): 386.

12. Aurel Croissant, "Riding the Tiger: Civilian Control and the Military in Democratizing Korea," *Armed Forces & Society* 30, no. 3 (2004): 357–81, 365–76.

13. Ibid., 368.

14. Sang-Yoon Bae, "Maritime Developments in South Korea," in *Maritime Power in the China Seas Capabilities and Rational*, ed. Dominic Sherwood (Canberra: Australian Defence Studies Centre, 1994), 51–60.

15. Robert Karniol, "Democratic Change Reaches ROK Military," *Jane's Defence Weekly*, 17 July 1993.

16. Ibid.

17. Carl J. Saxer, *From Transition to Power Alternation: Democracy in South Korea, 1987–1997* (New York: Routledge, 2002), 162.

18. Terence Roehrig, *The Prosecution of Former Military Leaders in Newly Democratic Nations: The Cases of Argentina, Greece and South Korea* (Jefferson, NC: MacFarland, 2002), 151.

19. Saxer, "Generals and Presidents: Establishing Civilian and Democratic Control," 395.
20. Byung-kook Kim, "Party Politics in South Korea's Democracy: The Crisis of Success," in *Consolidating Democracy in the South Korea,* ed. Larry J. Diamond and Byung-kook Kim (Colorado: Lynne Reinner, 2000), 53–86, 54.
21. Karniol, *Democratic Change*; Saxer, *Generals and Presidents: Establishing Civilian and Democratic Control,* 393–95.
22. Croissant, "Riding the Tiger: Civilian Control and the Military," 373.
23. It is important to note that the military still holds an important role in the national security apparatus. See Croissant, "Riding the Tiger: Civilian Control and the Military," 372.
24. During the Young-sam Kim administration there was time little or no oversight or ability for the bureaucracy to amend decisions made by the Blue House. See Yong-duck Jung "Administrative Reorganisation: The Case of the Kim Young-sam Regime," in *The White House and the Blue House: Government Reform in the United States and Korea,* ed. Cho Yong-Ho and George H. Frederickson (Maryland: United Press of America, 1997), 89–110, 91–95.
25. Gi-wook Shin, *The Paradox of Korean Globalisation* (Stanford: The Asia-Pacific Research Center, 2003), 10.
26. Samuel S. Kim, "Nationalism and Globalisation on South Korea's Foreign Policy," *New Asia* 14, no. 3 (2007): 17–18.
27. Samuel S. Kim, "Korean and Globalization (Segyehwa): A Framework for Analysis," in *Korea's Globalization,* ed. Samuel S. Kim (Cambridge: Cambridge University Press, 2000), 3.
28. Author conducted interview with Park, Jin (Kim, Young-sam's Press Secretary), April 2011.
29. Interview with Admiral An Byeong-tae, April 2011.
30. Ibid.
31. Young-sam Kim *Speech At the 49th Commencement of the Korean Naval Academy,* 24 March 1995; Young-sam Kim *Speech At the 51st Commencement of the Korean Naval Academy,* 12 March 1997.
32. Young-sam Kim *Speech At the 50th Commencement Ceremony of the Korean Naval Academy,* 13 March 1996.
33. Republic of Korea Ministry of National Defense, *Defense White Paper 1994–1995* (Seoul: Korea Institute of Defense Analysis, 1995), 106.
34. Ibid.
35. Heo Uk and Terence Roehrig, *South Korea's Rise: Economic Development, Power, and Foreign Relations* (Cambridge: Cambridge University Press, 2014), 36–40.

36. Samuel S. Kim, *The Two Koreas and the Great Powers* (New York: Cambridge University Press, 2006), 320–21.
37. Despite the depoliticization that occurred under his predecessor, Kim Dae-jung was keen to keep the ROKA onside despite their suspicion of the Sunshine Policy. See: Barany, *The Soldier and the Changing State*, 188.
38. Minister for Foreign Affairs and Trade Soon-young Hang *Foreign Policy Agenda of the Republic of Korea in the New Century*. Speech given at the Graduate School of International Studies: Korea University, 11 December 1998.
39. Ibid; Scott Snyder, "Strategic Thought Toward Asia in the Dae-jung Era Kim" in *South Korean Strategic Though Toward Asia*, ed. Gilbert Rozman, In-taek Hyun, and Shin-wha Lee (New York: Palgrave Macmillan, 2008), 77–99, 92.
40. While not the first South Korean president to dispatch troops on PKO, he was the first to deploy combat troops, when he sent a contingent of troops to assist the 1999 PKO mission in East-Timor (INTERFET). This was done despite considerable opposition within the conservative legislature. See Ian Bowers, "Korean Approaches to Peace Support and Stability Operations," in *Asia-Pacific Nations in International Peace Support and Stability Operations*, ed. Chiyuki Aoi and Yee Heng (New York: Palgrave Macmillan, 2014), 87–111.
41. Dae-jung Kim "Safeguarding the Nation: On the 50th Armed Forces Day," 1 October 1998, in *Government of the People: Selected Speeches of Kim, Dae-jung Vol. I* (Seoul: Office of the President of the Republic of Korea, 1999), 199.
42. Republic of Korea Ministry of National Defense, *Defense White Paper 1998* (Seoul: Korean Institute of Defense Analysis, 1999), 27.
43. Republic of Korea Ministry of National Defense, *Defence White Paper 2000* (Seoul: Republic of Korea Ministry of National Defense, 2001), 69.
44. Republic of Korea Ministry of National Defense, *Defense Data and Statistics 2001* (Seoul: Republic of Korea Ministry of National Defense, 2001), 28–32.
45. Ibid.
46. Republic of Korea Ministry of National Defense, *Defense White Paper 1998*, 237–38.
47. Michael Raska, *Military Innovation in Small States: Creating a Reverse Asymmetry* (Oxon: Routledge, 2016), 111.
48. Jiyul Kim and Michael J. Finnegan, "The Republic of Korea Approaches the Future," *Joint Forces Quarterly* 2 (Spring 2002): 37.
49. Chung-in Moon and Jin-young Lee "The Revolution in Military Affairs and the Defence Industry in South Korea," *Security Challenges* 4, no. 4 (2008): 122.

50. Victor Cha, "Strategic Culture and Military Modernization of South Korea," *Armed Forces and Society* 28, no. 1 (2001): 106.

51. Dae-jung Kim "Advancing into the World Through the Sea: At the 52nd Commencement Ceremony of the Korean Naval Academy," 16 March 1998, in *Government of the People: Selected Speeches of Kim, Dae-jung Vol. 1* (Seoul: Office of the President of the Republic of Korea, 1999), 31–34.

52. Ibid., 34.

53. Dae-jung Kim "Guarding the Turbulent Sea: At the 53rd Commencement Ceremony of the Korean Naval Academy," 12 March 1999, in *Government of the People: Selected Speeches of Kim, Dae-jung Vol. II* (Seoul: Office of the President of the Republic of Korea, 2000), 25.

54. Dae-jung Kim "In the Glorious Traditions of Admirals Yi Sun-shin and Chang-Po-go: At the 54th Commencement Ceremony of the Korean Naval Academy," 16 March 2000, in *Government of the People: Selected Speeches of Kim, Dae-jung Vol. III* (Seoul: Office of the President of the Republic of Korea, 2001), 73–74.

55. Dae-jung Kim "An Ever-Strong Security Stance: At the 55th Commencement Ceremony of the Korean Naval Academy," 19 March 2001, in *Government of the People: Selected Speeches of Kim, Dae-jung Vol. IV* (Seoul: Office of the President of the Republic of Korea, 2002), 69.

56. Heo Uk and Terence Roehrig, *South Korea Since 1980* (Cambridge: Cambridge University Press, 2010), 61–66.

57. Song-ho Sheen, "Strategic Thought Toward Asia in the Roh Moo-hyun Era," in *South Korean Strategic Though Toward Asia*, ed. Gilbert Rozman, In-taek Hyun, and Shin-wha Lee (New York: Palgrave Macmillan, 2008), 102.

58. Ibid.

59. Chung-in Moon, "China's Rise and Security Dynamics on the Korean Peninsula," in *Strategic Adjustment and the Rise of China*, ed. Robert S. Ross and Øystein Tunsjø (Ithaca, NY: Cornell University Press, 2017), 204–205.

60. Moo-hyun Roh Address by President Moo-hyun Roh on the 55th ROK Armed Forces Day, 1 October 2003.

61. Samuel S. Kim, *The Two Koreas*, 270.

62. Samuel S. Kim, *The Two Koreas*, 74–75; Roh, Moo-Hyun, *Address at the 53rd Commencement and Commissioning Ceremony of the Korean Air Force Academy*, 8 March 2005.

63. Chung-in Moon, "China's Rise and Security Dynamics on the Korean Peninsula," 206–7.

64. Song-ho Sheen, "Strategic Thought Toward Asia," 120.

65. Moo-hyun Roh *Address by the President Roh, Moo-hyun on the 84th March First Independence Movement Day*, 01 March 2003.

66. Presidential Commission on Policy Planning, *Korea's Future Vision and Strategy: Korea's Ambition to Become an Advanced Power by 2030* (Seoul: Seoul Selection, 2008), 317.
67. Moo-hyun Roh *Address by President Roh Moo-hyun on the 58th Anniversary of National Liberation*, 15 August 2003.
68. Chung-in Moon, "China's Rise and Security Dynamics on the Korean Peninsula," 206.
69. Moo-hyun Roh *Address at the 53rd Commencement and Commissioning Ceremony of the Korea Air Force Academy*, 8 March 2005.
70. Moo-hyun Roh *Address by President Roh Moo-hyun at the 57th Graduation and Commissioning Ceremony of the Korean Naval Academy*, 13 March 2003.
71. Moo-hyun Roh *President Celebrates Aegis Destroyer Launch*, 25 May 2007.
72. Moo-hyun Roh *Address by President Roh Moo-hyun at the 57th Graduation and Commissioning Ceremony of the Korean Naval Academy*, 13 March 2003.
73. Republic of Korea Ministry of National Defense, *Defense Reform 2020* (Seoul: Republic of Korea Ministry of National Defense, 2005), 12–13.
74. Moo-hyun Roh *Address by the President Roh, Moo-hyun on the 55th Armed Forces Day*, 1 October 2003.
75. Republic of Korea Ministry of National Defense, *Defense Reform 2020*, 12–13.
76. Ibid.
77. This breakdown of the significant points of Defence Reform 2020 was taken from Han Yong-sup, "Analyzing South Korea's Defense Reform 2020," *Korean Journal of Defense Analysis* 18, no. 1 (2006): 111–34, 116–18.
78. Republic of Korea Ministry of National Defense, *Defense Reform 2020*, 17.
79. Sang-yup Lee "Ships, Security, and Symbols: A Constructivist Explanation of South Korea's Naval Build-up" (Unpublished PhD Dissertation, Rutgers University 2013), 249.
80. Office of the President, *Global Korea: The National Security Strategy of the Republic of Korea* (Seoul: Office of the President, 2009), 11.
81. For a detailed description of Lee's North Korea policy see: Jae-jean Suh *The Lee Myung-bak Government's North Korea Policy: A Study on Its Historical and Theoretical Foundation* (Seoul: Korea Institute for National Unification 2009).
82. Sung-ki Jung "Lee Myung-bak to Revise Sunshine Strategy," *Korea Times*, 24 December 2007.

83. Song-ho Sheen "A Smart Alliance in the Age of Complexity; ROK-U.S. Alliance in the 21st Century," EAI Issue Briefing 009-02, 1.
84. The White House, Office of the Press Secretary, *Joint Vision for the Alliance of The United States of America and The Republic of Korea*, 16 June 2009.
85. President Roh rejected joining the PSI as he feared it could damage South Korea's foreign policy and provoke a diplomatic backlash from China.
86. The National Institute for Defense Studies, *East Asian Strategic Review 2009* (Tokyo: The Japan Times, 2009), 99.
87. Ibid., 100; Republic of Korea Ministry of National Defense, *Public Announcement of Defense Basic Reform Plan (2009–2020)* (Seoul: Republic of Korea Ministry of National Defense, 2009).
88. The National Institute for Defense Studies, *2009 East Asian Strategic Review*, 101.
89. Office of the President, *Global Korea: The National Security Strategy of the Republic of Korea*, 33.
90. Sang-ho Lee "Issue of the Oceanic Navy and Complement of Naval Force After Warship Cheonan-ham Incident," *Sejong Commentary No. 181* (2009).
91. Republic of Korea Ministry of National Defense, *"'10–'14 Gukbangjunggigyehoek* ['10–'14 Mid-term Defence Plan]," *Republic of Korea Ministry of National Defense, Press Release* (Seoul: Ministry of National Defence, 2009).
92. The National Institute of Defense Studies, *East Asian Strategic Review 2012* (Tokyo: National Institute of Defense Studies, 2012), 74.
93. Ibid., 77.
94. Ibid.
95. This concern was highlighted by several media reports which called into question the actions of the ROKN during the sinking and the Blue-water development policy. See Jee-ho Yoo "Navy to Get New Course After Loss of the Cheonan," *Korea Joongang Daily*, 24 May 2011.
96. Republic of Korea Ministry of National Defense, *"'12–'16 Gukbangjunggigyehoek* ['12–'16 Mid-term Defence Plan]," *Republic of Korea Ministry of National Defense, Press Release* (Seoul: Ministry of National Defence, 2011).

CHAPTER 8

Conclusion

In the introduction, this book asked how and why South Korea, a historically inward-looking nation with an existential threat on its only land border, began a sustained period of blue-water naval modernisation. By taking a multifaceted approach, the book identifies the drivers and constraints of this modernisation, its operational benefits and outstanding limitations. The core argument is that Republic of Korea Navy (ROKN) modernisation has been and is determined by the confluence of external strategic rationales and changes to the nature of South Korea as a state. The result is a ROKN which is benefitting from an overall increase in capabilities that have operational and strategic utility in both the littoral waters of the Korean Peninsula and the maritime strategic arena of East Asia. The ROKN is now one of the most powerful conventional naval forces in the world, yet it was understudied and largely ignored in the literature on contemporary Asian seapower. This book is the first monograph to fill this gap and reveals a navy with increasingly important and relevant operational and strategic capabilities.

Democratisation in 1988 and the election of a civilian president four years later opened the door for broader conceptions of South Korean security. While North Korea remains the predominant threat and primary determinant of South Korean foreign and security policy, Seoul developed a greater appreciation of the wider East Asian security environment and South Korea's position within it. The end of the Cold War, the introduction of United Nations Convention on the Law of the Sea

© The Author(s) 2019

I. Bowers, *The Modernisation of the Republic of Korea Navy*, Critical Studies of the Asia-Pacific,
https://doi.org/10.1007/978-3-319-92291-1_8

(UNCLOS) and South Korea's desire to become an active, responsible international stakeholder placed greater emphasis on the importance of naval power within South Korea's seapower and security calculus.

East Asia is a maritime theatre and there the ROKN, which had desired to expand its role, became a perfect tool with which South Korea could express and protect its new security and foreign policy interests. Of course, the threat from North Korea has not disappeared and the Korean People's Navy (KPN) constantly challenges the ROKN, which in turn must continuously alter its operations and capabilities to maintain deterrence and warfighting superiority. ROKN blue-water modernisation remains determined by this bifurcated requirement to maintain deterrence in the littoral waters of the Korean Peninsula while at the same time developing a regional operational capability. It is also informed by South Korea's push for a technology-intensive, independent military force. The pursuit of independence is an important consideration. The United States remains an extremely influential ally and retains wartime Operational Control (OPCON) over the South Korean military. Concerned about the direction of South Korea force development, previously, the United States tried to restrain South Korean naval modernisation. However, South Korea is seeking a gradual return of strategic autonomy and it is within this context that ROKN blue-water modernisation is taking place.

Considering these factors, ROKN modernisation encapsulates the development of South Korea into a modern, technologically advanced middle power. However, this book also argues that consistent long-term planning is required and while ROKN modernisation and an expanded naval role has current political support, the concept of South Korea as a seapower has not yet fully imbedded into the state's security culture and defence planning.

THREAT AND STRATEGY

Placing ROKN modernisation within South Korea's strategic environment is a complex exercise. South Korea faces an existential threat on its land border that requires constant attention and dominates their security planning. Yet at the same time, this threat has transformed South Korea into a geopolitical island. As it has no access to continental Asia, it is entirely reliant on the sea as a medium of trade and economic prosperity. This differentiates South Korea from its Northeast Asian neighbours, China and Japan. Neither of which face the threat of invasion and can therefore expend greater resources on the development of their naval power.

South Korea must confront a dilemma about how to maintain security within the context of North Korea, while at the same time ensuring that their Sea Lines of Communications (SLOC) and maritime interests are secure. Following the end of the Korean War, South Korea's solution was to maintain a limited naval force that could deter the minimal naval threat from North Korea, while simultaneously relying on the United States and its navy to maintain maritime security in East Asia and provide power projection capabilities in a time of war.

However, the strategic situation in the waters around the peninsula and in the wider East Asian maritime region presented a challenge to this formulation. First, in the 1970s the KPN with the introduction of submarines and anti-ship missiles began to gain the upper hand in the deterrent standoff between it and the ROKN. South Korea's response was to begin its own round of naval modernisation supported by its increasing economic and industrial capabilities. This dynamic has never ended and the ROKN has consistently modernised its forces within this context, first gaining superiority in the 1990s and then reacting to new challenges as they appeared. This book shows that the long-term deterrence relationship between the two countries has a dynamic where if either side introduces or uses new capabilities there is a subsequent response. The ROKN must constantly adjust its force posture and capabilities to continue to manage the North Korean threat.

This reaction dynamic was exposed following three surface battles and the sinking of the ROKS *Cheonan*. In the case of the surface engagements, the ROKN demonstrated operational superiority, yet was forced to adjust tactics and Rules of Engagement (ROE) to close specific vulnerabilities. The sinking of the *Cheonan* highlighted the difficulties faced by the ROKN in managing the shifting nature of the threat from North Korea. North Korea revealed a willingness to use a lethal capability during armistice conditions. By revealing its capabilities and intent, the KPN forced a change in ROKN operational priorities. Anti-Submarine Warfare (ASW) is an extremely difficult exercise, made even more challenging by the maritime geography on both sides of the peninsula and even though ROKN blue-water modernisation was in the process of increasing its ASW capacity it accelerated these efforts to limit the impact of the KPN's submarine capabilities.

The second challenge to South Korea's approach to seapower and national security was the end of the Cold War, which coincided with the dynamics of globalisation and economic interdependence coupled with increased geostrategic tensions in maritime East Asia. With some of the world's largest importers and exporters in the region reliant on the sea, its stability is a significant factor in East Asia's prosperity. At the same time, China's rise and moves towards the sea and the United States' relative decline in capabilities has created a situation where strategic competition is now occurring on the seas of the region. The introduction of the UNCLOS regime has also ignited a series of territorial and jurisdictional disputes compounded by historical animosities and energy competition.

Just because South Korea is faced with the threat from North Korea, it does not mean it is immune from, or can ignore the strategic environment that surrounds it. Since the 1970s South Korea has built much of its economy by exploiting the civilian aspects of seapower, using the sea as a medium for import and export, a lifeline for vital energy supplies and as a method of wealth production. However, the naval component of seapower was defined by North Korea and did not engage with the broader East Asian security environment.

A shift in early 1990s is observable when South Korea began to recognise that non-North Korea related threats to its security were at sea. With the introduction of UNCLOS, there has been a heightened emphasis on protecting its maritime territory from external influence. This threat is mainly focused on China and Japan and is informed by South Korea's own history where traditionally, it has been the victim of the machinations of its two larger neighbours. With ongoing disputes with both countries over exclusive economic zone (EEZ) boundaries and possession of territory, South Korea has recognised the need to protect what it perceives as its legal and historical claims to the seas around the peninsula. The ROKN is keenly aware that with China's naval build-up and Japan's response, South Korea is in an increasingly vulnerable position and needs to possess a force capable of deterring these two large powers from undertaking any acts detrimental to South Korea's interests.

There is also an understanding that South Korea's SLOC are vulnerable due to the potential for hostility in the East Asia. The disputes over Taiwan, the Senkaku, and Spratly Islands and the existing tension between China and the United States all serve to inform the direction of ROKN modernisation. South Korea does not have any interest in these disputes in so much as they are not directly involved, but it fears that being a third party, its SLOC to the Middle East may be disrupted and protection not granted by the warring parties. As such, South Korea has seen the need for an independent naval capability able to protect its interests in a potentially unstable regional environment.

NAVAL POWER AS A RESPONSE

It is this divergent threat environment that poses a dilemma for ROKN blue-water modernisation. Namely, how to continue to maintain a significant littoral capability to ensure that deterrence is effective, while at the same time developing a force capable of non-peninsular operations. The solution the ROKN hit upon was to focus on quality over quantity. ROKN force planners have chosen to leverage the multifunctionality of modern warships and diverse weapons complements to create operational potential in both scenarios.

ROKN blue-water modernisation plans have centred on developing a balanced, networked naval force with precision war-fighting capabilities. It is a cross-platform effort to replace old capabilities and introduce new ones. New destroyers, frigates, patrol boats and submarines reinforce the ROKN's ability to maintain deterrent superiority on the waters around the Korean Peninsula but also provide the ROKN with new capabilities and deterrent roles. These new platforms and systems have been well integrated into the ROKN's fleet and the navy now possesses an increasingly credible surface, subsurface and air warfighting capacity that is far superior to capabilities of the KPN.

North Korea's nuclear and ballistic missile program is an opportunity for the ROKN to demonstrate the value of its blue-water platforms to peninsular security. The three-ship class of KDX-III Aegis destroyers with their powerful sensors and tracking capabilities provide much-needed surveillance capacity for South Korea to monitor missile launches from North Korea. Equally, a substantial proportion of the blue-water initiative was focused on the development of new patrol boats and frigates that are primarily tasked with deterring North Korea. The advantage of these new platforms over previous vessels is a heavier and diverse weapon complement, advanced sensors and NCW capabilities which increase their lethality in warfighting scenarios.

ROKN force modernisation in relation to non-peninsular security faces a different set of challenges. The ROKN acknowledges that it will never be as powerful as its neighbours, China and Japan, and therefore is developing asymmetric forces capable of deterring either from taking action harmful to its interests. The centre piece of this strategy is the ROKN's submarine capability. These boats are powerful force multipliers and have utility in both peninsular and non-peninsular contexts. Their ability to engage land targets and surface vessels make them important for the ROKN's ability to project power into North Korea but their anti-ship capabilities make them dangerous foes for even superior opponents.

The ROKN's force structure highlights the ROKN's divergent mission sets. The structure is a derivation of one developed in 1985 which was designed to better manage the threat from the KPN. Divided into three fleets, each is charged with a geographic region around the peninsula, this structure is concerned with preventing infiltration and maintaining deterrence. Each fleet is composed of patrol craft, corvettes and frigates and has as a flag ship one KDX-I destroyer. As new capabilities are being introduced into these fleets, their ability to deter North Korea will improve, particularly in terms of ASW. These fleets can also play a vital role in ensuring South Korea's maritime sovereignty by maintaining a presence in its EEZ and supporting South Korea's Coast Guard. This is a vital mission considering the strength of South Korea's neighbours and China's record of using seapower for coercive strategic effect.

Outside of this structure are several flotillas dedicated to operating around the three fleets and reinforcing them when necessary. It is within this context that Maritime Task Flotilla 7 operates. Based at the new Jeju Naval Base, this flotilla is in many ways at the heart of ROKN blue-water modernisation. It is comprised of KDX-II and KDX-III destroyers and is charged with responding to contingencies around the peninsula and in the region. These dual tasking highlights how the ROKN is attempting utilise the mobility and multifunctionality of large modern platforms to meet its diverse operational requirements.

ALLIANCES, IDENTITY AND POLITICS

The external strategic environment is not a sufficient factor to explain how the ROKN began such a significant alteration in capabilities and expansion in operational roles. This book shows that changes in the alliance relationship with the United States, efforts by the ROKN and seapower advocates to explain the necessity of the naval component of seapower and alterations in South Korea's strategic outlook following democratisation combined to create an environment that facilitated ROKN blue-water modernisation.

The United States as South Korea's only ally plays an important role in the story of ROKN modernisation. It has moved from actively constraining South Korea's naval power following the end of the Korean War, to supporting and shaping it in the present day. This change can be explained by the shifting contexts of the US-South Korean alliance. Following the Korean War, Washington had near total control over South Korea military development and operations. The United States viewed the ROKN as almost extraneous to strategic requirements and equipped it with the minimal amount of ships needed to operate in the littoral against what was then a limited KPN. The presence of the US 7th fleet in East Asia and the overwhelming land threat posed by North Korea ensured that the ROKA and ROKAF received most capacity building assistance from the United States. ROKN modernisation advanced only when the United States judged that it was required to match the capabilities of North Korea.

As South Korean dependence on the United States began to end in the 1970s, the nature of Washington's influence over ROKN modernisation changed. The continued presence of the US 7th Fleet, ensured that the army-dominated governments in Seoul did not provide sufficient funds to expand the ROKN's roles. Deterrence in the littorals remained the primary mission, but the ROKN did benefit from the introduction of new indigenously constructed vessels that were designed to counter KPN capabilities. The United States became a commercial supplier of weapons and other naval systems and largely used their influence to persuade South Korea not to buy non-US equipment when possible.

The relationship changed again after the end of the Cold War. ROKN and South Korean military modernisation were shaped by the United States' embrace of RMA technologies. This was due to the requirement of maintaining interoperability. As the ROKN became more powerful and began to use modern naval weapon systems, the United States Navy (USN) became more interested in developing a closer working relationship. A powerful, modern ROKN is beneficial to US maritime strategic interests both around the Korean Peninsula and beyond. The relationship between the two navies is now closer than it ever has been. The United States has become an actor which now encourages and supports ROKN blue-water goals through the provision of high-end systems such as Aegis and increased joint training and exercises.

The removal of the United States as an impediment to ROKN blue-water modernisation did not automatically result in the ROKN being given the permission to develop a broader set of capabilities and roles. The ROKN and other advocates of seapower have had to actively persuade both the public and politicians of the necessity of such modernisation. Democratisation provided the window for the advocacy of seapower and gave the ROKN the opportunity to create a specific naval identity both within the public and political consciousness. The goal of these efforts is to cement support for the traditionally overlooked ROKN and provide the ideational justification for naval power to be imbedded into South Korea's security planning.

To achieve this, the ROKN began to use Korea's limited maritime history to provide the public with a frame of reference to understand what the role and goals of the ROKN were. Alongside this policy the ROKN began a strong public relations campaign, explaining to the populace through booklets, the internet and television about the importance of the ROKN and directly connecting a modern navy to the future development of South Korea as a state. However, while spreading the message to the public is important, of greater significance are the efforts of the ROKN and seapower advocates to influence the political and decision-making circles of South Korea. The major tool the ROKN has employed to do so are debates and conferences, which are designed to educate a political class, that has traditionally ignored the navy, about the value of the sea and the need for an advanced naval force.

The political support for the ROKN is the final element in explaining both its modernisation and move towards regional capabilities. The election of Kim Young-sam to the presidency of South Korea in 1993 was a milestone in the history of the country, as the first elected civilian leader since 1962 he brought with him to the office a series of policy reforms which would reshape the South Korean military into its present form. He began with the removal of the structures which had allowed the military and specifically the ROKA to hold power. At the same time, Kim initiated the policy of *Segyehwa* or globalisation which was aimed at pushing South Korea towards the international community in an economic, political and social sense. Without the domination of the army, the ROKN CNO was able to meet with the President in 1995 and presented a plan to modernise the ROKN in a way that would allow it to perform regional operations while maintaining its focus on the littoral waters of the peninsula. Blue-water modernisation matched the concept of *Segyehwa* and won the support of Kim.

Continued political support is vital to any form of naval force modernisation as it is an inherently long-term project. The administrations of Kim Dae-jung and Roh Moo-hyun which succeeded Kim Young-sam, had similar if more advanced policies which too met with the objectives of the ROKN's force improvement plans. Both presidents embraced the concepts of moving South Korea towards having stronger regional roles and at the same time adopted more conciliatory attitudes towards North Korea. While the former initiatives were not direct extensions of *Segyehwa* they were in the same spirit and allowed the ROKN to continue to push for greater modernisation within this policy context.

Both administrations also undertook defence reform initiatives aimed at developing an independent defence capability which would be able to address issues on the peninsula and at the same time would have the ability to deal with future threats. In this vein, while ROKN reform plans had been developed before these presidents came into office, their own defence reform plans matched the goals of the ROKN. The presidency of Lee Myung-bak highlights this importance, on his election he vowed to take a stronger line towards North Korea and to rejuvenate the US-South Korea alliance. As such his policies did not match those of predecessors and the ROKN lost political backing and therefore the momentum for blue-water modernisation. This momentum was regained under the Park Geun-hye government as a powerful multifunctional ROKN suited the peninsular and regional strategic environment and the governments security policies. Blue-water modernisation has only been possible because three successive administrations provided the political support for it. This ensured that the ROKN's ambitions could survive the scepticism of the Lee Myung-bak government and that the navy could demonstrate the value of a blue-water ROKN to a new administration facing an increasingly compex contemporary strategic environment.

PROBLEMS AND OPPORTUNITIES

By 2030, the ROKN will be a potent naval force. If procurement proceeds as planned, it will introduce a second Landing Platform Helicopter (LPH), up to nine new destroyers and a new class of indigenously designed and constructed submarines. It will be a navy that will have to be counted in calculations regarding strategic stability in East Asia.

However, several uncertainties exist regarding the future of ROKN modernisation and the role of the navy in South Korean security.

When North Korea sank the *Cheonan* in 2010 questions were raised in public and political circles over the direction of ROKN blue-water modernisation. Much of this criticism did not reflect the difficulties the ROKN faces in constantly maintaining deterrence and in conducting ASW operations. However, the ROKN was forced to temporarily stop referring to blue-water modernisation and the political support for it dried up causing the temporary suspension of long-term procurement plans. This suggests that the role of the ROKN and an expanded naval identity has not yet fully integrated into South Korean security planning. Although, blue-water modernisation is now back, and resources have been committed to further blue-water platforms, it remains to be seen if this will still be the case if another strategic shock occurs on or around the Korean Peninsula.

Second, the ROKN's plans for an effective regional blue-water force are constantly under-pressure due to resource constraints. This problem is more acute given the threat from North Korea and the increasing relative naval power in East Asia. While the ROKN can probably maintain deterrence within a Northeast Asia context, independent SLOC protection will be difficult to achieve. Such operations require a critical mass of platforms that can ensure training and maintenance requirements are met while at the same time maintaining a fighting force at sea. The ROKN has struggled with this due to a lack of platforms and multiple commitments around the Korean peninsula and beyond. Even with new platforms being introduced, the ROKN may find it difficult to sustain consistent regional operations while also maintaining deterrence around the Korean Peninsula.

The third area for both the ROKN and future South Korean governments to consider is the consequences of greater naval capacity. While South Korea contributed forces to the Vietnam War and the wars in Iraq and Afghanistan, it has shown itself unwilling to become involved in the maritime disputes in East Asia. It is arguable that with more capabilities comes more responsibility and South Korea may find it difficult to ignore US requests for a South Korean presence in the South China Sea, or even involvement in a conflict between the US and China. It was only when the ROKN began to modernise that more joint exercises and greater operational interaction occurred between the USN and ROKN. The United States now views the ROKN as a modern partner who can provide much-needed capabilities around the peninsula and the wider East Asian region. A blue-water navy provides South Korea with greater foreign policy tools but now decisions regarding their strategic posture in East Asia and the use of naval power will need to be considered.

Fourth, the future of ROKN modernisation lies in its embrace of technology. As a navy and country allied with the US, South Korea will face hard and expensive choices in developing and maintaining capabilities that will remain interoperable. The US is developing next-generation technologies such as artificial intelligence and unmanned autonomous craft and these capabilities will become more prominent in future naval operations.[1] How the ROKN embraces this future is an open question. The ROKN has demonstrated that its procurement strategy allows for the consistent modernisation of ship classes, however, it is still perfecting its C4I operational capabilities. It is becoming a networked force, but it will soon have to face the challenge of making the next leap in naval technology if it is to remain an interoperable and effective fighting force.

As I commit these words to paper, security on the Korean Peninsula is at something of a crossroads. North Korea's nuclear and missile program now directly threatens the US and consequently, the risk of war between the US and North Korea has heightened. At the same time, South Korea has led efforts to begin dialogue and negotiations, culminating in President Trump meeting Kim Jong-un in Singapore in June 2018. The future remains uncertain and potential outcomes range from war, to denuclearisation, to the maintenance of the status quo. Unless unification occurs, the ROKN will still be required to maintain year-round operations in the waters around the Korean Peninsula. Equally the East Asian maritime environment is likely to remain unstable and South Korea will need the tools to protect its strategic interests.

The naval component of seapower is often an expression of a state's ambition and desire to project power and influence away from home waters. The ROKN and its blue-water modernisation program reveal that South Korea is a modern and increasingly powerful state. Only time will tell if the ROKN can sustain its modernisation, but currently, it is on a path to becoming a military service that can serve a wide spectrum of South Korea's foreign policy and security requirements.

NOTE

1. Many of these concepts were included in the seemingly defunct Third
   Offset strategy. However, it is unlikely that the US will give up its pursuit
   of high-technology capabilities. See: Kathleen Hicks and Andrew Hunter,
   "What Will Replace the Third Offset? Lessons from Past Innovation
   Strategies," *Defense One*, 17 March 2017, http://www.defenseone.
   com/ideas/2017/03/what-will-replace-third-offset-lessons-past-innova-
   tion-strategies/136260/, accessed 11 March 2018.

SELECT BIBLIOGRAPHY

ARCHIVES

Central Intelligence Agency, Freedom of Information Act Electronic Reading Room.
Digital National Security Archive.
Gerald R. Ford Presidential Library.
National Security Archive, Korea Project.
Republic of Korea Presidential Archive.

PRIMARY SOURCES

Central Intelligence Agency. *Korean Fishing Areas in the Yellow Sea—Spawning Ground for Maritime Conflict.* GCK-RP 75–20, May 1975. Central Intelligence Agency Library. https://www.cia.gov/library/readingroom/docs/CIA-RDP86T00608R000600140005-7.pdf. Accessed 10 December 2017.
Ministry of Defense of Japan. *National Security Strategy December 17, 2013.* Tokyo: Ministry of Defense of Japan, 2013.
Ministry of Defense of Japan. *Defense of Japan 2017.* Tokyo: Ministry of Defense of Japan, 2017.
Ministry of National Defense. The People's Republic of China, *Full Text: China's Military Strategy,* 16 May 2015. http://eng.mod.gov.cn/Press/2015-05/26/content_4586805_4.htm.
Office of the President. *Global Korea: The National Security Strategy of the Republic of Korea.* Seoul: Office of the President, 2009.

© The Editor(s) (if applicable) and The Author(s) 2019   205
I. Bowers, *The Modernisation of the Republic of Korea Navy,* Critical Studies of the Asia-Pacific,
https://doi.org/10.1007/978-3-319-92291-1

Office of the Secretary of Defense. *Annual Report to Congress: Military and Security Developments Involving the People's Republic of China.* Washington, DC: Department of Defense, 2011.

Prime Minister of Japan. *National Security Strategy*, 17 December 2013. http://japan.kantei.go.jp/96_abe/documents/2013/__icsFiles/afield-file/2013/12/17/NSS.pdf. Accessed 3 March 2017.

Republic of Korea Defence Acquisition Program Administration. "*Seobukdoseo haesang jeollyeok 24sigan gamsichegye guchuk* [Construction of a 24-Hour Surveillance System for the Maritime Military Power of the Northwest Islands]." *Republic of Korea Defense Acquisition Program Administration Press Release*, 2 September 2013.

Republic of Korea Defense Acquisition Program Administration. "*Je82hoe bangwisaeopchujinwiwonhoe gyeolgwa* [Results of the 82nd DAPA Committee]." *Defense Acquisition Program Administration Press Release*, 12 August 2014.

Republic of Korea Defense Acquisition Program Administration. "*Je95hoe bangwisaeopchujinwiwonhoe gyeolgwa* [Results of the 95th Defense Business Promotion committee]," 15 May 2016.

Republic of Korea Defense Acquisition Program Administration. "*Gwanggaeto-III Batch-II tamsaekgaebal saeop gyeyak chegyeol* [Gwanggaeto-III Batch-II Conclusion of Exploratory Development Business Contract]." *Defence Acquisition Program Administration Press Release*, 24 June 2016.

Republic of Korea Defense Acquisition Program Administration. "*Je96hoe bangwisaeopchujinwiwonhoe gyeolgwa* [Results of the 96th DAPA Committee]." *Defense Acquisition Program Administration Press Release*, 30 September 2016.

Republic of Korea Defense Acquisition Program Administration. "*Bangwisaeopcheong, chagihowiham 3dangye saeop chaksu* [DAPA Launches Third Phase of Next Frigate]." *Defense Acquisition Program Administration Press Release*, 27 December 2016.

Republic of Korea Defense Acquisition Program Administration. "*HaegunjeonsulC4Ichegye seongneunggaeryangsaeop gaeyo* [Naval Tactical C4I System Performance Improvement Project Summary]," 30 November 2016. http://www.dapa.go.kr/user/boardList.action?command=view&page=1&boardId=I_36172&boardSeq=I_38914&id=dapa_kr_030303160000. Accessed 20 November 2017.

Republic of Korea Defense Acquisition Promotion Agency. "*Jangbogo-III Batch-I saeopchujinsanghwang* [Chang Bogo-III Batch-I Business Situation]," 23 December 2016. http://www.dapa.go.kr/user/boardList.action?command=view&page=1&boardId=I_6033&boardSeq=I_40979&id=dapa_kr_030302340000. Accessed 20 March 2018.

Republic of Korea Government. "*2007nyeondo gukjeonggamsagyeolgwa sijeong min cheoriyogusahange daehan cheorigyeolgwagoseo (Gukbangbu Sogwan)*"

[Report on the Completion of the 2007 National Assembly Audit Results and the Completion of the Corrective and Handling Requirements (Ministry of National Defense)]," January 2008.

Republic of Korea Government. "*Cheonanham pigyeoksageon baekse* [The Warship Cheonan Attack White Paper]." Seoul: Republic of Korea Government, 2011.

Republic of Korea Government. "*2010nyeondo gukjeonggamsagyeolgwa sijeong min cheoriyogusahange daehan cheorigyeolgwagoseo (Gukbangbu Sogwan)* [Report on the Completion of the 2010 National Assembly Audit Results and the Completion of the Corrective and Handling Requirements (Ministry of National Defense)]," April 2011.

Republic of Korea Government. "*2011nyeondo gukjeonggamsagyeolgwa sijeong min cheoriyogusahange daehan cheorigyeolgwagoseo* (Gukbangbu Sogwan) [Report on the Completion of the 2011 National Assembly Audit Results and the Completion of the Corrective and Handling Requirements (Ministry of National Defense)]," February 2012.

Republic of Korea Government. "*2012nyeondo gukjeonggamsagyeolgwa sijeong min cheoriyogusahange daehan cheorigyeolgwagoseo (Gukbangbu Sogwan)* [Report on the Completion of the 2012 National Assembly Audit Results and the Completion of the Corrective and Handling Requirements (Ministry of National Defense)]," March 2013.

Republic of Korea Government. "*2013nyeondo gukjeonggamsagyeolgwa sijeong min cheoriyogusahange daehan cheorigyeolgwagoseo (Gukbangbu Sogwan)* [Report on the Completion of the 2013 National Assembly Audit Results and the Completion of the Corrective and Handling Requirements (Ministry of National Defense)]," March 2014.

Republic of Korea Government. "*2015nyeondo gukjeonggamsagyeolgwa sijeong min cheoriyogusahange daehan cheorigyeolgwagoseo (Gukbangbu Sogwan)* [Report on the Completion of the 2013 National Assembly Audit Results and the Completion of the Corrective and Handling Requirements (Ministry of National Defense)]," April 2016.

Republic of Korea Government. "*2016nyeondo gukjeonggamsagyeolgwa sijeong min cheoriyogusahange daehan cheorigyeolgwagoseo (Gukbangbu Sogwan)* [Report on the Completion of the 2016 National Assembly Audit Results and the Completion of the Corrective and Handling Requirements (Ministry of National Defense)]," February 2017.

Republic of Korea Ministry of National Defense. *Defense White Paper 1994–1995*. Seoul: Korea Institute of Defense Analysis, 1995.

Republic of Korea Ministry of National Defense. *Defense White Paper 1998*. Seoul: Korean Institute of Defense Analysis, 1999.

Republic of Korea Ministry of National Defense. *Defense Data and Statistics 2001*. Seoul: Republic of Korea Ministry of National Defense, 2001.

Republic of Korea Ministry of National Defense. *Defence White Paper 2000.* Seoul: Republic of Korea Ministry of National Defense, 2001.

Republic of Korea Ministry of National Defense. *"Jajugukbanggwa Uriui Anbo* [Self-reliant National Defense Capability and Our Security]." Seoul: Republic of Korea Ministry of National Defense, 2003.

Republic of Korea Ministry of National Defense. *Participatory Government Defense Policy.* Seoul: Republic of Korea Ministry of National Defense, 2003.

Republic of Korea Ministry of National Defense. *Defense Reform 2020.* Seoul: Republic of Korea Ministry of National Defense, 2005.

Republic of Korea Ministry of National Defense. *2008 Defense White Paper.* Seoul: Republic of Korea Ministry of National Defense, 2008.

Republic of Korea Ministry of National Defense. *"'10 – '14 Gukbangjunggigyehoek* ['10–'14 Mid-term Defence Plan]." *Republic of Korea Ministry of National Defense, Press Release.* Seoul: Ministry of National Defence, 2009.

Republic of Korea Ministry of National Defense. *Public Announcement of Defense Basic Reform Plan (2009–2020).* Seoul: Republic of Korea Ministry of National Defense, 2009.

Republic of Korea Ministry of National Defense. *2010 Defense White Paper.* Seoul: Republic of Korea Ministry of National Defense, 2010.

Republic of Korea Ministry of National Defense. *"'12 – '16 Gukbangjunggigyehoek* ['12–'16 Mid-term Defence Plan]." *Republic of Korea Ministry of National Defense, Press Release.* Seoul: Ministry of National Defence, 2011.

Republic of Korea Ministry of National Defense. *2012 Defense White Paper.* Seoul: Republic of Korea Ministry of National Defense, 2012.

Republic of Korea Ministry of National Defense. *2016 Defence White Paper.* Seoul: Republic of Korea Ministry of National Defense, 2016.

Republic of Korea National Defense Committee. *"Gukgunbudaeui somallia haeyeok pagyeon donguian geomto* [Review of the Motion to Dispatch Korean Military Forces to Somalia Waters]." Seoul: National Defense Committee, 2009.

Republic of Korea Navy. *"Haegun* [Navy]." Seoul: Republic of Korea Navy, 1998.

Republic of Korea Navy. *"Haegun haeoemugi doip gwallyeon* [Naval Overseas Weapons Acquisitions]." Seoul: Republic of Korea Navy, 2005.

Republic of Korea Navy. *"Haegun* [Navy]." Gyeryong: ROKN Troop Information and Public Relations Office, 2011.

Republic of Korea Navy. *"(Nuguna al su Issneun!) Haegunjakjeon Deuryeodabogi* [As Anyone Can See! Look Into Naval Operations]." Seoul: Republic of Korea Navy, 2011.

Republic of Korea Navy. "Chagi giroebuseolham(MLS-II) Nampoham tjinsu [Next Minelayer (MLS-II), the Warship Nampo Launched]." *Republic of Korea Navy Press Release,* 27 May 2015.

Republic of Korea Navy. "*Gandanhago pyeonhage ilgeul su inneun haegungaideubuk* [An Easy and Simple to Read Navy Guide Book]." Gyeryong: Navy Headquarters, 2016.

Republic of Korea Navy. "*214Geup Jamsuham (KSS-II) 9Beonham 'sindolseokam' Jinsu* [9th 214 Class Submarine (KSS-II) Shin Dol-seouk Launch]." *News Release,* 7 September 2017.

Republic of Korea Navy. "*Nojeokbongham (LST-II 4Beonham) jinsusik geohaeng* [Warship No Jeok Bong (LST-II 4th vessel) Launching Ceremony]." *Republic of Korea Navy Press Release,* 2 November 2017.

Republic of Korea Navy Headquarters. "*2008nyeondo haegunjeongchaek bogoseo* [2008 Naval Policy Report]." Gyeryong, ROKN Headquarters.

Republic of Korea Navy Headquarters. "*21 Segireul hyanghan haegun* [The Navy Heading Toward the 21st Century]." Nonsan: Republic of Korea Navy Headquarters, 1998.

Republic of Korea Navy Headquarters. "*Haegun bijeon 2020* [Navy vision 2020]." Gyeryong, Republic of Korea Navy Headquarters, 1999.

Republic of Korea Navy Headquarters. "*Daehanminguk haegu = The Republic of Korea Navy* [The Republic of Korea Navy = The Republic of Korea Navy]." Chungnam: Republic of Korea Navy Headquarters, 2008.

Republic of Korea Navy Headquarters. "*Haegun bijeon 2030* [Navy Vision 2030]." Gyeryong, Republic of Korea Navy Headquarters, 2008.

ROK-US Combined Forces Command. *Air-Ground Operations-Korea. CFC PUB 3-2.2,* 15 June 2002.

Statement by the Spokesperson of the Ministry of Foreign Affairs of the Republic of Korea on the South China Sea Arbitration Award. ROK Ministry of Foreign Affairs, 13 July 2016. http://www.mofa.go.kr/eng/brd/m_5676/view.do?seq=316765. Accessed 10 August 2017.

The State Council. The People's Republic of China. *China's Military Strategy.* 27 May 2015. http://english.gov.cn/archive/white_paper/2015/05/27/content_281475115610833.htm. Accessed 20 June 2016.

The White House. Office of the Press Secretary. *Joint Vision for the Alliance of The United States of America and The Republic of Korea,* 16 June 2009.

"Text of Agreed Minute." November 19, 1954, The Department of State Bulletin 31, no. 805 (Washington, DC: Government Printing Office, 1954).

Trilateral Information Sharing Arrangement Concerning the Nuclear and Missile Threats Posed by North Korea Among the Ministry of National Defense of the Republic of Korea, the Ministry of Defense of Japan, and the Department of Defense of the United States of America. http://www.defense.gov/pubs/Trilateral-Information-Sharing-Arrangement.pdf?source=GovDelivery. Accessed 1 February 2015.

United Kingdom Ministry of Defence. *British Maritime Doctrine, BR 1806 3rd Edition.* London: The Stationary Office, 2004.

United States Department of Defense. *Asia-Pacific Maritime Security Strategy.* Washington, DC: United States Department of Defense, 2016.

United States Department of the Navy. *Forward, Engaged Ready; A Cooperative Strategy for 21st Century Seapower.* Washington, DC: US Department of the Navy.

United States Department of the Navy. *Naval Operations Concept 2010: Implementing the Maritime Strategy.* Washington, DC: United States Department of the Navy, 2010.

United States Joint Chiefs of Staff. *Joint Intelligence Estimate for Planning, Vol. II, FY 1973 Through FY 1980, Book VII East Asia and The Western Pacific.* Washington, DC: US Department of Defense, 1970.

United States Joint Chiefs of Staff. *Joint Strategic Objective Plan for FY 1973 Through FY 1980, Vol II Analyses and Force Tabulations, Book VII Free World Forces, Part II Major Objectives for Free World Countries, Section 3, The Pacific/Asia Area.* Washington, DC: US Department of Defense, 1970.

United States Navy. *Program Guide 2013.* Washington, DC: Department of the Navy, 2013.

United States Senate, Committee on Armed Services. *Department of Defense Authorization of Appropriations for Fiscal Year 2014 and the Future Years Defense Program: U.S. Pacific Command,* 9 April 2014. http://www.armed-services.senate.gov/imo/media/doc/DODauthorizationFY2014_full-committee_hearings_2013.pdf. Accessed 14 January 2015.

SPEECHES AND REMARKS

Admiral Scott H. Swift. *Republic of Korea Navy International Seapower Symposium Seoul, Republic of Korea September 5, 2017 as Prepared for Delivery.* http://www.cpf.navy.mil/leaders/scott-swift/speeches/2017/09/rok-sea-power-symposium.pdf. Accessed 3 March 2018.

House Appropriations Committee. *Statement of General Curtis M. Scaparrotti Commander, United Nations Command; Republic of Korea and United States Combined Forces Command; and United States Forces Korea in Support of U.S. Pacific Command's Testimony Before the House Appropriations Committee-Defense Subcommittee,* 26 April 2017.

Kim, Dae-jung. *Advancing in to the World Through the Sea: At the 52nd Commencement Ceremony of the Korean Naval Academy,* 16 March 1998.

Kim, Dae-jung. *Safeguarding the Nation: On the 50th Armed Forces Day,* 1 October 1998.

Kim, Dae-jung. "Guarding the Turbulent Sea: At the 53rd Commencement Ceremony of the Korean Naval Academy," 12 March 1999.

Kim, Dae-jung. *In the Glorious Traditions of Admirals Yi Sun-shin and Chang-Po-go: At the 54th Commencement Ceremony of the Korean Naval Academy*, 16 March 2000.

Kim, Dae-jung. "An Ever-Strong Security Stance: At the 55th Commencement Ceremony of the Korean Naval Academy," 19 March 2001.

Kim, Young-sam. *Address by President Kim, Young-sam at the 48th Graduation and Commissioning Ceremony of the Korean Naval Academy*, 4 March 1994.

Kim, Young-sam. *Speech at the 49th Commencement Ceremony of the Korean Naval Academy*, 24 March 1995.

Kim, Young-sam. *Speech at the 50th Commencement Ceremony of the Korean Naval Academy*, 13 March 1996.

Kim, Young-sam. *Speech at the 51st Commencement of the Korean Naval Academy*, 12 March 1997.

Locklear, Samuel J. *Statement of Admiral J. Locklear, U.S. Navy Commander, U.S. Pacific Command Before the Senate Armed Services Committee on U.S. Pacific Command Posture*, 16 April 2015. Washington, DC: Senate Armed Services Committee. http://www.armed-services.senate.gov/imo/media/doc/Locklear_04-16-15.pdf. Accessed 19 April 2015.

Minister for Foreign Affairs and Trade Hang Soon-young. *Foreign Policy Agenda of the Republic of Korea in the New Century*. Speech Given at the Graduate School of International Studies: Korea University, 11 December 1998.

Roh, Moo-hyun. *Address by the President Roh, Moo-hyun on the 84th March First Independence Movement Day*, 1 March 2003.

Roh, Moo-hyun. *Address by President Roh Moo-hyun at the 57th Graduation and Commissioning Ceremony of the Korean Naval Academy*, 13 March 2003.

Roh, Moo-hyun. *Address by President Roh Moo-hyun on the 58th Anniversary of National Liberation*, 15 August 2003.

Roh, Moo-hyun. *Address by President Roh Moo-hyun on the 55th ROK Armed Forces Day*, 1 October 2003.

Roh, Moo-hyun. *Address at the 53rd Commencement and Commissioning Ceremony of the Korea Air Force Academy*, 8 March 2005.

Roh, Moo-hyun. *Address by the President Roh, Moo-hyun at the 61st Graduation and Commissioning Ceremony of the Korean Naval Academy*, 2 March 2007.

Roh, Moo-hyun. *President Celebrates Aegis Destroyer Launch*, 25 May 2007.

Senate Armed Services Committee. *Statement of General Thomas A. Schwartz, Commander in Chief United Nations Command/Combined Forces Command & Command United States Forces Korea Before the 107th Congress Senate Armed Service Committee*, 5 March 2002, 17.

Senate Armed Services Committee. *Statement of General Vincent K. Brooks, Commander, United Nations Command; Commander United States-Republic of Korea Combined Forces Command; and Commander, United States Forces Korea Before the Senate Armed Services Committee*, 23 February 2016.

The White House Office of the Press Secretary. *Remarks by President Obama, President Park of the Republic of Korea, and Prime Minister Abe of Japan*, 25 March 2014. http://www.whitehouse.gov/the-press-office/2014/03/25/remarks-president-obama-president-park-republic-south-korea-and-prime-minister. Accessed 12 January 2015.

MONOGRAPHS & EDITED VOLUMES

Barany, Zoltan. *The Soldier and the Changing State*. Princeton: Princeton University Press, 2012.

Bechtol, Bruce E. *Red Rogue: The Persistent Challenge of North Korea*. Washington, DC: Potomac Books, 2007.

Bitzinger, Richard. *Arming Asia: Technonationalism and Its Impact on Local Defense Industries*. Oxon: Routledge, 2017.

Chung, Eui-sung. *Ultramodern Conventional Submarine KSX As a Leverage for the Future Defense of the Korean Peninsula*. Seoul: Korea Institute of Maritime Studies, 2007.

Clark, Bryan, Peter Haynes, Jesse Sloman, and Timothy Walton. *Restoring American Seapower: A New Fleet Architecture for the United States Navy*. Washington, DC: Centre for Strategic and Budgetary Assessments, 2017.

Cole, Bernard. *The Great Wall at Sea 2nd Edition: China's Navy in the Twenty-First Century*. Annapolis: Naval Institute Press, 2010.

Edwards, Paul M. *Small United States and United Nations Warships in the Korean War*. Jefferson: McFarland & Co, 2008.

Foreign Relations of the United States 1952–1954, Vol. XV, Korea Part 2. Washington, DC: Government Printing Office, 1984.

Foreign Relations of the United States 1955–1957, Korea, Vol. XXIII, Part 2. Washington, DC: Government Printing Office, 1992.

Foreign Relations of the United States 1958–60, Japan; Korea, Vol. XVIII. Washington, DC: Government Printing Office, 1994.

Foreign Relations of the United States 1964–68, Vol. XXIX, Part 1 Korea. Washington, DC: U.S. Government Printing Office, 2000.

Foreign Relations of the United States, 1969–1972, Vol. XIX, Part 1, Korea. Washington, DC: U.S. Government Printing Office, 2010.

Foreign Relations of the United States, 1969–1976, Vol. E-12, Documents on East and Southeast Asia. Washington, DC: Government Printing Office, 2013.

Friedman, Norman. *The Naval Institute Guide to World Naval Weapons Systems 1997–1998*. Annapolis: Naval Institute Press, 1997.

Friedman, Norman. *Seapower as Strategy: Navies and National Interests*. Annapolis: Naval Institute Press, 2001.

Gearson, Michael, and Daniel Whiteneck. *Deterrence and Influence: The Navy's Role in Preventing War*. Virginia: Centre for Naval Analyses, 2009.

Glosserman, Brad, and Scott A. Snyder. *The Japan-South Korea Identity Clash: East Asian Security and the United States*. New York: Columbia University Press, 2015.

Jane's Information Group. *Jane's Fighting Ships 2012–2013*. Coulsdon: Jane's Information Group, 2012.

Kim, Jung-ik. *The Future of the U.S.-ROK Military Relationship*. London: Macmillan Press, 1996.

Kim, Samuel S. *The Two Koreas and the Great Powers*. New York: Cambridge University Press, 2006.

Kim, Suk-kyoon. *Maritime Disputes in Northeast Asia: Regional Challenges and Cooperation*. Boston: Brill Nijhoff, 2017.

Kirchberger, Sarah. *Assessing China's Naval Power: Technological Innovation, Economic Constraints and Strategic Implications*. Berlin & Heidelberg: Springer, 2015.

Koo, Min-gyo. *Island Disputes and Maritime Regime Building in East Asia: Between a Rock and a Hard Place*. New York: Springer, 2009.

Lee, Seok Woo, and Hee Eun Lee. *The Making of International Law in Korea: From Colony to Asian Power*. Leiden: Brill Nijhoff, 2016.

Mahan, Alfred T. *The Influence of Sea Power Upon History 1660–1783*. 12th ed. Boston: Little Brown and Company, 1947.

Marine Corps Intelligence Activities. *North Korea Country Handbook*. Quantico: Marine Corps Intelligence Activity, 1997.

Marolda, Edward J. *Ready Seapower: A History of the U.S. Seventh Fleet*. Washington, DC: Naval History and Heritage Command, 2011.

McDevitt, Michael A. *Report on the KIMS-CNA Conference "The PLA Navy's Build-Up and ROK-USN Cooperation"*. Alexandria: Centre for Naval Analysis, 2009.

Michishita, Narushige. *North Korea's Military Diplomatic Campaigns, 1996–2008*. Oxon: Routledge, 2010.

Newton, Robert E. *The Capture of the USS Pueblo and its Effect on SIGINT Operations, United States Cryptological History, Special Series Crisis Collection Vol. 7*. Maryland: Centre for Cryptologic History National Security Agency, 1992.

Office of the President of the Republic of Korea. *Government of the People: Selected Speeches of Kim, Dae-jung Vol. I*. Seoul: Office of the President of the Republic of Korea, 1999.

Office of the President of the Republic of Korea. *Government of the People: Selected Speeches of Kim, Dae-jung Vol. II*. Seoul: Office of the President of the Republic of Korea, 2000.

Office of the President of the Republic of Korea. *Government of the People: Selected Speeches of Kim, Dae-jung Vol. III.* Seoul: Office of the President of the Republic of Korea, 2001.

Office of the President of the Republic of Korea. *Government of the People: Selected Speeches of Kim, Dae-jung Vol. IV.* Seoul: Office of the President of the Republic of Korea, 2002.

Paine, Lincoln. *The Sea and Civilisation: A Maritime History of the World.* London: Atlantic Books, 2013.

Patalano, Alessio. *Post-war Japan as a Sea Power: Imperial Legacy, Wartime Experience and the Making of a Navy.* London: Bloomsbury, 2015.

Perkins, William. *Alliance Airborne Anti-Submarine Warfare: A Forecast for Maritime Air ASW in the Future Operational Environment.* Kalkar: Joint Air Power Competence Centre, 2016.

Presidential Commission on Policy Planning. *Korea's Future Vision and Strategy: Korea's Ambition to Become an Advanced Power by 2030.* Seoul: Seoul Selection, 2008.

Raska, Michael. *Military Innovation in Small States: Creating a Reverse Asymmetry.* Oxon: Routledge, 2016.

Roehrig, Terence. *The Prosecution of Former Military Leaders in Newly Democratic Nations: The Cases of Argentina, Greece and South Korea.* Jefferson, NC: MacFarland, 2002.

Rottman, Gordon L. *Korean War Order of Battle: United States, United Nations, and Communist Ground, Naval, and Air Forces, 1950–1953.* Westport: Praeger, 2002.

Rüger, Jan. *The Great Naval Game Britain and Germany in the Age of Empire.* Cambridge: Cambridge University Press, 2007.

Saxer, Carl J. *From Transition to Power Alternation: Democracy in South Korea, 1987–1997.* New York: Routledge, 2002.

Schneller, Robert J. *Anchor Resolve: A History of the U.S. Naval Forces Central Command Fifth Fleet.* Washington, DC: Naval Historical Center, 2005.

Scobell, Andrew, and John M. Sanford. *North Korea's Military Threat: Pyongyang's Conventional Forces, Weapons of Mass Destruction, and Ballistic Missiles.* Carlisle: Strategic Studies Institute, 2007.

Seth, Michael J. *A History of Korea from Antiquity to the Present.* Plymouth: Rowman and Littlefield, 2011.

Shin, Gi-wook. *The Paradox of Korean Globalisation.* Stanford: The Asia-Pacific Research Center, 2003.

Speller, Ian. *Understanding Naval Warfare.* Oxon: Routledge, 2014.

Suh, Jae-jean. *The Lee Myung-bak Government's North Korea Policy: A Study on Its Historical and Theoretical Foundation.* Seoul: Korea Institute for National Unification, 2009.

The National Institute for Defense Studies. *East Asian Strategic Review 2009*. Tokyo: The Japan Times, 2009.

The National Institute of Defense Studies. *East Asian Strategic Review 2012*. Tokyo: National Institute of Defense Studies, 2012.

Till, Geoffrey. Seapower: A Guide for the Twenty-First Century. 2nd ed. Oxon: Routledge, 2009.

Todd, Daniel, and Michael Lindberg. *Navies and Shipbuilding Industries: The Strained Symbiosis*. Westport: Praeger, 1996.

Turnbull, Stephen. *The Samurai Invasion of Korea, 1592–98*. Oxford: Osprey Publishing, 2008.

Uk Heo, and Terence Roehrig. *South Korea Since 1980*. Cambridge: Cambridge University Press, 2010.

Uk Heo, and Terence Roehrig. *South Korea's Rise: Economic Development, Power, and Foreign Relations*. Cambridge: Cambridge University Press, 2014.

Vego, Milan. *Maritime Strategy and Sea Control: Theory and Practice*. Oxon: Routledge, 2016.

Watson, Robert J. *History of the Joint Chiefs of Staff, Vol V: The Joint Chiefs of Staff and National Policy 1953–1954*. Washington, DC: Office of Joint History 1998.

Wertheim, Eric. *The Naval Institute Guide to Combat Fleets of the World*. 16th ed. Annapolis: Naval Institute Press, 2013.

Wooley, Peter J. *Japan's Navy: Politics and Paradox*. London: Lynne Rienner, 1999.

JOURNAL ARTICLES

Benbow, Tim. "The 'Operational Level' and Maritime Forces." *The RUSI Journal* 160, no. 5 (2015): 52–59.

Bowers, Ian. "Power Asymmetry and the Role of Deterrence in the South China Sea." *Korean Journal of Defense Analysis* 29, no. 4 (2017): 551–573.

Cha, Victor. "Strategic Culture and the Military Modernization of South Korea." *Armed Forces and Society* 28, no. 1 (2001): 99–127.

Cohen, Joshua. "The Korea People's Army Naval Force." *Naval Forces* 35, no. 3 (2014): 14–16.

Croissant, Aurel. "Riding the Tiger: Civilian Control and the Military in Democratizing Korea." *Armed Forces & Society* 30, no. 3 (2004): 357–381.

Fravel, Taylor M. "China's Strategy in the South China Sea." *Contemporary Southeast Asia* 33, no. 3 (2011): 292–319.

Gearson, Michael S. "Conventional Deterrence in the Second Nuclear Age." *Parameters* 39, no. 3 (Autumn 2009): 32–48.

Han, Yong-sup. "Analyzing South Korea's Defense Reform 2020." *Korean Journal of Defense Analysis* 18, no. 1 (2006): 111–134.

Heginbotham, Eric. "The Fall and Rise of Navies in East Asia: Military Organisations, Domestic Politics and Grand Strategy." *International Security* 27, no. 2 (2002): 86–125.

Holmes, James R. "China Fashions a Maritime Identity." *Issues and Studies* 42, no. 3 (September 2006): 87–128.

Huntington, Samuel P. "Conventional Deterrence and Conventional Retaliation in Europe." *International Security* 8, no. 3 (1993–1994): 32–56.

Huxley, Tim, and Benjamin Schreer. "Standing up to China." *Survival* 57, no. 6 (2015): 127–144.

Johnston, Alastair Iain. "Thinking About Strategic Culture." *International Security* 19, no. 4 (1995): 32–64.

Kim, Ellen, and Victor Cha. "Between a Rock and a Hard Place: South Korea's Strategic Dilemmas with China and the United States." *Asia Policy* 21, no. 1 (January 2016): 101–121.

Kim, Jiyul. "Strategic Culture of the Republic of Korea." *Contemporary Security Policy* 35, no. 2 (2014): 270–289.

Kim, Jiyul, and Michael J. Finnegan. "The Republic of Korea Approaches the Future." *Joint Forces Quarterly* 2, no. 30 (Spring 2002): 33–40.

Kim, Samuel S. "Nationalism and Globalisation on South Korea's Foreign Policy." *New Asia* 14, no. 3 (2007): 17–18.

Koda, Yoji. "The Emerging Republic of Korea Navy: A Japanese Perspective." *The Naval War College Review* 60, no. 2 (Spring 2010): 13–34.

Laird, Melvin R. "A Strong Start in a Difficult Decade: Defense Policy in the Nixon—Ford Years." *International Security* 10, no. 2 (Fall 1985): 5–26.

Lee, Jamie Shinhee. "Linguistic Constructions of Modernity: English Mixing in Korean Television Commercials." *Language in Society* 35, (2006): 59–91.

Moon, Chung-in and Jin-young Lee. "The Revolution in Military Affairs and the Defence Industry in South Korea." *Security Challenges* 4, no. 4 (Summer 2008): 117–134.

Park, Hwee-rhak. "South Korea's Failure to Implement 'Defence Reform 2020'." *The Korean Journal of International Studies* 12, no. 2 (2014): 379–401.

Park, Sang-hoon. "Korea's Security Policy." *Institute for Foreign Affairs and National Security Review* 4, no. 3 (1996): 15.

Patalano, Alessio. "Japan as a Seapower: Strategy, Doctrine, and Capabilities Under Three Defence Reviews, 1995–2010." *The Journal of Strategic Studies* 37, no. 3 (2014): 403–411.

Patalano, Alessio, and James Manicom. "Rising Tides: Seapower and Regional Security in Northeast Asia." *The Journal of Strategic Studies* 37, no. 3 (2014): 335–344.

Rhodes, Edward. "Conventional Deterrence." *Comparative Strategy* 19, no. 3 (2000): 221–253.

Roh, Young-koo. "Yi Sun-shin, An Admiral Who Became a Myth." *The Review of Korean Studies* 7, no. 3 (2004): 15–36.

Ross, Robert S. "China's Naval Nationalism: Sources, Prospects, and the U.S. Response." *International Security* 34, no. 2 (Fall, 2009): 46–81.

Saxer, Carl J. "Generals and Presidents: Establishing Civilian and Democratic Control in South Korea." *Armed Forces & Society* 3, no. 3 (2004): 383–408.

Shin, Kyoung-ho, and Paul S. Cicanntell. "The Steel and Shipbuilding Industries of South Korea: Rising East Asia and Globalisation." *American Sociological Association* 15, no. 2 (2009): 167–192.

Tritten, James John. "Is Naval Warfare Unique?" *Journal of Strategic Studies* 12, no. 4 (1989): 494–507.

Van Dyke, Jon M., Mark J. Valencia, and Jenny Miller Garmendia. "The North/South Korea Boundary Dispute in the Yellow (West) Sea." *Marine Policy* 27, no. 2 (2003): 143–158.

Vego, Milan N. "On Naval Power." *Joint Forces Quarterly* 50, no. 3 (2008): 8–17.

Yoon, Suk-joon. "Expanding the ROKN's Capabilities to Deal with the SLBM Threat from North Korea." *The Naval War College Review* 70, no. 2 (Spring 2017): 49–74.

Book Chapters

Bae, Sang-yoon. "Maritime Developments in South Korea." In *Maritime Power in the China Seas: Capabilities and Rationale*, edited by Dominic Sherwood, 51–60. Canberra: Australian Defence Studies Centre, 1994.

Bekkevold, Jo Inge, and Ian Bowers. "A Question of Balance: Warfighting and Naval Operations other the War." In *International Order at Sea: How It Is Challenged, How It Is Maintained*, edited by Jo Inge Bekkevold and Geoffrey Till, 241–259. London: Palgrave MacMillan, 2016.

Bowers, Ian. "South Korea." In *Asia-Pacific Nations in International Peace Support and Stability Missions*, edited by Chiyuki Aoi and Yee-Kuang Heng, 87–111. New York: Palgrave MacMillan, 2014.

Bowers, Ian, and Bjørn Gronning. "Protecting the Status Quo: Japan's Response to China's Rise." In *Strategic Adjustment and the Rise of China: Power and Politics in East Asia*, edited by Robert Ross and Øystein Tunsjø, 137–168. New York: Cornell University Press, 2017.

Forbes, Andrew, and Sukjoon Yoon. "Old and New Threats from North Korea against the Republic of Korea." In *Korean Maritime Strategy: Issues and Challenges*, edited by Geoffrey Till and Sukjoon Yoon, 17–54. Seoul: Korea Institute for Maritime Strategy, 2011.

Gooch, John. "Maritime Command: Mahan and Corbett." In *Seapower and Strategy*, edited by Colin S. Gray and Roger W. Barnett, 27–46. London: Tri-Service Press, 1989.

Gray, Colin S., and Roger W. Barnet. "Introduction." In *Seapower and Strategy*, edited by Colin S. Gray and Roger W. Barnett, ix–xiv. London: Tri-Service Press, 1989.

Grygiel, Jakub. "Geography and Seapower." In *Twenty-First Century Seapower: Cooperation and Conflict at Sea*, edited by Peter Dutton, Robert S. Ross, and Oystein Tunsjø, 18–41. Oxon: Routledge, 2012.

Jung, Yong-duck. "Administrative Reorganisation: The Case of the Kim Young-sam Regime." In *The White House and the Blue House: Government Reform in the United States and Korea*, edited by Yong-Ho Cho and George H. Frederickson, 89–110. Maryland: United Press of America, 1997.

Kim, Byung-kook. "Party Politics in South Korea's Democracy: The Crisis of Success." In *Consolidating Democracy in the South Korea*, edited by Larry J. Diamond and Byung-kook Kim, 53–86. Colorado: Lynne Reinner, 2000.

Kim, Duk-ki. "ROKN's Requirements for Countering North Korea's Potential Nuclear and Ballistic Missile Threats." In *The Evolution of the Maritime Security Environment in Northeast Asia and ROKN-USN Cooperation*, 161–173. Seoul: Korea Institute for Maritime Studies, 2016.

Kim, Joo-hong. "The Armed Forces." In *The Park Chung Hee Era: The Transformation of South Korea*, edited by Byung-kook Kim and Ezra F. Vogel, 168–199. Cambridge: Harvard University Press, 2011.

Kim, Samuel S. "Korean and Globalization (Segyehwa): A Framework for Analysis." In *Korea's Globalization*, edited by. Samuel S. Kim, 1–28. Cambridge: Cambridge University Press, 2000.

Kim, Young-il. "Status of Korean Navy's Tactical C4ISR Systems Acquisition and Issues on Interoperability between ROK-U.S. Combined Naval Operations." In *Bytes and Bullets: Information Technology Revolution and National Security on the Korean Peninsula*, edited by Alexander Y. Mansourov, 179–201. Hawaii: Asia Pacific Centre for Security Studies, 2005.

Lee, Guen. "Strengthening the National Assembly's Influence on South Korean Foreign Policy." In *Domestic Constraints on South Korean Foreign Policy*, edited by Scott A. Snyder, Guen Lee, Young Ho-kim, and Jiyoon Kim, 4–19. Washington, DC: Council on Foreign Relations, 2018.

Lee, Seok Woo. "South Korea's Maritime Challenges and Priorities." In *Maritime Challenges and Priorities in Asia*, edited by Joshua H. Ho and Sam Bateman, 219–230. Oxon: Routledge, 2012.

McDevitt, Michael. "Final Report." In *Workshop Report: The Future of ROK Navy-US Navy Cooperation*, edited by Michael McDevitt, 1–9. Alexandria: Centre for Naval Analysis, 2007.

McDevitt, Michael. "The Maritime Relationship." In *The U.S.-South Korea Alliance Meeting New Security Challenges*, edited by Scott Snyder, 21–42. London: Lynne Reinner, 2012.

Moon, Chung-in. "South Korea Recasting Security Paradigms." In *Asian Security Practice Material and Ideational Influence*, edited by Muthiah Alagappa, 265–287. Stanford: Stanford University Press, 1988.

Moon, Chung-in. "China's Rise and Security Dynamics on the Korean Peninsula." In *Strategic Adjustment and the Rise of China*, edited by Robert S. Ross and Øystein Tunsjø, 196–229. Ithaca: Cornell University Press, 2017.

Redford, Duncan. "Introduction." In *Maritime History and Identity: The Sea and Culture in the Modern World*, edited by Duncan Redford, 1–10. London: I.B. Tauris, 2014.

Roehrig, Terence. "South Korea's Counterpiracy Operations in the Gulf of Aden." In *Global Korea: South Korea's Contributions to International Security*, edited by Scott Bruce, John Hemmings, Balbina Y. Hwang, Terence Roehrig, and Scott A. Snyder, 28–44. Washington, DC: Council of Foreign Relations, 2012.

Rozman, Gilbert, In-taek Hyun, and Shin-wha Lee. "Overview." In *South Korean Strategic Thought Toward Asia*, edited by Gilbert Rozman, In-taek Hyun, and Shin-wha Lee, 1–32. New York: Palgrave Macmillan, 2008.

Schottenhammer, Angela. "The East Asian Maritime World, c. 1400–1800: Its Fabrics of Power and Dynamics of Exchanges—China and Her Neighbours." In *The East Asian Maritime World 1400–1800: Its Fabrics of Power and Dynamics of Exchanges*, edited by Angela Shottenhammer, 1–86. Weisbaden: Harrassowitz Berlag, 2007.

Sheen, Song-ho. "Strategic Thought Toward Asia in the Roh Moo-hyun Era." In *South Korean Strategic Though Toward Asia*, edited by Gilbert Rozman, In-taek Hyun, and Shin-wha Lee, 101–126. New York: Palgrave Macmillan, 2008.

Snyder, Scott. "Strategic Thought Toward Asia in the Kim, Dae-jung Era." In *South Korean Strategic Though Toward Asia*, edited by Gilbert Rozman, In-taek Hyun, and Shin-wha Lee, 77–99. New York: Palgrave Macmillan, 2008.

Speller, Ian, Deborah Sanders, and Michael Mulqueen. "Introduction." In *Small Navies: Strategy and Policy for Small Navies in War and Peace*, edited by Michael Mulqueen, Deborah Saunders, and Ian Speller, 1–14. Surrey: Ashgate, 2014.

Sullivan, William D. "Chapter 1: Old Issues and New Threats." In *Korean Maritime Strategy: Issues and Challenges*, edited by Geoffrey Till and Yoon Sukjoon, 3–16. Seoul: The Korea Institute for Maritime Strategy, 2011.

Tangredi, Sam J. "Globalization and Sea Power: Overview and Context." In *Globalization and Maritime Power*, edited by Sam J. Tangredi, 1–24. Washington, DC: National Defense University, 2002.

Till, Geoffrey. "Editorial Introduction." In *Seapower: Theory and Practice*, edited by Geoffrey Till, 1–6. Essex: Frank Cass, 1994.

REPORTS AND ANALYSIS

Erickson, Andrew. "Numbers Matter: China's Three Navies Each Have the World's Most Ships." *The National Interest*, February 26, 2018. http://nationalinterest.org/feature/numbers-matter-chinas-three-navies-each-have-the-worlds-most-24653?page=show. Accessed 3 March 2018.

Feffer, John. "Ploughshares into Swords: Economic Implications of South Korean Military Spending." *Korea Economic Institute Academic Paper Series 4*, No. 2, February 2009.

Grove, Eric. "The Ever-Increasing Importance of Sea Power." *ISN, ETH Zurich*, April 7, 2014. https://www.files.ethz.ch/isn/188136/ISN_177612_en.pdf. Accessed 5 March 2018.

Lee, Sang-ho. "Issue of the Oceanic Navy and Complement of Naval Force After Warship Cheonan-ham Incident." *Sejong Commentary No. 181*, 2009.

Morris, Lyle J. "Indonesia-China Tensions in the Natuna Sea: Evidence of Naval Efficiency over Coast Guards?" *The RAND Blog*, July 5, 2016. https://www.rand.org/blog/2016/07/indonesia-china-tensions-in-the-natuna-sea-evidence.html. Accessed 12 February 2018.

Roehrig, Terence. *Korean Dispute over the Northern Limit Line: Security, Economics or International Law?, Issue 3 of Maryland Series in Contemporary Asian Studies.* Maryland: University of Maryland at Baltimore, 2008.

Roehrig, Terence. "The Origins of the Northern Limit Line Dispute." *North Korea International Document Project, E-Dossier #6, The Origins of the Northern Limit Line Dispute*, May 2012.

Rubel, Robert C. Navies and Economic Prosperity—The New Logic of Sea Power. *Corbett Paper No. 11*, Kings College London, London, 2012.

Sheen, Song-ho. "A Smart Alliance in the Age of Complexity; ROK-U.S. Alliance in the 21st Century." *EAI Issue Briefing* 009-02.

Watanabe, Takeshi. "Reform of South Korea's Defense Acquisition Program Administration." *NIDS Commentary No. 41*, 25 December 2014. http://www.nids.mod.go.jp/english/publication/commentary/pdf/commentary041e.pdf. Accessed 5 May 2016.

Wie, Sung hwan, Chang Su Kim, Perry Wood, David Carlson, and Christopher Yung. *Prospects for U.S.-Korean Naval Relations in the 21st Century.* Virginia: Centre for Naval Analyses, 1994.

Yung, Christopher, Chang Soo Kim, Sung Hwan Wie, and Tomoyuki Ishizu. *Trilateral Naval Cooperation: Japan, US, Korea—A Workshop Report.* Virginia: Centre of Naval Analyses, 1996.

PRESS RELEASES

"Chief of Naval Operations Change of Command Ceremony (26th & 27th)." *Navy News,* 21 March 2008. Link No Longer Available.
Essenmacher, Abraham. "US, ROK Navies Strengthen Partnership Through ASW Cooperation." *Commander, US Pacific Fleet,* 27 April 2015. http://www.cpf.navy.mil/news.aspx/030536. Accessed 15 November 2017.
"Last US Ship Transferred to ROK Navy Decommissioned in Ceremony Highlighting Naval Partnership." *Commander, US Naval Forces Korea Public Affairs,* 29 December 2016. http://www.navy.mil/submit/display.asp?story_id=98304. Accessed 3 March 2017.
"Naval Forces Korea Commander Highlights US, ROK Cooperation at Symposium." *Commander, US Naval Forces Korea Public Affairs,* 6 June 2016. http://www.pacom.mil/Media/News/News-Article-View/Article/792527/naval-forces-korea-commander-highlights-us-rok-cooperation-at-symposium/. Accessed 15 November 2017.
"Navy Introduces New Slogan, Marching Song to Mark 63rd Anniversary." *Ministry of National Defence News,* 21 November 2008. http://www.mnd.go.kr/user/boardList.action?command=view&page=1&boardId=O_47261&boardSeq=o_1000000010030&titleId=&siteId=mndEN&id=mndEN_020100000000. Accessed 2 August 2010.
Republic of Korea Ministry of Foreign Affairs. "Korea-China Fisheries Agreement Comes into Effect." *Press Release,* 29 June 2001. http://www.mofa.go.kr/eng/brd/m_5676/view.do?seq=296187. Accessed 10 January 2018.
Reynolds, Brian G. "USN Hosts ROKN 45th Submarine Warfare Committee Meeting." *Commander, US Pacific Fleet,* 12 May 2017. http://www.cpf.navy.mil/news.aspx/140017. Accessed 15 November 2017.

DEFENCE INDUSTRY LITERATURE

Hanwha Systems. *PKG Combat Management System.* http://www.hanwhasystems.com/views/eng/front/business/biz213.jsp. Accessed 3 March 2018.
LIG Nex1. *SONAR Surveillance System.* https://www.lignex1.com/eng/product/product02_03.jsp. Accessed 5 January 2018.
LIG Nex1. *130mm Guided Rocket System.* https://www.lignex1.com/eng/product/product01_02.jsp. Accessed 9 February 2018.

LIG Nex1. *Air and Surface Short Range Surveillance Radar, SPS-540K.* https://www.lignex1.com/eng/common/download.jsp?filePath=/upl oad/2016/09/27/2016092715073755221.pdf&fileName=SPS540K.pdf. Accessed 3 March 2018.

LIG Nex1. *Anti-Ship Missile, C-Star.* https://www.lignex1.com/eng/common/ download.jsp?filePath=/upload/2016/09/27/2016092714320532795. pdf&fileName=Cstar.pdf. Accessed 20 March 2018.

Lockheed Martin. *Lockheed Martin to Bring Aegis Ballistic Missile Defense to the Latest US Korea and Japan Destroyers.* https://www.lockheedmartin.com/ us/news/press-releases/2016/august/160815-mst-aegis-ballistic-missile-defense-to-latest-us-korea-and-japan-destroyers.html. Accessed 10 December 2017.

Rosoboronexport *Naval Systems. Uran-E.* http://roe.ru/eng/catalog/naval-systems/shipborne-weapons/uran-e/. Accessed 1 December 2018.

Ultra Electronics. *MDLMS, Multi Data Link Management System: Ultra Electronics Advanced Tactical Systems* (PPT Presentation, 2017). http://www. ultra-ats.com/files/mdlmspresentation17-s-0382.pdf. Accessed 1 February 2018.

Popular Media Articles

"50 N. Korean Submarines Vanish from Radar." *The Chosun Ilbo*, 24 August 2015. http://english.chosun.com/site/data/html_dir/2015/08/24/2015082401139. html. Accessed 14 September 2015.

"ADEX 2017: ROK Marine Corps Showcasing Bigung for the 1st Time." *Army Recognition*, 18 October 2017. https://www.armyrecognition.com/ adex_2017_online_show_daily_news/adex_2017_rok_marine_corps_show-casing_bigung_for_the_1st_time.html. Accessed 19 November 2017.

"Allies' Navy Forces Launch Combined Maritime Operations Center in Jan." *Yonhap News Agency*, 21 May 2017. http://english.yonhapnews.co.kr/ search1/2603000000.html?cid=AEN20170520001600315. Accessed 15 November 2017.

"*Badaui wangja marinboi Park Taehwan seonsu, haegun hongbodaesaro wichok* [Prince of the Sea, Marine Boy Park Tae-hwan Appointed Navy PR Ambassador]." *Republic of Korea Navy News Release*, 31 May 2013.

Bermudez, Joseph S. "New North Korean Helicopter Frigates Spotted." *38 North*, 15 May 2014. https://www.38north.org/2014/05/jbermu-dez051514/. Accessed 1 December 2017.

Bermudez, Joseph S. "The Korean People's Navy Tests New Anti-Ship Cruise Missile." *38 North*, 8 February 2015. https://www.38north.org/2015/02/ jbermudez020815/.

Bermudez, Joseph S. "North Korean Special Operations Forces: Hovercraft Bases (Part I)." *Beyond Parallel CSIS*, 25 January 2018. https://beyondparallel.csis.org/north-korean-special-operations-forces-hovercraft-bases-part-1/. Accessed 28 January 2018.

Bermudez, Joseph S. "North Korean Special Operations Forces: Hovercraft Bases (Part II)." *Beyond Parallel CSIS*, 5 February 2018. https://beyondparallel.csis.org/north-korean-special-operations-forces-hovercraft-bases-part-ii/. Accessed 8 February 2018.

Bermudez, Joseph S. "North Korean Special Operations Forces: Hovercraft Bases (Part III)." *Beyond Parallel CSIS*, 15 February 2018. https://beyondparallel.csis.org/north-korean-special-operations-forces-hovercraft-bases-part-iii/. Accessed 20 February 2018.

Blanke II, Harry H. "Korea Theatre Command and Control Enhancements Support Decisive Actions." *Signal*, November 2006. https://www.afcea.org/content/korea-theater-command-and-control-enhancements-support-decisive-actions. Accessed 4 February 2018.

"Boeing, Saab Compete to Win S. Korea's Maritime Patrol Aircraft Deal." *Yonhap News Agency*, 22 October 2017. http://english.yonhapnews.co.kr/search1/2603000000.html?cid=AEN20171022000200320. Accessed 10 January 2017.

"Chinese Fishing Vessels Ram Korean Coast Guard Boat." *Maritime Executive*, 10 October 2010. https://www.maritime-executive.com/article/chinese-fishing-vessel-rams-korean-coast-guard-boat#gs.0LOK=_Q. Accessed 10 February 2018.

Chun, Young-gi, and Bong-moon Kim. "Korea's Statues Without Limitations: Kim Jong-pil Remembers: 70." *Korea Joongang Daily*, 6 October 2015. http://mengnews.joins.com/view.aspx?aId=3009977. Accessed 10 November 2017.

Cohen, Zachary, and Ryan Browne. "US Detects 'Highly Unusual' North Korean Submarine Activity." *CNN*, 2 August 2017. http://edition.cnn.com/2017/07/31/politics/north-korea-ejection-test-submarine-activity/index.html.

Collins, Lisa. "Between a Rock and a Grey Zone: China-ROK Illegal Fishing Disputes." *AMTI*, 6 July 2016. https://amti.csis.org/rock-grey-zone-china-rok-illegal-fishing-disputes/.

"Dokdo Class LPD—ROK Navy." *Navy Recognition*. https://navyrecognition.com/index.php/134-republic-of-korea-navy-vessels-ships-and-equipment/rok-navy-aircraft-carriers-a-amphibious-vessels/869-dokdo-class-lph-lpx-landing-platform-helicopter-amphibious-assault-ship-lph-6111-roks-marado-baengnyeongdo-ieodo-republic-of-korea-rok-navy-hanjin-heavy-industries-hhi-datasheet-pictures-photos-video-specifications.html. Accessed 17 January 2017.

Dominguez, Gabriel. "South Korean Navy Receives New Minelayer." *IHS Jane's Defence Weekly*, 12 June 2017. http://www.janes.com/article/71328/south-korean-navy-receives-new-minelayer. Accessed 10 March 2018.

Dominguez, Gabriel. "South Korea to Start Building Training Ship in August." *IHS Jane's Defence Weekly*, 17 July 2017. http://www.janes.com/article/72347/south-korea-to-start-building-training-ship-in-august. Accessed 20 November 2017.

Dominguez, Gabriel. "ROKN Commissions 18th and Final PKG-A-Class Patrol Vessel." *IHS Jane's Defence Weekly*, 25 January 2018. http://www.janes.com/article/77348/rokn-commissions-18th-and-final-pkg-a-class-patrol-vessel. Accessed 10 February 2018.

"*Dongbuga haeyanganbohwangyeong byeonhwae ttareun hangukaegunui dojeongwa gwaje* [Challenges and Tasks of the Republic of Korea Navy Due to Changes in the Northeast Asia Maritime Security Environment]." *Korea Institute for Maritime Strategy*. http://www.kims.or.kr/%EC%A0%9C41%ED%9A%8C-%EA%B5%AD%EC%A0%9C/. Accessed 12 November 2017.

"Egypt Receives New Warship Donated by South Korea." *APA News*, 26 October 2017. http://apanews.net/en/pays/egypte/news/egypt-receives-new-warship-donated-by-south-korea. Accessed 17 February 2017.

"Endless, Wasteful Brawls." *The Korea Times*, 8 October 2013. http://www.koreatimes.co.kr/www/opinion/2017/08/202_143904.html. Accessed 10 August 2017.

Eshel, Tamir. "Seoul to Equip Its New Maritime Helicopters with Israeli Spike Missiles." *Defense Update*, 6 January 2014. http://defense-update.com/20140106_seoul-equip-new-maritime-helicopters-israeli-spike-missiles.html#.U3y0WsJOUdV. Accessed 10 March 2017.

Gady, Franz-Stefan. "US, ROK Navies Hold Military Drill Off Korean Peninsula." *The Diplomat*, 16 October 2017, https://thediplomat.com/2017/10/us-rok-navies-hold-military-drill-off-korean-peninsula/. Accessed 3 March 2018.

Goldrick, James. "Just How Long Can Submarines Remain Operational." *The Strategist*, 7 March 2016. https://www.aspistrategist.org.au/just-how-long-can-submarines-remain-operational/. Accessed 20 March 2018.

"HHI Launched "Soyang" First 10,000 Tons AOE-II Class Fast Combat Support Ship for ROK Navy." *Navy Recognition*, 29 November 2016. http://www.navyrecognition.com/index.php/news/defence-news/2016/november-2016-navy-naval-forces-defense-industry-technology-maritime-security-global-news/4619-hhi-launched-soyang-first-10-000-tons-aoe-ii-class--fast-combat-support-ship-for-rok-navy.html. Accessed 15 March 2018.

Hicks, Kathleen, and Andrew Hunter. "What Will Replace the Third Offset? Lessons from Past Innovation Strategies." *Defense One*, 17 March 2017.

http://www.defenseone.com/ideas/2017/03/what-will-replace-third-off-set-lessons-past-innovation-strategies/136260/. Accessed 11 March 2018.

Hong, Song-kyu. "ROK Daily: ROK National Assembly Confronts Military over Response Deficiencies." *Seoul Sinmun Online*, 21 September 2011. http://wnc.eastview.com/wnc/article?id=32816050. Accessed 5 March 2014.

Im, Jang-hyuk. "Navy Secretly Moves Base to Busan." *Korean JoongAng Daily*, 3 December 2007. http://koreajoongangdaily.joins.com/news/article/Article.aspx?aid=2883441. Accessed 5 February 2011.

Jane's Information Group. "South Korean Navy Improves Its Air-Defence Capabilities." *International Defence Review*, 1 November 2004.

"*Je17hoe hamsangtoronhoe gongdong gaechoe gyeolgwa* [Results of the 17th Shipboard Co-hosted Debate]." *Korea Institute for Maritime Strategy*. http://www.kims.or.kr/notice_16_6_7/. Accessed 12 November 2017.

Jeong, Yong-soo. "China Tried Muscling South Korea in the Yellow Sea." *Korea Joongang Ilbo*, November 30, 2013. http://koreajoongangdaily.joins.com/news/article/article.aspx?aid=2981288. Accessed 2 April 2014.

Jeong, Yong-soo, and Sarah Kim. "Korean Navy Conducts Drill Close to Ieodo." *Korea Joongang Ilbo*, 4 December 2013. http://koreajoongangdaily.joins.com/news/article/article.aspx?aid=2981469. Accessed 10 March 2016.

Jeong, Yong-soo, and Myo-ja Ser. "Korea Upgrades Submarine Command Structure." *Korea JoongAng Daily*, 3 February 2015. http://koreajoongangdaily.joins.com/news/article/article.aspx?aid=3000459. Accessed 10 August 2017.

Jeong, Yong-soo, and Myo-ja Ser. "North has New and Fast Submersible." *Korea Joongang Daily*, 28 May 2015. http://koreajoongangdaily.joins.com/news/article/article.aspx?aid=3004696. Accessed 3 February 2018.

Jung, Sung-ki. "Anti-Piracy Naval Unit Inaugurated." *The Korea Times*, 3 March 2009. http://www.koreatimes.co.kr/www/nation/2017/08/205_40629.html. Accessed 27 April 2016.

Karniol, Robert. "Democratic Change Reaches ROK Military." *Jane's Defence Weekly*, 17 July 1993.

Karniol, Robert. "Acquiring a Global Viewpoint." *Jane's Defence Weekly* 22, No. 18, 5 November 2004.

Kim, Min-Seok, and Myo-ja Ser. "South Korea Navy Dominating." *Korea JoongAng Daily*, 13 May 2008. http://koreajoongangdaily.joins.com/news/article/article.aspx?aid=2889732. Accessed 2 February 2018.

Kim, Sarah. "Plan to Build Three More Aegis Destroyers is OKed." *Korea JoongAng Daily*, 11 December 2013. http://koreajoongangdaily.joins.com/news/article/article.aspx?aid=2981846. Accessed 20 March 2014.

Kim, Su-jeong, and Gwang-lip Moon. "With Reforms Its Blue House Versus the Generals." *Korea JoongAng Daily*, 30 March 2011. http://

koreajoongangdaily.joins.com/news/article/article.aspx?aid=2934132. Accessed 16 November 2012.

"KIMS Founding Purpose." *Korea Institute for Maritime Strategy.* http://www. kims.or.kr/en/history/. Accessed 19 February 2018.

Lee, Chi-dong. "S. Korean Navy Deploys 4 More Wildcat Choppers." *Yonhap News Agency,* 15 July 2017. http://english.yonhapnews.co.kr/search1/2603000000. html?cid=AEN20170705004000315. Accessed 2 February 2018.

Lee, Hong Liang. "Busan Port Aims for 20m TEU Container Volume in 2017." *Seatrade Maritime News,* 24 January 2017. http://www.seatrade-maritime. com/news/asia/busan-port-aims-for-20m-teu-container-volumes-in-2017. html. Accessed 10 February 2018.

Lee, Hyo-won. "2014 South Korean Box Office: 'Roaring Currents' Takes All-Time Record, Stellar Year for Hollywood." *The Hollywood Reporter,* 21 December 2014. https://www.hollywoodreporter.com/news/2014-south-korean-box-office-759768. Accessed 13 March 2018.

Lee, Seok-jong. *Haegun, "Jeongnyejeok Dokdobangeohullyeon* [Navy, Regular Dokdo Defense Training]." *National Defense Daily,* 18 December 2017. www.kookbang.dema.mil.kr/kookbangWeb/view.do?bbs_id=BBSM-STR_000000000005&ntt_writ_date=201712229&parent_no=5. Accessed 16 February 2018.

Lennon, Brad. "North Korea: 3 US Aircraft Carriers Creating 'Worst Ever' Situation." *CNN,* 20 November 2017. https://edition.cnn. com/2017/11/12/politics/us-navy-three-carrier-exercise-pacific/index. html. Accessed 1 March 2018.

Madan, Tanvi. "The Rise, Fall and Rebirth of the 'Quad'." *War on the Rocks,* 16 November 2017. https://warontherocks.com/2017/11/rise-fall-rebirth-quad/. Accessed 10 February 2018.

"Marine Corps to Deploy 30 Amphibious Helicopters By 2023." *Yonhap News Agency,* 28 December 2018. http://english.yonhapnews.co.kr/news/2016 /12/28/0200000000AEN20161228004800315.html. Accessed 20 March 2018.

McDevitt, Michael. "Beijing's Dream: Becoming a Maritime Superpower." *The National Interest,* 1 July 2016. http://nationalinterest.org/blog/the-buzz/ beijings-dream-becoming-maritime-superpower-16812. Accessed 3 March 2018.

"Navy Pushes Blue-Water Operations." *The Korea Herald,* 7 February 2013. http://m.koreaherald.com/view.php?ud=20130207000954&ntn=0. Accessed 10 March 2013.

"Navy Revives 'Ocean Going Slogan." *Korea Times,* 17 February 2012. http:// koreatimes.co.kr/www/news/nation/2012/02/113_105079.html. Accessed 17 November 2017.

"Navy to Get New Unit for Submarines by 2015." *Korea Herald*, 16 February 2012. http://www.koreaherald.com/view.php?ud=20120216000901. Accessed 20 April 2012.

"New Patrol Boat to Be Named After Killed Soldier." *The Korea Times*, 15 June 2007. https://www.koreatimes.co.kr/www/common/printpreview.asp?categoryCode=205&newsIdx=4797. Accessed 3 March 2017.

Oh, Kwang-sup. "*Dongbugajiyueogui gunsajeongse gwallyeon haegun hamsangtoronhoe yeollyeo* [Opening Navy Shipboard Debate on Military Affairs in Northeast Asia]." *MBC News*, 1 November 1992. http://imnews.imbc.com/20dbnews/history/1992/1918429_19402.html. Accessed 1 March 2014.

O'Carroll, Chad. "Exclusive: New Low-Visibility Corvette Spotted in North Korea." *NK News*, 8 November 2016. https://www.nknews.org/2016/11/exclusive-new-low-visibility-corvette-spotted-in-north-korea/. Accessed 3 February 2018.

Panda, Ankit. "Meet North Korea's Speedy, Stealthy Boats." *The Diplomat*, 29 May 2015. https://thediplomat.com/2015/05/meet-north-koreas-speedy-stealthy-boats/. Accessed 26 January 2018.

Panda, Ankit. "North Korea's New KN19 Coastal Defense Cruise Missile: More Than Meets the Eye." *The Diplomat*, 26 July 2016. https://thediplomat.com/2017/07/north-koreas-new-kn19-coastal-defense-cruise-missile-more-than-meets-the-eye/. Accessed 2 August 2017.

Panda, Ankit. "China and South Korea: Examining the Resolution of the THAAD Impasse." *The Diplomat*, 13 November 2017. https://thediplomat.com/2017/11/china-and-south-korea-examining-the-resolution-of-the-thaad-impasse/. Accessed 10 December 2018.

Park, Boram. "USFK's Naval Forces Move Headquarters to S. Korean Base in Busan." *Yonhap News Agency*, 19 February 2016. http://english.yonhapnews.co.kr/news/2016/02/19/0200000000AEN20160219009000315.html. Accessed 15 November 2017.

Park, Boram. "S. Korea, UNC Crack Down on Illegal Chinese Fishing in Neutral Waters Between Koreas." *Yonhap News Agency*, 10 June 2016. http://english.yonhapnews.co.kr/northkorea/2016/06/09/0401000000AEN20160609003852315.html. Accessed 15 September 2017.

Park, Byong-su. "S. Korean Navy Vessel Attempted to Damage N. Korean Patrol Boat." *Hankyoreh*, 14 October 2014. http://english.hani.co.kr/arti/english_edition/e_northkorea/659698.html. Accessed 10 January 2018.

Park, Jin-hai. "Donghae-1 Natural Gas Field." *The Korea Times*, 3 November 2015. http://www.koreatimes.co.kr/www/news/biz/2015/11/123_190136.html. Accessed 3 February 2018.

Park, Ju-min. "South Korea Vows Greater Force Against China Fishing Boats." *Reuters*, 11 October 2016. https://www.reuters.com/article/

us-southkorea-china-fishermen/south-korea-vows-greater-force-against-china-fishing-boats-idUSKCN12B09O. Accessed 10 February 2018.

Rahmat, Ridzwan. "South Korea to Bolster Northern Limit Line Security with Four More PKX-B Vessels." *Jane's Navy International,* 28 June 2017. http://www.janes.com/article/71874/south-korea-to-bolster-northern-limit-line-security-with-four-more-pkx-b-vessels. Accessed 27 December 2017.

Rahmat, Ridzwan. "South Korea to Equip KSS-3 Class with Indigenous Submarine Combat System." *IHS Jane's Defence Weekly,* 10 October 2017. http://www.janes.com/article/74795/south-korea-to-equip-kss-3-class-with-indigenous-submarine-combat-system. Accessed 20 March 2018.

"Renewed Calls by Minister for Reforms in the Military." *Korea JoongAng Daily,* 2 June 2011.

"Republic of Korea Navy (ROKN) Seeking New Anti-Submarine Warfare (ASW) Helicopter." *Naval News,* 13 November 2017. http://www.navalnews.net/south-koreas-defense-acquisition-program/. Accessed 20 March 2018.

Roblin, Sebastian. "A Short History of North Korea's Long Mini-Submarine Spy Campaign." *War Is Boring,* 25 March 2017. https://medium.com/war-is-boring/a-short-history-of-north-koreas-long-mini-submarine-spy-campaign-958b4ac7024b. Accessed 4 April 2017.

"ROK Navy Future ASR-II Submarine Rescue Vessel Passes Capability Test." *Navy Recognition,* 28 December 2017. http://www.navyrecognition.com/index.php/news/defence-news/2017/december-2017-navy-naval-forces-defense-industry-technology-maritime-security-global-news/5829-rok-navy-future-asr-ii-submarine-rescue-vessel-passes-capability-test.html. Accessed 15 March 2018.

"ROKN Selects Rheinmetall MASS System for LST-II-Class Ships." *Naval Technology,* 2 May 2012. https://www.naval-technology.com/news/newsrokn-selects-rheinmetall-mass-system-for-lst-ii-class-ships/. Accessed 3 March 2018.

Ser, Myo-ja, and Yong-soo Jeong. "Assembly Increases Defense Budget for 2016." *Korea Joongang Ilbo,* 4 December 2015. http://mengnews.joins.com/view.aspx?aId=3012354. Accessed 21 March 2018.

"S. Korea's U.S. Energy Imports Soar This Year." *Yonhap News Agency,* 20 December 2017. http://english.yonhapnews.co.kr/business/2017/12/20/0501000000AEN20171220009300320.html. Accessed 10 February 2018.

"S. Korea, U.S., Japan Agree to Bolster 3-Way Cooperation." *The Korea Herald,* 17 April 2015. http://www.koreaherald.com/view.php?ud=20150417000168. Accessed 20 April 2015.

"S. Korean Navy's Aegis Destroyers to Get Upgraded Missile Launch Systems." *Yonhap News Agency,* 29 May 2016. http://english.yonhapnews.co.kr/search1/2603000000.html?cid=AEN20160529004000315. Accessed 30 November 2017.

"S. Korean Navy Seeks Aviation Command, New Task Fleet." *Yonhap News Agency*, 10 October 2017. http://english.yonhapnews.co.kr/northkorea/20 17/10/19/98/0401000000AEN20171019004652315F.html. Accessed 25 January 2018.

"S. Korea, US to Share Underwater Data on N. Korean Waters." *KBS World Radio*, 28 August 2016. http://world.kbs.co.kr/english/news/news_Po_ detail.htm?No=121419&id=Po. Accessed 15 November 2017.

"South Korea Fires Warning Shots at North Patrol Boat Near Border." *Reuters*, 25 October 2015. https://www.reuters.com/article/us-northkorea-southko-rea-shooting/south-korea-fires-warning-shots-at-north-patrol-boat-near-bor-der-idUSKCN0SJ03L20151025. Accessed 10 January 2018.

"South Korea, Japan Agree Intelligence-Sharing on North Korea Threat." *Reuters*, 23 November 2016. https://www.reuters.com/article/us-southko-rea-japan-military/south-korea-japan-agree-intelligence-sharing-on-north-ko-rea-threat-idUSKBN13I068.

"The Dokdo Class: An LHD for the ROK." *Defence Industry Daily*. https://www.defenseindustrydaily.com/aegis-awd-lhd-for-rok-03431/. Accessed 1 February 2016.

"Three Chinese Fishermen Killed in Confrontation with South Korea Coastguard." *Reuters*, 30 September 2016. https://www.reuters.com/arti-cle/us-southkorea-china-fishermen/three-chinese-fishermen-killed-in-con-frontation-with-south-korea-coastguard-idUSKCN1200DQ. Accessed 10 March 2017.

Watts, Johnathan. "South Korean Coastguard Stabbed to Death while Seizing Chinese Boat." *The Guardian*, 12 December 2011. https://www.theguard-ian.com/environment/2011/dec/12/south-korean-coastguard-stabbed-boat. Accessed 10 February 2018.

Yoo, Jee-ho. "Navy to Get New Course After Loss of the Cheonan." *Korea Joongang Daily*, 24 May 2011. http://koreajoongangdaily.joins.com/news/article/article.aspx?aid=2920854. Accessed 4 February 2017.

DISSERTATIONS

Cho, Young-joo. "The Naval Policy of the Republic of Korea: From the Beginnings to the Twenty-First Century." Unpublished PhD Diss., University of Hull, 2003.

Collins, Robert T. "Commander Combined Naval Component Command; A Significant Change in a Command Relationship." Unpublished MA Thesis, US Naval War College, 1996.

Lee, Sang-yup. "Ships, Security, and Symbols: A Constructivist Explanation of South Korea's Naval Build-up." Unpublished PhD Diss., Rutgers University, 2013.

Olsen, Edward. "Prospects for an Increased Naval Role for the Republic of Korea in Northeast Asian Security." Unpublished MA Thesis, US Naval War College, 1989.

Suh, Jimmy J. "Effects of the Subsurface Domain on the Security of the Korean Peninsula." Unpublished MA Thesis, Naval Postgraduate School, 2017.

TECHNICAL ARTICLES & STATISTICS

AMI International. *Sejong the Great (KDX-3) Class Destroyer*, 21 November 2017. http://amiinter.com/wnpr/html2pdf/examples/viewproject.php?newcontID=717&countryID=34. Accessed 16 December 2017.

Central Intelligence Agency. "Country Comparison: Imports." *The World Factbook*, Continuously Updated. https://www.cia.gov/library/publications/resources/the-world-factbook/rankorder/2078rank.html. Accessed 3 February 2018.

"Cheonwangbong Class Landing Ship Tank." *Naval Technology*. https://www.naval-technology.com/projects/cheonwangbong-class-landing-ship-tank-lst/. Accessed 3 March 2018.

"Chunghaejin [Cheong-Hae-Jin] ASR." *Global Security*. https://www.globalsecurity.org/military/world/rok/asr-21.htm. Accessed 15 March 2018.

Defense Security Cooperation Agency. *Fiscal Year Series as of September 30, 2015*. Washington, DC: Department of Defense, 2010.

Food and Agricultural Organisation of the United Nations. *FAO Yearbook: Fishery and Aquaculture Statistics*. Rome: Food and Agricultural Organisation of the United Nations, 2017.

Food and Agriculture Organisation of the United Nations. *Fishery and Aquaculture Profiles Republic of Korea*, June 2017. http://www.fao.org/fishery/facp/KOR/en. Accessed 4 January 2018.

"Georeoon-gil & bijeon [The Path & Vision]." *Republic of Korea Navy, Jeju Civilian-Military Complex Port*. http://jejunbase.navy.mil.kr/jeju-navy/sp.jsp?p=13. Accessed 20 March 2018.

"Gumdoksuri Class." *Naval-Technology*. http://www.naval-technology.com/projects/pxk-gumdoksuri/. Accessed 19 February 2018.

"Gwanggaeto the Great Class / KDX-I Class Destroyer." *Naval Technology*. http://www.naval-technology.com/projects/gwanggaeto-the-great-class-kdx-i-class-destroyer/. Accessed 10 March 2018.

"Haesong I." *Missile Threat, CSIS Missile Defense Project*, 10 November 2017. https://missilethreat.csis.org/missile/haeseong-i/. Accessed 4 February 2018.

"Haesong II." *Missile Threat, CSIS Missile Defense Project*, 10 November 2017. https://missilethreat.csis.org/missile/haeseong-ii/. Accessed 4 February 2018.

International Institute of Strategic Studies. *The Military Balance 1975–1976*. London: International Institute of Strategic Studies, 1975.

International Institute of Strategic Studies. *The Military Balance 1992–1993*. London: Brassey's, 1992.

International Institute for Strategic Studies. "Chapter Two: Comparative Defence Statistics." *The Military Balance* 118, no. 1, 2018: 19–26. London: International Institute for Strategic Studies.

Korea Energy Economics Institute. *2016 Energy Info. Korea*. Ulsan: Korea Energy Economics Institute, 2017.

"Korea's New Coastal Frigates: The FFX Incheon Class." *Defense Industry Daily*, 23 August 2016. http://www.defenseindustrydaily.com/ffx-koreas-new-frigates-05239/. Accessed 19 February 2018.

Korea National Oil Company. *Operations: E&P Worldwide*. https://www.knoc.co.kr/ENG/sub03/sub03_1_1_4.jsp. Accessed 3 February 2018.

Korea Shipowners Association. *Korean Seaborne Trade Volume*. http://www.shipowners.or.kr/eng/ks_industry/ks_industry2.php. Accessed 19 March 2018.

Korean Coast Guard. *Junggugeoseondansokyeonhwang* [Status of Chinese fishing boat control], December 26, 2017. http://www.index.go.kr/potal/main/EachDtlPageDetail.do?idx_cd=1622. Accessed 10 January 2018.

"MADEX 2017: Hyundai Heavy Industries HDM-4000 MLS II-class Minelayer of the ROK Navy." *Navy Recognition*, 25 October 2017. http://www.navyrecognition.com/index.php/news/naval-exhibitions/2017/madex-2017/5656-madex-2017-hyundai-heavy-industries-hdm-4000-mls-ii-class-minelayer-of-the-rok-navy.html. Accessed 26 January 2018.

"Nongo Surface Effect Ship." *Global Security*. https://www.globalsecurity.org/military/world/dprk/p-nongo.html. Accessed 26 January 2018.

"Organization, Navy Corps Organization." *Republic of Korea Navy Website*. http://www.navy.mil.kr/mbshome/mbs/eng/subview.do?id=eng_010200000000. Accessed 13 March 2018.

Republic of Korea Joint Chiefs of Staff. *Gunsayongeohaesol* [Military Glossary]. http://www.jcs.mil.kr/user/indexSub.action?codyMenuSeq=71157&siteId=jcs&menuUIType=sub. Accessed 19 January 2018.

"ROKN Chang Bogo Class Submarines." *Naval Technology*. http://www.naval-technology.com/projects/chang-bogo-class-submarine-south-korea-rokn/. Accessed 20 March 2018.

SIPRI. *SIPRI Arms Transfer Database: Trade Registers*. http://armstrade.sipri.org/armstrade/page/trade_register.php. Accessed 21 February 2018.

The International Monetary Fund. *World Economic Database*, October 2017.

The World Bank. *GDP (Current US$) Korea, Rep. 1960–2016*. https://data.worldbank.org/indicator/NY.GDP.MKTP.CD?locations=KR. Accessed 10 February 2018.

The World Bank. *World Development Indicators, Republic of Korea*, 3 January 2018. https://data.worldbank.org/country/korea-rep. Accessed 19 March 2018.

"Top 50 World Container Ports." *World Shipping Council*. http://www.world-shipping.org/about-the-industry/global-trade/top-50-world-container-ports. Accessed 3 March 2018.

United Nations Conference on Trade and Development. *Review of Maritime Transport 2017*. Geneva: United Nations Conference on Trade and Development, 2017.

United States Energy Information Administration. *Country Analysis Brief: South Korea*, 19 January 2017. https://www.eia.gov/beta/international/analysis_includes/countries_long/Korea_South/south_korea.pdf. Accessed 10 February 2018.

United States Navy. *MW 08_Multi-Beam Air and Surface Surveillance Radar, Military Applications Summary Bulletin AD-A233 492*, 6 September 1989.

United States Navy Judge Advocate General's Corps. "Korea, Republic of: Summary of Claims, DoD 2005.1-M." *Maritime Claims Reference Manual*, October 2014. http://www.jag.navy.mil/organization/documents/mcrm/Korea,South2014.pdf. Accessed 10 February 2018.

Websites

Korean Institute for Maritime Strategy Homepage. http://kims.or.kr/.

Republic of Korea Defense Acquisition Program Homepage. http://dapa.go.kr/mbshome/mbs/dapa_kr/index.jsp.

Republic of Korea Ministry of Foreign Affairs Homepage. http://www.mofa.go.kr/eng/index.do.

Republic of Korea Ministry of National Defense Homepage. http://mnd.go.kr/.

Republic of Korea Navy Homepage. http://www.navy.mil.kr/.

Republic of Korea Navy YouTube Page. https://www.youtube.com/user/MsRoknavy/videos.

Republic of Korea Navy Facebook Page. https://www.facebook.com/ilovenavy/.

SLOC Study Group—Korea Homepage. http://www.sloc.co.kr/.

Site Rank Data. www.siterankdata.com/navy.mil.kr.

INDEX

© The Editor(s) (if applicable) and The Author(s) 2019
I. Bowers, *The Modernisation of the Republic of
Korea Navy*, Critical Studies of the Asia-Pacific,
https://doi.org/10.1007/978-3-319-92291-1

Printed by Printforce, the Netherlands